China-Russia-India Relations in 21st Century

China-Russia-India Relations in 21st Century

Deepak Yadav

Kaveri Books
New Delhi – 110 002

First Published in 2014

ISBN: 978-81-7479-155-9

Published by
Kaveri Books
4832/24, Ansari Road
New Delhi-110002 (India)
Tel: 011- 47072321
E-mail : info@kaveribooks.com
kaveribooks@gmail.com
Website: www.kaveribooks.com

Typeset in AGaramond Font at
Delta Book World, New Delhi - 110 002

PRINTED IN INDIA

Preface

This book intends to show how Soviet Union and China in the past and Russia and China at present faced ups and downs in their bilateral relations. Despite being the followers of same communist ideology which gives call for all communist countries to unite, Soviet Union and China had a bitter relationship throughout 1960s and 1970s and considered each other as enemy number one. But in the present day world politics, they are considered allies and strategic partners.

The book mainly tries to deal with Russia-China relations in the post-Soviet period. Even after disintegration of Soviet Union, Russia with a territory of more than 17 million square km. is the world's largest country while China with more than1.3 billion people is the most populous country in the world. It covers the period from 1991 to 2007. However as and when required to substantiate an argument, some later developments have been also discussed.

Chapter one deals with the historical background of Russia-China relations. It gives a broad view of how they managed their co-operation despite the presence of ideological differences. In 1950, just after a month of the establishment of People's Republic of China (PRC), USSR signed the Treaty of Friendship, Alliance and Mutual Co-operation with it. The first half of 1950s could be termed as honeymoon period between the two. However differences started surfacing up in the second half of 1950s and early 1960s mainly over ideological issues. These tensed relations finally culminated into border clashes between USSR and China.

However in late 1980s relations between the two returned to normalcy, especially after Gorbachev visited China in 1989. After the disintegration of Soviet Union, Russia is no longer follows communist ideology in its foreign policy and it is national interest which is the guiding light to the new Russia.

Chapter two attempts to analyze the areas of common concern and divergent views on various issues of national and international importance. Among the issues on which both Russia and China have similar views includes separatism, religious fundamentalism, opposition to US hegemonistic policy and humanitarian intervention. Both countries favour multipolar world based on just and equal international order etc. Issues where both countries have divergent view includes extensive illegal Chinese migration to the Russian Far East and Siberia, cultural divide, China's reluctance to accept Russia as a regional hegemon in Central Asia and conflict of interest in the region.

Chapter three provides detailed and systematic account of Russo-China economic relations and defence co-operation with the help of tables. Russian arms sale to China accounts for major portion of bilateral trade between the two. Russia provides the state- of- art weapons to China at the reasonable cost without any strings attached.

Chapter four deals with Russo-China relations in the context of Central Asia with special emphasis on SCO. Russia considers Central Asia as its backyard and enjoyed the role of regional hagemon in the region. China is investing extensively in the Central Asia to meet its ever growing energy quest for oil and natural gas and has emerged as the largest donor to Central Asia. SCO is created to counter US and NATO's influence in the region as well as to establish stability in the region and to fight terrorism. This chapter also includes the discussion regarding former Russian Prime Minister Yevegeny Primakov's dream of Russia -China - India Triangle.

Chapter five, which is conclusion, sums up the issues discussed in this book.

Contents

PREFACE 5

ABBREVIATIONS 11

1. INTRODUCTION 13
   - Russia-China Relations: Historical Background
   - Development of Relations after Distintegration of USSR
   - Post 1991 Partnership
   - Russian Policies Towards China during Yeltsin Regime
   - On Taiwan Question
   - December 1992: First Russo-Chinese Summit
   - The Second Summit: from 'Good Neighbourliness' to 'Constructive Partnership'
   - 1996: from 'Constructive Partnership' to 'Strategic Co-operation'

2. POLITICAL RELATIONS BETWEEN RUSSIA AND CHINA 64
   - Areas of Common Concern
   - NATO's Eastward Expansion
   - Dynamics of the Russia-China Security Dialogue in 1996-1998
   - Arms Sales to China: Motives and Risks
   - China's Approach to the NATO Expansion: Compatibility with the Russian Interests

- NATO's Involvement in Kosovo and its Impact on Russia-China Ties
- Russia, China and The Multipolar World Order
- A Shared Perspective
- Chinese Perspective
- Arms Factor
- Alliance Politics-Sanghai Co-operation Organization (SCO)
- Problem Areas Between Russia and China
- The Issues of Chinese Emigration to the Russian Far East
- China's Complaint Regarding Quality of Goods from Russia
- Russia Calls China as 'King of Cloning'
- The Siberian Pipeline Struggle
- Overlapping Interests, Tensions and Limitations between Russia and China

3. ECONOMIC RELATIONS AND DEFENCE CO-OPERATION BETWEEN RUSSIA AND CHINA 166
   - Economic Co-operation
   - Defence Co-operation
   - Why Russia and China Have not Formed an Anti-American Alliance
   - Border Stability and Arms Control
   - Impediments to Deeper Geopolitical Cooperation between Russia and China
   - Non-military Economic Ties Remain Limited
   - Still a Top-Down Process
   - Anti-U.S. Co-operation: Rhetoric versus Reality
4. RUSSO-CHINA RELATIONS IN THE REGIONAL CONTEXT: CENTRAL ASIA AND SCO 209
   - Russia and China in Central Asia
   - The Beginning of Shanghai Five
   - Annual Summit Meetings of the Shanghai Five
   - China's Policy towards Central Asia: Initial Emphasis on Transport, Trade and Economic Links
   - Russia Remain Big Brother in Central Asia
   - Islamic Extremism and Militancy a Common Threat

- China's Campaign to Develop its Western Regions
- Potential Rivalry between Russia and China in Central Asia
- Russia Moves to Strengthen CIS Collective Security
- Post-September 11, 2001 Developments in the Central Asia
- US Military Presence in Central Asia
- SCO and CSTO Presence in Central Asia
- Energy Security: SCO Energy Club
- Co-operation between NATO and SCO
- China's Response to Russia-Georgia Conflict
- Background of the Conflict
- China-Georgia Relations
- Russia-China-India Triangle
- The Soviet Times
- Russia-India Relations
- Russia-India-China Emerging Triangle: Myth and Reality
- Implications for India

5. CONCLUSION 285

APPENDICES 294

BIBLIOGRAPHY 340

INDEX 357

Abbreviations

ABM	-	Anti-Ballistic Missile
ASEAN	-	Association of South East Asian Nations
CBM	-	Confidence Building Measure
CCP	-	Chinese Communist Party
CDPSP	-	Current Digest of Post Soviet Press
CICA	-	Conference on Interaction and Confidence Building Measures in Asia
CIS	-	Commonwealth of Independent States
CPSU	-	Communist Party of Soviet Union
CSTO	-	Collective Security Treaty Organization
CTBT	-	Comprehensive Test Ban Treaty
EU	-	European Union
GLONASS	-	Global Navigational Satellite System
HAL	-	Hindustan Aeronautics LimitedI
CBM	-	Inter Continental Ballistic Missile
LBM	-	Long Range Ballistic Missiles
MBTs	-	Main Battle Tanks
MFN	-	Most Favoured Nation
NAFTA	-	North American Free Trade Area
NATO	-	North Atlantic Treaty Organization
NMD	-	National Missile Defence

NPT	-	Nuclear Proliferation Treaty
PLA	-	People's Liberation Army
PRC	-	People's Republic of China
R&D	-	Research and Development
SAFTA	-	South Asian Free Trade Area
SCO	-	Shanghai Cooperation Organization
SWB	-	Summary of World Broadcast
TMD	-	Theatre Missile Defence
UNSC	-	United Nations Security Council
USSR	-	Union of Soviet Socialist Republics
WTO	-	World Trade Organization
XUAR	-	Xinjiang Uighur Autonomous Region

1 Introduction

Relations between Moscow and Beijing have gone full circle in the past half century, from alliance to containment and now to strategic partnership. To understand the ebbs and flows in Moscow's China policy it is necessary to look into the Soviet history.

History which is characterized as chronicle of the past provides the solid base for building up future relationships. In International Relations, there is no permanent 'friend or foe', today's bitter enemy can become tomorrow's staunchest ally. It is interest which runs supreme, and Russia and China are not exceptions to it. Despite being communist countries both Soviet Union and China counted each other as enemy number one and targeted each other with their nuclear weapons. But today Russia and China no longer consider each other as enemy and both countries have developed "very deep" relations in the strategic field.

China has the largest population in the world, while Russia is the largest nation in terms of territory. Both are permanent members of the United Nations Security Council. Obviously, the significance of Sino-Russian relations extends far beyond the interests of the two nations. It also affects the stability of Asia and the world at large.

Soviet-China relations before disintegration of USSR were characterized by a number of ups and downs. In February 1950 just four months after establishment of the PRC the two countries signed the treaty of Friendship, Alliance and Mutual Cooperation. The first half of the 1950s was the honeymoon period. However, by the late 1950s differences in national interest and ideology emerged leading to serious disputes in early 1960s which developed in to acute conflict and border clashes in 1969. Hence in the late 1960s and 1970s the USSR regarded China as one of its main rivals and stationed approximately one million troops and one third of its SS-20 intermediate-range ballistic missile along the Sino-Soviet border, threatening to make a 'surgical' first strike on China', nuclear bases. Under serious threat, China had to prepare for a military intrusion from north. However, in 1980s two countries came to realization that these were not in the interests of either side and they made effort to alleviate the situation. These efforts resulted in the normalization of the relations during a state visit to Beijing by the then Soviet President Mikhail Gorbachev in May 1989. (Qimao, 1999, pp. 206-207)

Historical Background

Relations between Russia and China the world's two largest states from the point of view of territory and population respectively have always had a strong impact on the course of global and regional politics. During the 1960s and 70s there have been sharp ups and downs in their relations. Soviet pilots fought on the side of Chinese when China was attacked by militarist Japan. During the Second World War thousands of Chinese helped the Soviet Union both at the front and the rear. (Ragachev, 1997, p. 25).

Russo-Chinese relations exert a powerful influence on Asian world politics. Today, a strong and increasingly stable bilateral detente seems to have emerged, but change is the law of life and neither state's future is mechanistically predicable. The relations between Russia and China have always exerted to impact on the larger regional and global political scenario. During the historical processes of formation and expansion of two large empires or state systems they came to share the largest land boundary running into 7500km. The fact, that the two shared a long border, which was also disputed, inter alia generated nascent and actual apprehensions and distrusts regarding each others, motives and objectives. At the same time two were also compelled to extensively interact and deal with each other.

Mao Zedong made numerous references to the 'unequal' relationship between Chinese communist party and the Soviet Union during Stalin's era which started with his refusal during the Chinese civil war to provide greater support to communist rebels, in spite of the ideological bond. Stalin was indeed initially reluctant to repudiate the Sino-Soviet Treaty of August 1945, signed with the Guondnang, and with it, the commitments of the Yalta arrangements in the Far East. Negotiations for a new treaty did not go smoothly and Mao, who was in Moscow during the winter of 1949-1950, had to cool his heads for nearly two and a half months. People's Republic of China had to accept the disparity of power with its Soviet 'protector' and the Mao admitted later that he had hardly any choice but to allow Stalin in 1950 to get away with beating Manchuria and Xinjiang as 'semi colonies of the USSR by prohibiting citizens of third countries from entering these two regions and by preserving its economic interests. Already in 1939, a treaty had been signed between nationalist China and Soviet government for economic collaboration in Xinjiang for ten years, providing for instance, Soviets with exclusive right in the exploration of oilfields and some universal resources.

The Chinese leadership realized their move from a subordinate position vis-à-vis the USSR to a more trusted allies only when they came to North Korea's assistance and resist American forces. It did not go without rebuff. This was reflected in Nehru's words to John. F. Dulles, during the latter's visit to New Delhi in May 1953, that the 'Soviet Union wants to keep China dependent upon the Soviet Union as its spokesman and does not want China's admission to the UN in reality.

Stalin's death in March 1953 facilitated a re-appraisal of Sino-Soviet relations, taking into account the Chinese resentment over Moscow's patronizing attitude. The visit of China by a Soviet party and state delegation headed by Khrushchev on 29 September and 12 October 1954 for fifth anniversary of the PRC played a substantial role in the adoption of the 'Panchasheel' as the basis for relations of between the USSR and its allies. It is clear that China and Russia today share a number of common interests. Countries are struggling to protect their actual (Chechnya, Xinjiang) or virtual (Taiwan) common integrity, reform their old command economy, alleviate poverty and maintain a stable society. Moscow and Beijing are also concerned by what they perceive in this post-cold war world as Washington's arrogance and domination, in particular on matters related to global and regional security.

Some agreements forced upon the Chinese in 1950-51, largely in line with the Sino-Soviet Treaty of 1945, such as the establishment of four jointly owned companies and existence of Soviet bases at Dairen and Port Arthur, were addressed, by the dismantling of the former and the evaluation of the latter. Along with it Soviet agreed to give new loans adding up to 520 million rubles. The Belgrade declaration of June 1955, issued at the end of Khrushchev's visit to Tito's Yugoslavia and acknowledging that every country had the right to choose its own path to socialism, seemed to auger well for the further establishment of more trusting relations, even if Mao Zedong was to comment to a Yugoslavian delegation in September 1956 that "liberty, equality and fraternity were a slogan of the bourgeoisie which had a direct resonance on Sino-Soviet relations since the shadow of the father and son relationship of the past had not completely give way to a brotherly relationship (Rubinstein, 1956: 4-6). China blamed the interventionist attitude of Moscow regarding the popular uprising in Poland of the summer of 1956 as a main frustration of 'Great Power of Chauvinism' in trying to exert pressure on the Polish leaders and even threatening to resort the use of military force. (Jain, 1983:304-315).

For Mao Zedong, the unity of the communist camp came nevertheless first and he did support the Soviet military intervention in Hungary. Beijing was of the view that this country should not be abandoned to the 'reactionary forces' even if there was no love lost for Stalin, Mao had not shared Khrushchev's unrestrained criticism of the former Soviet leader at the 20th Congress of the CPSU, done furthermore without consulting the Chinese leadership, and which had only weakened the communist camp and lead to the events in Poland and Hungary. In a conversation with Khrushchev in 1958, Mao Zedong stigmatized the unrestrained criticism of Stalin, explaining that 'out of Stalin's ten fingers, three were rotten. (Jain, 1983: 304-305).

By the mid fifties, the two communist giants had started to fight for influence in Asia. The Soviet leadership had made it clear that it wanted to emulate Chinese activism in developing relationships with a number of non-communist countries of the Asian continent. While Chinese had in this endeavor a platform with the Bandung Conference, the Soviets in turn also hoped to achieve the same by hiring India as a 'Spring board' for multiplying contacts with the states of Asia so as o counterbalance China's hegemonic proclivity.

The joint Soviet-Chinese Declaration of January 1957 emphasizing the complete unity of USSR and the PRC as an important factor in unifying the whole socialist camp and Mao's agreement to participate in Moscow international conference of communist parties in November 1957, on the occasion of the Fortieth anniversary of the Russian October Revolution, were just a lull in the growing tension. Soon Mao's wrath was triggered by the two Soviet proposals: the establishment of a short-wave radar station in China to maintain communications with the Soviet submarines operating against the US in the Pacific Ocean and the setting up of a joint Sino-Soviet submarine flotilla operating under the Russian command. Mao interpreted the first proposal as a Soviet attempt o gain a new military bare in China and the second an unacceptable substitute for an earlier Chinese request for Soviet technology and documentation in order to enable PRC to build its own nuclear power submarines. The Chinese assured the USSR of attempting to put China under its military control as, in 1962, they were to accuse Moscow of the same imperialist logic in shipping missiles to Cuba. (Anderson, 1997:315-323).

It was out of question that the Chinese would accept to share the ownership of a submarine fleet and to have a radar station which would not be the property of China, built with investments of the Chinese government, even if jointly exploited. In July 1956, Mao vented in rage at Soviet ambassador Pavel Yudin regarding the ostensible resumption of unequal treatment of China by the Soviet leadership. The shelling in August 1958 of the coastal islands of Quemoy and Matsu in the straits of Taiwan did not go down well with the Soviet leaders since it went against the relaxation of tension with the US favored by Moscow. The Chinese leadership, rallying behind Mao's metaphor that 'the east wind is now stronger than the west wind' were increasingly restive in giving support to 'wars of national liberation and 'anti-imperialist struggles'. Moscow feared that inconsiderate foreign policy initiative of the PRC would only push a number of Asian countries into the western rings or could even escalate to a destructive war if the super powers were to intervene on opposing sides. (Anderson, 1997: 315-323).

Mao was increasingly critical of Khrushchev's revisionism and of his perceived fascination for peaceful coexistence with the capitalist west. When in July 1958, a leftist camp against the Iraqi-pro-western government sparked a brief but intense crisis in Middle East, leading to landing of British and American troops in Lebanon and Jordan, the Chinese officials urged the USSR to take a firm stand against 'American imperialist aggression'. Contrary to Beijing's wishes, Khrushchev quickly decided there was little to be gained by risking a direct East-West confrontation. He preferred to propose on July 19, a summit conference to which the American, British, French and also Indian leaders would be invited to discuss the crisis in the Middle East. If this proposal was aborted it nevertheless reflected the growing warmth between Moscow and Delhi whereas the relations with Beijing were cooling off. Another instance of a diplomatic move favoring India was when in June 1957, Moscow supported, unsuccessfully, the participation of India in the disarmament commission which was to meet in London in August of the same year.

The positive recognition of India's active policy in favour of nuclear disarmament stood in sharp contrast with the increasingly dubious attitude of Soviets vis-à-vis Chinese nuclear weapons programme they had agreed to back when it was launched in 1955. A secret defence technology agreement, which provided for broad Soviet assistance to China in the development of a nuclear device, was signed in October 1957. Soon after, Soviet nuclear weapon scientists and engineers were dispatched to China. Sensitive information were transferred and equipment sold for Uranium processing and enrichment. Soviet leaders turned things around when they formally notified their Chinese counter parts, on 20 June 1959 that no prototype bombs or detailed technical blueprints would be provided. (Ziegler, 1994:529-544).

The Soviets were less and less prone to take at face value the Chinese growing ranting and ravings on India with regards to the Tibetan insurrection of March 1959, if the Soviet leadership considered that the Chinese could legitimately put down the counter revolutionary rebellion, they accused China of playing into the hands of imperialist powers. Moscow blamed Beijing for unleashing its own propagandist campaign against Nehru whom the Soviet considered a far sighted statesman able to recognize the vital importance of India's friendship with socialist camp. They called the Chinese authorities that, in the first place, the responsibility fell on them for letting the Dalai Lama escape to India. Moscow also stressed the fact that Nehru never disputed that Tibet was not part of China and that the imperialist powers would only benefit from a sharp deterioration in Sino-Indian relations. In spite of ruthless and suppression of the Tibetan rebellion and an agitated political class in India, Nehru had indeed avoided to go overboard and developed a rather resigned outlook fearing, an influx of Chinese into Tibet and within ten or twenty years time, there would be little left of the old Tibet.

Within few days of this ill-breaking meeting with Eisenhower at Camp David, Khrushchev headed a Soviet party delegation including Suslav and Gromyko, to Beijing in early October 1959 for the tenth anniversary of the founding of PRC. There he warned the Chinese that the socialist camp should avoid any moves that could be exploited by the reactionaries to push the world back to the tracks of a heightened Cold War and that the principles of peaceful co-existence between the two global systems were more than just a temporary tactical maneuver. At this point of time Moscow and Beijing were holding increasingly divergent views not only on foreign policy matters but also on domestic policy. The Soviet disfavored the cult of personality developing around Mao and labeled as disastrous the 'Peoples, commune' and 'Great leap forward'- which were the first serious attempts to depart from the Soviet model of development and to display their incomparable revolutionary order.

In the initial post-Soviet period, Russia hoped to establish equal partnership relations with the developed world, especially the west with the initiation of a systematic transformation to democracy and market economy the ideological divide between the two socialist and capitalist systems came to an end. Russia expected to be taken as a natural partner by the west on equal basis. This was evident in the foreign policy concept of 1993 which said "the war of ideologies have keen concluded, the ground work is being laid for equal partnership with neighboring leading democratic and economically developed countries on the basis of standing up for our values and interests through real interaction and not by rushing from confrontation of Utopias.

The socialist ideology was totally removed from Russian foreign policy during this period. Earlier ideology of communism was one of the determining factors of Soviet foreign policy. "It is a vital necessity for Russia's foreign policy orientation to proceed not from ideological principles or party demands, but from fundamental national interests". Thus even though commonwealth of independent states (CIS) was given top priority in the Concept of 1993, Russia's actual primary objective was partnership and relationship with US. The concept itself says "for the foreseeable fulltime, the relations with the US will retain a prominent place on the scale of Russian foreign policy priorities, corresponding to the position and weight of US in the world affair. It also said 'Relying on the existing agreements in the military, political and economic and financial spheres, Russia will strive towards the stable development of relations with the USA, with a view towards, strategic partnership and inclined towards alliance. (Kuhrt, 2007:213-243).

Russian foreign policy concept of 1993 termed CIS as 'Near Abroad', and was given top priority. However immediate concern of Russia was to ensure that various agreements signed during the Gorbachev period were not annulled. Moreover, Russia needed western aid and technology to sustain its economy. Thus, on the one hand Russia hoped that strategic partnership or even alliance with the only superpower status of the US in the aftermath of the demise of the Soviet power. In April 1993, President Yeltsin and the US President Clinton had their official meeting during which Clinton offered $1.6 billion credit to Russia's which was much less than was promised to Gorbachev by the west and US. More surprisingly by 1998 Yeltsin and Clinton met fourteen times but without much headway on the economic assistance front. (Kuhrt, 2007:213-243).

Foreign aid had become very essential for Russia as its economy was in bad shape after 'shock therapy' treatment by Yelstin. Russia had inherited a drastic decline in industrial and agricultural output from USSR. The economy was dominated by military industrial complexes which accounted for up to third of the industrial output. For example the shares of military industrial complexes were almost 75% of industrial output in St. Petersburg, and in Moscow over 50%. Inflation was a major problem in December 1992, wholesale prices were thirty four times higher in December 1991. In fuel and energy sector, prices increased 80 fold and in consumer products more than twenty four fold. The picture got further worsened in 1993 after the introduction of internal convertibility, the exchange rate of rubble against dollar faced steep decline, resulting in soaring up of prices of imported goods. Also living standards fell to all time low and a huge population automatically slipped below poverty line.

The history of Moscow-Beijing military-technical cooperation goes back to the 1950s when the two communist giants, the Soviet Union and newly formed People's Republic of China, signed the treaty of alliance. Moscow extended massive aid to its communist ally that laid to the foundation of the latter's heavy industry. However in July 1960 thousands of Soviet technicians and experts were suddenly withdrawn from China in protest against their political education by the latter. The following two and half decades were marked by intense political and ideological rivalry and antagonism between two coupled with serious border dispute which erupted in bloody conflicts over the Usuri river island in March 1969. (Rogachev, 1997, pp. 149-150).

Beginning in the late 1960s, the ideological rivalry between Soviet Union and China about who is the true communist came on surface. Soviet leadership tried to orchestrate unified socialist -response to China's challenge. The international Department of CPSU Central Committee held regular meetings with its counterparts in the East European Socialist Countries and Mangolia to coordinate propaganda on China question, including symposia, research and media campaign in the third countries. (Wishnick, 2001: 50).

To resolve the true communist issue the international communist conference was called on June 7, 1969 at Moscow. Addressing the conference, Brezhnev bemoaned the Communist Party of China's "departure from Marxism-Leninism", "break with internationalism" and "organization of armed conflicts". He urged his fellow communists to fight against imperialism and cooperate in defense of Marxist-Leninist ideas. (Brezhnev, 1969, pp. 10-13).

By the 1970s, the Chinese leadership had articulated an alternative vision of the world that ran counter to Soviet postulates on proletarian internationalism. In April 1974, Deng Xiaoping outlined China's view of international relations, the "theory of three worlds". According to this international relations proceeded from 3 groups of states:- the superpowers (first-world); the West, and East European States and Japan (second world); and developing states (third world, including China). The Soviet leadership blamed China for "deideoloziation" of international relations' and to sponsor a block spearheaded in the first place against the USSR and world socialism". (Ellision, 1982, pp. 309-312).

The ideological rift between Moscow and Beijing formally ended with the restoration of party-to-party ties during the May 1989 Deng-Gorbachev summit. For the Chinese, the turnaround came following the resolution of what Deng Xiaoping called the "three big obstacles" the militarization of northern border, Afghanistan, and Vietnam in the late 1980s. This was followed by Moscow's repeated offers to update China's Soviet built industrial plants of the 1950s and the nuclear power industry. (Nelson, 1993:149-151).

By mid 1980s rethinking began in Moscow as well as in Beijing. The Soviet leadership and analyst began to doubt the wisdom of the 'siege mentality" over defence preparedness and total reliance on military security. It was acutely realized that excessive defence expenditure was draining the resources of the country. This realization along with other factors laid the basis for rethinking in Moscow on its general strategic policy and posture and also relations with China.

In 1980s China had began to demonstrate signs of an opening towards Moscow. The Kremlin responded positively, hoping that an opening to China could weaken the Sino-American axis which had developed during the 1970s. For the first time since Brezhnev had attempted to create a rapprochement in 1964 an improvement in Soviet-China relations seemed possible. The Soviet invasion of Afghanistan, however, had stalled any rapprochement. In January 1980 the Chinese declared that the invasion meant that any negotiation would be inappropriate. (Pipe, 1998, pp. 178-180).

The military buildup along the border damaged the Soviet Union both economically and strategically. The split with China opened a second front in the west's confrontation with the Soviet Union that was exploited by both Beijing and Washington throughout the 1970s and 1980s. China isolated the Soviet Far East by shifting its trading relations. The number of Soviet ground forces in the Far East, and Central Asia had increased between 1965 and 1980s (Anderson, 1997, pp. 9-11). These prevailing conditions forced Gorbachev to normalize relations with China to stop West and US to play 'China card' against it.

In March 1981, Moscow proposed to Chinese a series of measures to build confidence. Although the Chinese rebuffed the proposal, a series of meeting did take place between the officials of the Soviet and Chinese foreign ministries. As the result of those meeting things became clearer that Sino-Soviet relations changed for the better again as the post-Mao leadership concentrated its energy on modernization of the country, an objective that required a more constructive relationship with Soviet Union. By September 1981 Moscow had proposed the resumption of negotiations on the outstanding issues of the border. Soviet initiatives were renewed in March 1982 at Tashkent. Brezhnev announced that the USSR wished to negotiate on issues of border, but dictated clearly that he would not make concession on the situation of Afghanistan. By the early 1980, the Soviet leadership was convinced that Sino-American forces were attempting to encircle USSR. There was every incentive to try to 'break down' the Sino-American rapprochement and reverse the trends of the 1970s. (Anderson 1997, pp. 9-11).

In addition, the Soviet leadership was also influenced by the growing relationship between Washington and Tokyo. Moscow was anxious about the growing industrial and military power of Japan and what appeared to be its inevitable anchorage in an alliance with USA. This development provided a greater degree of urgency to the necessity of certain strategic developments such as on securing of Sea of Okhostk for the deployment of Soviet SLBMs.

When Aradopov died in March 1984 practically all this foreign policy initiatives had ended in failure. There was little progress on the Polish issue; more Soviet troops were in Afghanistan, but with little prospects of victory. In 1978, Deng Ziaoping, the new Chinese leader, introduced a reform programme that called for four modernizations. High priority in the policy was given to economic development Moscow hoped that for a longtime to come, China would concentrate on its domestic reconstruction which would make peace with neighbouring countries a preconditions. It was for instance noted that from 1979 to 1989 PRC was reported to have reduced its deference expenditure by 7 per cent. (Ditmer, 2001, pp-399-401).

*S*oviet foreign policy during the Cold War exhibited considerable variability, notwithstanding the fundamental antagonism between the communist world and the West. East-West relations were at times close to military confrontation and at times cooperative. The arms race was interspersed with arms control agreements. Former friends became enemies and intervention gave way to "new thinking"-in a world during the Soviet period there were multiple forces at play that constantly pushed Moscow in new direction. Donaldson and Nogee found seven general variables that they believe influenced the changing direction of Soviet foreign policy:

1) Change in the structure in the international system from multipolarity to bipolarity;
2) Growth of polycentrism in international communist movement followed by collapse of the movement altogether;
3) The development of military technology that makes possible the total destruction of an adversary;
4) The achievement of military parity between the USSR and USA, followed by collapse of USSR as a superpower;
5) Transition of Soviet regime from a totalitarian system to an authoritarian oligarchy and then to a fragmented polity;
6) The failure of command economy;
7) The differences reflected in the leadership of different personalities, from Stalin to Khrushchev to Brezhnev to Gorbachev.

As we survey Russian foreign policy in making after demise of USSR in the post-Cold War era both Nogee and Donaldson identify five broad underlying factors that collectively explain much of changes and variability in Russian foreign policy:

1) The change in the structure of the international system away from bipolarity;
2) Decline in Russian military capability;
3) Russia's transformation from command economy to market economy;
4) Russia's integration in to the global economy and its increasing reliance on the global market;
5) Russia's political leadership and domestic politics especially as manifested in the struggle between Yeltsin and Russian nationalists, followed by Putin's effort to restore the power of the state and its central control.

The debate over Russian foreign policy in 1990s tended to focus on a single stark polarity - Atlanticism vs Eurasianism. This in turn was a debate over the attitude towards meaning of West and East. In East main actor was China and a rhetoric of a Russo-China "strategic partnership" was an attempt to establish a counterbalance to an increasingly fraught relationship with the West.

Second reason behind tilt to East was due to its "geo-economics". Despite economic crisis in Asian Tiger countries the region stood in stark contrast to Russia's constant struggle to come to terms with modernity and modernization. The chronic underdevelopment of Russian Far East would require investment from Asian countries above all Japan and China as would the effective exploitation of the energy reserves in Sakhalin. (Kuhrt, 2007:2-5).

The third reason is a 'geo-ideological' one in which the East not only represent the spiritual alternative to western modernism but a broader alternative to the West in general. (Sakwa, 2000:175-175).

Development of Relations after Disintegration of USSR

a) Post-1991 Partnership

While the paths of the two countries seemed o have converged in May 1989 at the time of Gorbachev visit to China in the midst of the pro-democracy demonstrations in Tiananmen Square, the domestic choices made both in Beijing and in Moscow after this short lived reconciliation between the two communist giants were 20 poles apart that many observers wondered whether in the post 1989 period, Sino-Russian relations would not be more complicated than Sino-Western relations.

Freshly democratized Yeltsin's Russia faced so many challenges that it saw in China co-operative counter weight to the pressure and lecturing of the west. Isolated Beijing first found in Moscow one of the few remaining capitals agreeing (not allowed) to sell weapons to China, then later a 'strategic partner' ready to join its campaign against the US missile defence programme and prepared to close its eyes to China's infringements on human rights.

The care of Russia is important, as it was the first country, 1996, to try out the for China's new multi-polar foreign policy: the establishment of 'partnership relation' with the major or regional powers. In the following years, a dozen countries and regional organizations concluded partnership agreement with the PRC. For instance in 1997 France and then the US signed 'global partnership or constructive strategic partnership, declarations with China.The concept of partnership is perfectly adopted to the more fluid and flexible political and strategic relations that regional powers are to develop in the post-cold water ear. The ideas and objectives underlining this new concept is that other regional or major powers should establish with China relations that are neither antagonistic or confrontational, nor so close that they might be perceived by the rest of the world as an "alliance" against a third power.

From the beginning of the post-Soviet era, the Sino-Russian partnership has clearly been a 'strategic' one paving the way to the building, with the signing on July 16, 2001 of the new Russo-China bilateral Treaty of Friendship and Co-operation of what can be qualified as a 'privileged partnership': Today Russia has become if not China is only 'only at least its closest 'partner' well ahead of smaller countries friendly to China such as North Korea, Thailand, Iran, Burma, and of course other regional powers such as Brazil and India, not to mention the allies of the US (France, Japan). Immediately after the emergence of Russia as a sovereign republic, there were initial debates about its geopolitical orientations. The debates are reminiscent of the 19th century on the question of Russia's destiny: whether it lay with the west or Russia had a unique destiny. One school of thought called westernizes adhered to Russian ideology that gives priority to "modernizations and cordial relations with Europe. They believed that "enlightened elites could westernize the country, as was the case with Peter the Great.

The Atlantists firmly believed that Russia's transformation required close cooperation with the west. They also saw Atlantic foes as the natural parteners for Russia's entry into the civilized world. Andrei Kozyrev, the first foreign minister, German corporation, the head of the centre for strategic studies and liberal democratic reflections in Duma belonged to this category. They argued that "Strategic partnership with other UNSC permanent members, NATO, G 7 and deep ties with EU are important.

The other school of thought is the great Russians who also based their philosophy on arguments of the 19th century. Russophiles believes that the goal of the state is to lay the foundations of the birth of great Russia. Their thinking was influenced by the Greek Orthodox Christianity which was unique. This made them to conclude that Russia had a different destiny to become a world leader. The property included Alexander Solzhenistin a foreign affair expert, Surgei Baburin, Koustantin Zatlin and vice speaker of Duma Vladimir Shirinovsky. They strummed the Byzantine traditions based on the Orthodox Church which earlier considered Russia as the "Third Rome". (Groom and Light, 1994:17).

The Eurasiansts formed the third school of thought. They based their philosophy on the post-revolutionary emigrant movement developed in the Soviet Union led by Lev Gurmilev. For them Russia's geo-strategic interesting are neither than those of the whole area of CIS. They considered US as the most expansionist and hostile power vis-à-vis Russia. They believed that there was no real conflict of interests with Asian powers; hence Russia should create a block of countries in Eurasia dissatisfied with American dominance. Some Eurasianists suggested that Russia should assume the role of a bridge, connecting Europe and Asia and many insisted that Kremlin concentrate its attention on the East, not the west. The Eurasists argued that Russia's symbol was the two headed eagle and one should look east. Many adherently of this school of thought were connected with, old Soviet institutes devoted to the study of Asian affairs.

At the same time, Sergei Gonchavov, Head of socio-Soviet section at institute of Far East of the Russian Academy of Sciences in and early as 1992 objected Moscow's preoccupation with the West "as developmental model and a business partner and warned Kremlin not to neglect other regions such as China, and the Islamic world, that were of great importance to Russia.

Regarding Asia in general and China in particular, the Foreign Policy concept 1993 document asked for a realistic assessment of the nature of relations with China must consider the differences in ideology and the socio-political system two countries and must also proceed from the principle of no alternative for Russia other than good neighborly intensive and substantial relations with it. In the past cooperation with Peoples Republic of China (PRC) and USSR costed too much to both countries and was one of the main reasons for our alimentation from the region. Moreover, by maintaining all round lies with Beijing, we should also borrow a quite a bit from PRC for implementing our own economic systems.

So, Russia took note of the differences in the Russian and Chinese ideology as Russia adopted capitalism while China remains socialist. Nevertheless the prosperity of trade and profitable commercial ties compelled Russia to opt for a policy of accommodation with C. The foreign policy concept 1993 further elaborated that "on the whole our relations with China must be such that third countries are not tempted to are it against Russia, just as China is not tempted to play the Russian card in its relations with other countries. Russia needs a well planned and circumspect policy, which would give us the opportunity of foreign policy maneuvering in matters where our positions diverge. In sphere of military and technical co-operation we should measure commercial interests against the task of maintaining stability in the region and not permitting the recreation of situation from the cold war times, when the USA armed Taiwan while we armed communist China.

During the initial period after the disintegration of USSR, Russia decided to move away from the third world countries. It was felt that third world countries could not contribute to the economic development of Russia. The debts owed by third world countries to the USSR were very high.

Russia's role in the world affairs during the transitional period was very limited. As in the early 1990s Russia decided to integrate with the Euro-Atlantic spurting. Moreover west did not see Russia as equally and treated her as spent force. The foreign aid did not match expected levels. The former foreign minister of Russia rightly remarked, "In foreign policy we expected that a radical shift away from confrontation in favour of rapprochement with the west would automatically change the west's leadership to Russia and Mobilize concentrated political support and economic aid for us. There unrealistic expectations lift a mark on the first draft of the foreign policy concept of 1993.(Kuhrt,2000:121-138).

The economic crisis of 1998 affected Russia badly and Yeltsin appointed Yevegeny Primakov as prime minister to deal with the crisis. Primakov started cracking down oligarchs which included Yelstin supporters also. This resulted in removal of Primakov and appointed Putin as new prime minister. But before his removal

Primakov gave new orientation to Russian foreign policy by giving priority to the third world. At the time, when India was alimented in the world after conducting five nuclear tests at Pokhran in Rajasthan, Primakov proposed a trilateral alliance between India, Russia and China. On the eve of New Year, Yeltsin resigned and nominating Putin as acting president who has already proved his worth by ruthlessly crushing Chechen rebellion.

b) Russian Policies towards China during Yeltsin Regime

The new Russia's relations with China did not at first look promising. Diplo-matic activity was initially focused on the main economic powers of the West, which appeared to downgrade China as a potential partner: Kozyrev remarked: 'Whether we have a stabilization fund, and whether we enter the world economy depends on the G-7.... With all due respect, China is not a world economic leader for the time being.(SWB,SU/1321 A1/4 5th March,1992).

Nevertheless, one year into Yeltsin,s incumbency, the new state's first summit was held in Beijing, rather than in Tokyo. The Beijing summit laid the founda-tions for a qualitatively new relationship largely devoid of ideological considera-tions and continued Gorbachev's policy of engagement with China. The assertion that it was 'largely by default that China became the chief object of Russian diplomacy in Northeast Asia is not borne out by the evidence. While courting the West and Japan for economic reasons, the diplomatic ball had already started rolling in China's direction as early as December 1991, when Vladimir Lukin (as Chair of the RSFSR parliamentary committee on International Affairs) visited Beijing to show his understanding for 'China's concern that the exit of the USSR would leave the United States as the lone hegemon'(Nguyen,1993:285-301).

The Foreign Ministry of Russia (MID in Russian language) was accused of continuing and even exaggerating its Soviet predecessor's 'Euro-Americocentrism', while 'displaying a tendency to relegate the South and East to a minor position (Goncharov,

1993:102-115). Others pointed to the fact that states such as China, Turkey and India were attempting to integrate into the world economy but 'without losing face and while protecting their own interests', while partnership with the West, and in particular Japan, entailed substantial strategic concessions and playing the role of junior partner.

The reasons for the MID's shunning of China are best described as a combination of lack of expertise (i.e. Kunadze and Kozyrev's backgrounds) and the fact that in these early months Yeltsin had placed too much of the burden of foreign policy making on the shoul-ders of the MID. It was not until the appointment of Pavel Grachev as Defence Minister in May 1992 and the establishment of a presidential Security Council (also in May), that the Foreign Ministry's pre-eminent role in Russian foreign policy began to come under scrutiny. Igor' Rogachev, an old China hand, was made ambassador to Beijing, but in the Kremlin there were few high level champi-ons of rapprochement with China (a notable exception was Evgeni Primakov, head of the SVR, who early on drew attention to the need for a balanced policy in the East). Instead, in the first half of 1992 official policy towards China displayed a breathtaking degree of naiveté and clumsiness. Thus in March 1992 Kozyrev concluded that relations should be based on 'pragmatism', a pragmatism that in his view included developing 'nongovernmental ties with Taiwan at the same level as most other countries without damage to political relations with China, (Buszyinski, 1992:172).

Nevertheless, the Chinese model of reform, in particular the free economic zones, such as the successful example of Shanghai, was championed by some as a model to emulate, in particular in order to revive Russia's ailing Far East; their common border and mutually complementary economies made a perfect 'fit'. Just as Gorbachev had been seeking a 'way to bind the Soviet Union and China on the basis of common developments in domestic politics' so too did Yeltsin

Come to realize that this was the surest way to convince both the Chinese leader-ship and his domestic critics that the pro-

Western policy had been but a lull in the traditional, centuries-old friendship of two neighbours(Buszyinski,1992:172-175). Thus, the director of the Institute of the Far East, Mikhail Titarenko, wrote: 'in Russia as in China the close connection between the internal economic reforms and open foreign policy defines the possibilities for their joint cooperation. (Titarenko, 1995:27-36).

The industrial lobbyist and centrist politician Arkadii Volskii espoused reform: 'Our situation is much closer to the Chinese experience than to the experience of any other country. We should study their experience in conducting land reform, as well as their experience in state support of the private sector with the help of laws, taxation, investments, etc. We should also study the Chinese experience of setting up free-trading economic zones. (Bazhanov,1992:166-167). Conservative elements were keen to point out that the relationship with China 'does not threaten us with the fate of a raw materials appendage to somebody's industrial machine'. Others highlighted the importance of the fact that China had good relations with both the USA and Russia, thus serving as 'a theoretical model of an independent foreign policy for Russia' (Muradian, 1992:39-50).

Hearings on Russian foreign policy held to scrutinize Kozyrev's draft of the 'Foreign Policy concept' addressed the issue of China's place in this 'concept'. Vladimir Lukin advocated a balanced policy: 'Russia's relations with China are of particular importance, and due to their priority these relations must be placed on an equal footing with our European and American orientations. The draft concept allotted priority status to relations with countries of the Asia-Pacific region as well as Southern and Western Asia, because, it argued, these countries were of great significance: for establishing our Eurasian status and in terms of achieving a balance in relations with the West and for diversifying foreign economic activity, and also as countries that, due to their geopolitical position, have a direct influ-ence on the situation in the CIS (Kozyrev, 1992:1-10).

At the beginning of 1990, nearly two years before the collapse of the Soviet Union, Deng Xiaoping asserted: 'Whatever changes take place in the Soviet Union, we should steadily expand relations with it, including political relations on the basis of the five principles of peaceful co-existence and refrain from arguing over ideological differences.' (Kui, 1996:7). Nevertheless, the leadership in Beijing had not bargained for the collapse of the Soviet Union and the ascendancy of Yeltsin's, whose democratic credentials did not find favour with the regime in Beijing. China warned of a possible return to Tsarist imperialism, suspicious that Moscow could switch allegiance to the government on Taiwan, and fearing the overspill into Chinese society of reformist ideas. (Sherman, 2000:166-67).

The Tiananmen experience, when students inspired by Gorbachev demonstrated against the regime, was still fresh in the leadership's mind. In addition, the new Russia's apparent intention to make itself an integral part of the West both politically, economically posed the question of whether Moscow would join in the inter-national condemnation of China's human rights record. At first it seemed China's fears might be realized, as Kozyrev declared Russia's first priority as being 'to ensure all human rights and freedoms in their entirety,I believe that these questions are not an internal matter of states but rather their obliga-tions under the UN Charter, international covenants and conventions.' In any case, by 1993 in Russia 'concern about human rights in the People's Republic of China shrank to the circle of a few government officials and academics'. (SWB, SU/ 1294 C1/2, 3rd Feb.1992).

Once it was clear that Russia's 'flirtation' with the West was over, the Chinese simply restated their original philosophy. Li Peng, in a report to the National People's Congress (NPC) in 1992 spoke of China's 'good-neighbour policy' as 'an important component of China's foreign policy'. The following year, again reporting to the NPC, Li noted that 'friendly relations between China and its neighbouring countries are established on the basis of national interest, regardless of whatever differences there may be between their ideologies and political systems'. (Xuetong, 1995:12) Prior to the 1995 parliamentary elections a Chinese Foreign Ministry spokesman stated that whatever the outcome China would adhere to the current course of 'constructive partnership'(Kuhrt,2007:25-35).

Chinese interests in cooperation with Russia were based on practical as well as strategic issues. Wan Li, the head of the Chinese parliament emphasized that 'China's economic development needs a peaceful international environment. Therefore, China is willing to live on good terms with all other countries.' Essential components of China's security strategy were defence modernization, the establishment of a regional security mechanism, and the development of 'good-neighbour' relations. The friendly relations between China and its neigh-bouring countries are established 'on the basis of national interest, regardless of whatever differences there may be between their ideological and political spheres'. (Xuetong,1995:13). As David Lampton wrote, 'Beijing's foreign policy framework has been stable because it has its origins in China's domestic goals and needs rather than in the international system itself.'(Lampton 1995:63-75).

As we have seen, the issue of human rights did not hold sway over Russian foreign policy for long. The official report on Kozyrev's visit to Beijing in March 1992 emphasized that while the two sides had different understandings of human rights they were 'not inclined to let these differences put a brake on inter-governmental relations'. Accompanying Kozyrev on his trip was the Chairman of the State Committee for Foreign Economic Relations, Petraven, who expressed concern at the fall in trade between the two countries in 1991 in com-parison to 1990. He noted, however, that the volume of decentralized and border trade had increased. An agreement on trade and economics as well as on MFN status for Russia was signed. In May Deputy Prime Minister Aleksander Shokhin made a trip to Beijing for further talks on economic issues. (Gill and Kim, 1995:147).

In August 2002, there was an eight-day visit to Russia by Qin Jiwei, Chinese Defence Minister, to discuss arms cuts in the APR, troop reductions on the joint border and arms sales. While problems on the demilitarization and demarcation of the border remained, the infrastructure for dialogue was being established, an infrastructure noticeably lacking in relations with Japan. At this time the furor over the Kuril islands was reaching crisis point and it seemed less and less likely that Yeltsin's trip to Japan could bring either political or economic benefits. In this context the frequent military contacts between Russia and China and the pressing problem of border demarcation and demilitarization and control and monitoring of cross-border trade, setting up customs posts and so on, entailed contact on an almost daily basis. The military exchanges facilitated the establishment of trust and cooperation, a feature distinctly lacking in Russia's dealings with Japan. During 1992 (not including the December summit meeting) there were at least ten visits exchanged between Russia and China concerning some aspect of military cooperation, whether arms sales, exchange of aircraft personnel, or discussions on nuclear technology. (Kuhrt, 2000:35-45).

Apart from Kozyrev's brief sojourn in Beijing in the early part of the year there had been few meetings in the economic and political sphere – it was the military and the industrialists who were setting the agenda. It was not until November, in meetings to prepare for the summit that wider issues of cooperation began to appear. Importantly, in his meeting with Kozyrev, Chinese Foreign Minister Qian Qichen stressed that China and Russia had common interests in preserving stability in Central Asia and that China's plans to establish economic relations with these states would take into account their close links with Russia. Kozyrev appeared grateful too that Qian understood the need to curb Islamic fundamentalism in Central Asia and the importance of the CIS in this regard. (Xinhua, SWB, SU/1549/ A1/2,27 Nov.1992).

As Yeltsin faced growing criticism from the Supreme Soviet of his and Kozyrev's pro-Western policy, the chance to make political capital out of the forthcoming visit to China, and shortly afterwards India, was tempting. Yeltsin now set about criticizing Kozyrev's ministry, emphasizing the need for a 'multi-vector' foreign policy that would pay equal attention to both East and West. However, the growth in trade turnover with China was unexpectedly high, so that the Foreign Ministry was now able to parry charges that the economic crisis was hampering trade by pointing to the flourishing economic relationship. 1992 saw trade rise to a record high of US$5.8 billion, imports of Chinese goods making up the larger part of this figure. While China's trade with Russia was minimal compared to trade turnover with the United States and Japan, Russia represented an important market for cheap consumer products from the adjacent.(Garver,1998:126).

c) On Taiwan Question

The Russian MID had seriously underestimated the sensitivity of the Taiwan issue for bilateral relations. In January 1992, a delegation from Taiwan visited Moscow, prompting speculation that this might herald a change in the Kremlin's China policy. In an attempt to limit the damage, the Russian MID issued a state-ment insisting that the delegation had been invited privately and not by the government and emphasizing that El'tsin's administration viewed Taiwan as an inalienable part of China.[34] However, this was not the end of the matter. On 9 September 1992 a committee was established to deal with cultural and commer-cial affairs with Taiwan, headed by the industrialist Oleg Lobov. The committee was apparently 'non-governmental', but as Evgenii Bazhanov has pointed out, 'China wanted to know why Yeltsin had created an unofficial committee by decree and why it comprised so many government officials'. (Bazhanev, 2000:177). Yeltsin acted swiftly, and issued a clear statement.

In relations with Taiwan the Russian Federation proceeds from the premise that there is only one China. The PRC government is the only lawful government representing the whole of China. Taiwan is an inalienable part of China. The Russian Federation does not maintain official interstate rela-tions with China. (ITAR-TASS, Sept.19, 1992).

Nevertheless, only two days after Yeltsin's decree Lobov went ahead with the visit, issuing a statement prior to his departure to the effect that maintaining and develop-ing economic and trade relations with the PRC was important, but that the trip to Taiwan would not 'cause any indignation on the part of Beijing'. As one journal- ist noted, Yeltsin's decree closed 'an unfortunate page in our relations, when a semi-official agency for contacts with Taiwan was created under Russian Federation governmental structures without the knowledge of the Ministry of Foreign Affairs and subsequently disbanded'. (SWB, SU/1491/A1/6 Sept.23, 1992).

d) December 1992: First Russia-Chinese Summit

Just before leaving for Beijing Yeltsin noted that some accused his government of 'Americanization, of looking towards the West all the time, that is why we are now making the second break-through into the Asian-Pacific Ocean region after the visit to the Republic of Korea'. Later, at a press conference in the Chinese capital, Yeltsin expressed surprise at the calm reaction to the summit from Tokyo, revealing the extent to which Russia was now viewing this visit as com-pensation for the lack of success in the relationship with Tokyo.(SWB, FE/1567 A1/Dec.18,1992).

Certainly there were many agreements signed at the summit, twenty four to be precise, but none of these were in themselves spectacular. In many cases they simply codified what was already the status quo. However, various subcommittees were established which would hold regular consultations and sustain the level of diplomatic activity: these included an intergovernmental commission on trade–economic and scientific–technical cooperation. The Chinese pressed for the commission to tackle the problems of cross-border trade such as increasing transport capacities and the number of passport controls. These moves were important because they sought to increase government control over spontaneous trading activity, which of course could lose the government important tax and excise revenue. In addition, Shokhin noted the significance of establishing control over the transfer of military technology, as there had been several cases of private individuals attempting to conclude deals on private visits. (SWB, FE/1569 A1/8,21st Dec.1992).

The new course of Russian foreign policy in Asia was re-emphasized on Yeltsin's visit to India at the beginning of 1993 where he stressed that Russo-Chinese rap-prochement did not in any way mean a choice between one or other country: 'Russian–Chinese relations are part of the main channel of our Asian policy. The principle of squeezing some other country out of it is absolutely unacceptable. . . 'Bearing in mind the old animosity between China and India, this statement may well have been intended to calm Indian fears of being downgraded by Moscow in favour of Beijing. However, the deliberate vagueness of the statement could also be interpreted as a sign to Japan that Russia intended to keep its options open in Asia. The final draft of the Foreign Policy Concept further underlined the point: 'Russia's relations with China should be such that third countries will not be tempted to use China against Russia, and vice-versa, that China will not be tempted to use the "Russian card" in its relations with other countries.' (SWB, SU/1770 C2/1, 18th Aug.1993).

High-level exchanges of visits in 1993 were again dominated by senior offi-cials from the military and industrial spheres. Meetings in the political sphere were confined to a meeting between Kunadze and the head of the PRC chan-cellery for political questions, and a brief meeting between Kozyrev and the Chinese ambassador to Moscow. April saw the visit to Russia of the Commander-in-Chief of China's navy and it is likely that at this time negotia-tions were begun on the sale to China of Kilo class submarines. In May the com-mander of the Leningrad Military district visited Beijing to discuss further military cooperation. June saw a further visit of Chinese naval officials to Moscow for talks on the submarine deal, and at the beginning of July Russian naval officials were then invited to Beijing as guests of the Chinese Ministry of Defence. A five-day visit to Russia by Colonel-General Liu Huaqing, vice-chairman of the Central Military Commission, included visits to Vladivostok to inspect the Pacific Fleet and meetings with Shokhin and Chernomyrdin to discuss industrial and scientific cooperation and defence conversion. In August, the Chinese Chief of General Staff of the PLA arrived, moving Grachev todeclare that relations with the PRC were 'one of the priorities of Russia's military policy'. (SWB,SU/1740 A1/2,14 July,1993).

The frenzy of military contacts obscured unresolved issues such as the increase in Chinese pirate attacks on Russian vessels in the East China seas. A Foreign Ministry spokesman noted that Russian offers of talks to discuss the safety of sea-lanes were going unheeded by the Chinese. An increase in illegal Chinese migration to the Russian Far East was also causing tension that required urgent attention.

Thus, while 1994 was again marked by a substantial number of visits by military officials, there was an increase in discussions of political and economic questions, including the question of the border regime. Trade turnover in 1993 was the highest ever, reaching more than $7 billion in total. However, it was clear that a high pro-portion of the turnover consisted of cross-border trade, and the clampdown by Russian authorities on Chinese 'shuttle merchants' meant that 1994 showed a significant downturn in trade turnover, reflecting the sharp fall in imports of Chinese goods. The fact that turnover fell well below the high of 1993 until the year 2000, when it reached just over $8 billion, was evidence of the still primitive nature of Sino-Russian trade. Shokhin was outspoken in his condemnation of Chinese trading methods: 'Without a departure from the barter scheme, which allows a couple of Chinese companies to dictate prices and choice of goods, we shall fail to keep trade with China on a proper level.' (FBIS-SOV-94-104,May 31,1994).

e) Second Summit: from 'Good-neighbourliness' to 'Constructive Partnership'

According to the joint declaration issued at the summit meeting of September 1994, Russo-Chinese relations had now reached the stage of 'constructive partnership, genuinely equal relations of good-neighbourliness, friendship and mutually profitable cooperation, based on the principles of peaceful coexis-tence'. It was emphasized that these relations did not have the character of an alliance and were not 'directed against a third country'. However, the construc-tive partnership could not disguise the fact that trade had fallen drastically from a high of over $7 billion to only $5 billion (the MFEA had projected $8 billion.) This was due mainly to a sharp fall in imports of Chinese goods. The two sides emphasized that economic relations still had 'enormous potential, the effective use of which is capable of playing an important role in the economic development of both countries'. As if to compensate for the miserable state of economic relations, the declaration contained a particularly detailed section on international relations including a clause on the 'inadmissibility of displays of expansionism, hegemonism, the politics of force or the creation of opposing blocs'. (Kuhrt,2000:121-135).

Those who wished to place a positive gloss on the declaration, such as the conservative newspaper *Pravda,* wistfully speculated whether the words 'friendship' and 'constructive partnership' were a 'return to the Russian–Chinese political lexicon from the romantic era of the distant 1950s'. Once again Lukin stressed that the only way to ensure substance and interdepen-dence in the economic relationship was to make Russia and China so dependent on each other that any split would be 'unacceptably painful to both countries'. (At hearings on Russian foreign policy in 1992 Lukin had described this as a relationship of 'irreversible mutual dependence'.) Addressing Chinese business circles in Beijing that year, Viktor Chernomyrdin, noting the drop in trade turnover, had called for 'new forms of interaction', namely investments by the Chinese, joint exploration of Russian natural resources, and construction of infrastructure facilities in the Russian Far East. (FBIS-SOV-94-104, May 31, 1994).

The summit planned for autumn 1995 failed to take place due to Yeltsin's illness, but there were numerous exchanges of visits encompassing all aspects of bilateral relations. No doubt with one eye on the upcoming parliamentary elec-tions, Gennadii Ziuganov, leader of the KPRF, and Grigorii Iavlinskii of Iabloko, both made trips to China before the end of the year. May saw the visit to Beijing of the Defence Minister Grachev, who called for the creation of a multilateral security alliance, a proposal swiftly rebutted by his Chinese hosts, who were no doubt wary of the similarity to Brezhnev's conception of an Asian collective security pact mooted in 1969. Meanwhile border issues were becom-ing pressing: demilitarization was making little progress due to differences over the exact location of the demilitarized zone, while the launch of the Border Guards' campaign, 'Operation Foreigner' the previous year had had further adverse effects on cross-border trade.

Nevertheless, on the occasion of Li Peng's trip to Moscow in June 1995 it was claimed that 'complete political unanimity' existed between the 'two great powers'. Russia reiterated its stance as a staunch supporter of the 'one China' concept, while China endorsed Russia's invasion of Chechnya by stating that it had 'complete understanding of the actions taken by the Russian side to preserve the country's unity'. It was becoming increasingly common for Russian politicians to refer to the two countries as the 'two great powers': as Chernomyrdin and Li Peng declared, 'the two great powers have no need of lectures to run their own lives'. This approach was demonstrated by Russia's refusal to vote in favour of a European Union resolution in the United Nations condemning China's human rights record. The reason given for the vote at the time was that Russia could not disre-gard the explanations of the Chinese that adoption of the resolution would have a 'destabilizing character for the internal situation in China. Finally, the MID briefing noted that 'as distinct from other countries, Russia and China have, over the last three years conducted an open bilateral dialogue on human rights' (SWB, SU /2811/ B/6 8th June, 1995).

f) 1996: from Constructive Partnership' to 'Strategic Co-operation'

Thus in his annual address to the Federal Assembly in February 1996, Yeltsin was able to take comfort in the relationship with China, while warning of geopo-litical changes for Russia linked to NATO expansion. While expressing disquiet at attempts to undermine or directly interfere with 'legitimate Russian interests in the CIS', he referred by way of contrast to the agreement on confidence-building measures around the Sino-Russian border. The 'eastern' orientation of Russian foreign policy was now firmly entrenched, and Yeltsin was to be aided in this by his new Foreign Minister Evgeni Primakov, appointed in January 1996. Primakov was an orientalist and a staunch advocate of a balanced foreign policy: 'A power like Russia, with enormous interests in Asia and the Middle East, cannot walk on just one – "Western leg". (12 October 1998, at www.vladivostoknews.ru).

1996 proved another testing time for Russian foreign policy, as April saw the renewal of the US–Japan alliance in the wake of Chinese military posturing in the Taiwan straits. Russia's relations with Japan were in stasis and following hard on the heels of plans for NATO expansion, the pledge to renew another Cold War alliance seemed a double blow. The third Sino-Russian summit in April 1996 was thus held against this backdrop, in an atmosphere of unprece-dented cordiality, with the two sides declaring their intention to develop rela-tions of an 'equal, trusting partnership aimed at strategic cooperation in the twenty-first century'.

By the time of the fourth summit in April 1997, spurred on by the relatively high trade figures of 1996 – $6.8 billion – both sides now pledged to increase trade turnover by the end of 1997 to at least US$7 billion (the figure reached in 1993), and to $20 billion by the end of the century. However, the decision to conduct trade in convertible currency (from 1996) may have been the reason for the sharp fall in Chinese exports to Russia the following year. The highlight of the 1997 summit was the

'Russo-Chinese Joint Declaration on a Multipolar World and the Formation of a New World Order'. Among other issues, the two sides affirmed their opposition to any attempts by one state to 'strive for hege-mony or conduct politics from a position of force and monopolise international affairs'. Nevertheless, despite the concurrence of views on international issues there were growing signs of strain as the economic relationship struggled to keep pace with the political and military one.

Hopes of reaching the trade turnover of $7 billion by the end of 1997 were dashed, the final total according to Goskomstat amounting to a mere $5.24 billion.[72] Of this figure, only $1.26 billion accounted for Chinese imports, although according to the Primore regional administration's department for foreign trade, undocumented illegal imports accounted for an additional $3.6 billion a year. China's huge trade turnover with Japan of $60 billion, and with the USA of $43 billion in 1997, highlighted the small volume of its trade with Russia. (12 October 1998, at www.vladivostoknews.ru.).

Thus, towards the end of 1997 both sides began criticizing the low level of trade. China was disappointed by the Russians' growing lack of enthusiasm for their often shoddy consumer goods, while Russia was irritated by China's rejection of a Russian bid to supply equipment to the Three Gorges hydroelectric project. In addition, there had been optimism that Russia would be able to earn billions of dollars by building nuclear power plants in China, but due to fears that haggling over prices might mean China would put out the projects to general tender, Russia simply lowered its prices. Viktor Mikhailov, Minister for Atomic Energy, bemoaned this state of affairs, complaining of Beijing's new-found 'cold pragmatism'.

Meanwhile, there were high hopes of the Russo-Japanese 'meeting without neckties' in Krasnoiarsk in December 1997. A closer relationship with Japan would mean that Russia's Asian policy would no longer be 'walking on one Chinese leg', to borrow Primakov's phrase. Whether Japan could offer more than China in economic and political terms was a different matter. It was, in any case, clear that there would be no rejection of China in favour of Japan, for the core of the Sino-Russian relationship could not be reduced to economic relations alone. The disappointing economic relationship was offset by the attention paid to global issues at the following year's summit in November 1998. In particular the joint declaration emphasized the problems that could arise from globalization and interdependence, as well as 'attempts at using currency and financial levers to impose political and economic conditions which infringe upon the legitimate national interests of a particular country.(ITAR-TASS, 23 November 1998, FBIS-SOV-98–327).

Russia and China also signalled their intention to increase efforts to curb ethnic separatism and religious extremism. As we shall see, these concerns were voiced increasingly often as the crisis in Kosovo deepened. The final Sino-Russian summit of Yeltsin's incumbency, just a few weeks before his resignation, was informed by both Kosovo and the second invasion of Chechnya. The Joint Declaration that came out of the 1999 summit made little or no mention of bilateral economic or political issues: with the US announcement of its intention to abrogate the ABM treaty and the events in Kosovo, both Beijing and Moscow were caught off-guard. However, there were signs that Russia and China were becoming increasingly vocal about the US role in international affairs, and the use of force to safeguard human rights (Kosovo). The Declaration specifically pointed to 'attempts to weaken the role of the United Nations' as well as 'the seeking of excuses to give irresponsible interpretations of the substance and principles of the UN Charter and finally, 'the jeopardizing of the sovereignty of independent states using the con-cepts of "human rights are superior to sovereignty" and "humanitarian inter-vention" The two sides drew attention to the development of the Shanghai Five', specifically the meeting of law-enforcement heads and defence ministers, to be held in 2000, as well as the eventual meeting of foreign ministers (in line with the Bishkek Declaration of August 1999). The final section declared their mutual support for the preservation of state unity, sovereignty and territorial integrity.(FBIS-SOV-1999–1210 ,10 December 1999).

The trade in arms would seem at first glance to be one of the few bright spots in the two countries' economic relationship. Kozyrev's sojourn in Beijing in March 1992 was brief, and his remarks on human rights seemed at odds with Moscow's apparent willingness to continue arms transfers, as evidenced by the CIS Chief of Staff Valeri Samsonov, who the previous month had rushed to Beijing to reassure the Chinese that deliveries would not be affected by the USSR's collapse. After Kozyrev and Aven's trips to Beijing, the exchange of visits by Chinese and Russian military officials increased at a startling pace. April saw the visit to Russia of the head of the PLA's General Logistics Department, Zhao Nanqi, to discuss arms purchases while the Deputy Commander of the Russian Air Force travelled to the PRC for an exchange of air force personnel. As Bates and Kim point out, military cooperation consisted of three components: talks on demilitarizing the border, which had begun way back in 1989; the 'institutional-ized military relationship' which had already begun in 1990 with fairly high-level visits; the third component was discussion of technology and weapons transfers. At least ten exchanges of visits took place in 1992 on matters related to defence and military technology, including a visit by Viktor Mikhailov, the Minister for Atomic Energy in November (Gill and Kim,1993:122-135).

After a visit by China's Defence Minister, Egor Gaidar, acting Russian Premier, noted the dynamism of Sino-Russian military and technical ties as evidence that both were now overcoming their previously confrontational relations, which would strengthen their geopo-litical positions in the long term. Domestic factors in both countries were pointing to the wisdom of maintain-ing arms deliveries: since Tiananmen the Chinese had lost American and French supplies. Moreover, when in December 1992 a furor erupted over France's sale of 60 Mirage fighter aircraft to Taipei this must have been an important signal to Moscow that its decision not to sell arms to Taiwan and to draw a veil over human rights issues by continuing, and even upgrading arms sales, was the right way to forge a new relationship with China. Moreover, by 1992 'China's economy was booming and the government, and especially the PLA had money to address some of the PLA's deficiencies'. Hence Yeltsin's statement at the December 1992 summit: 'We proceed from the basis that today China is one of the most solvent countries in the world.' Strangely, Shokhin appeared to con-tradict Yeltsin's confidence in China's solvency: 'It is very difficult to predict the volume of this cooperation in 1993 and its dynamics, because the Chinese side is short of hard currency and the Russians do not want to exchange armaments for jackets and sports shoes.' (*SWB,* FE/1569 A1/8, 21 December 1992).

The biggest single arms deal was the sale to China of 26 Su-27s, a deal con-cluded in 1990 under Gorbachev, although the contract was not agreed until nearly a year later, and the aircraft were not delivered until 1992. A second batch of 22 Su-27s was ordered between 1992 and 1993, but was not delivered until 1995–96, as the delivery was delayed by unresolved issues regarding payment terms: 'Russia insisted that 70 per cent or more of the payment be made in hard currency, compared to 35 per cent for the first batch of Su-27s in 1992.' The new Deputy Defence Minister, Andrei Kokoshin, visited China in October 1992 and helped lay the foundation for transferring production rights to the Chinese. In an interview shortly after his appointment, he had drawn atten-tion to the severe problems facing the defence industry.(*SWB,* SU/1556 A1/1, 6 December 1992).

By the time of the December 1992 summit, arms exports were described by the MID as 'a major lever of the transformation of Russia's economy on the basis of market relations'. At the same time, it was noted that other major arms-exporting countries needed to 'step back and open up more export possibilities for Russia'. In general, there was widespread concern that Russia had 'yielded' its position as a major arms supplier to countries like the United States. This was depicted not only as a financial, but also a serious strategic loss. Viktor Glukhikh, chairman of Gazprom vowed that Russia would never leave the world arms market, declaring Russia's yielding of its former 'positions' as 'abnormal'. According to Glukhikh, in 1989 the USSR led the global market in arms exports, with a share amounting to 38.7 per cent. By January 1993, this had dropped to 17 per cent, while the USA had increased its share of arms exports over the same period from 30 per cent in 1989 to 56 per cent in 1992. (ITAR-TASS, *SWB,* SU/1593 C2/3, 22 January 1993.)

The drive for hard currency earnings to prop up the ailing defence industry led Mikhail Malei, adviser on defence conversion to remark: 'To Russia, the export of military hardware will be profitable even if we sell it cheaper than world prices by a factor of six. According to Sergey Kortunov the principle of 'sell to anybody who pays' was already being given priority in the Gorbachev period.Yeltsin was convinced of the necessity of exporting arms to China, declaring that Russia was 'prepared to trade on all fronts, including in the area of the latest up-to-date weapons'. China's interest in purchasing arms was detailed in a 'secret report' of the Chinese Communist Party's Military Commission, which instructed the government to increase purchases of weapons from the former Soviet Union and increase China's sales to Third World countries. The report noted that this strategy would mean saving valuable currency reserves, adding that the military budget for 1992 had been increased by 40 per cent from the pre-vious year. (SWB, FE/1568 A1/6,19th Dec.1992).

However, there were signs that the Russian foreign policy establishment was not at first entirely happy with the defence industry's drive to sell more weapons to China. In an article published at the beginning of December 1992, Kozyrev warned of the dangers of 'pursuing "easy dollars" from military deliv-eries without taking into account the political consequences'. He concluded optimistically that Russia was 'gradually accustoming Western partners to the thought that they will have to make room in the markets, including the high-technology and arms markets'. Kozyrev made the same point again in Febru-ary 1993 in a speech to the Supreme Soviet, noting the need to monitor 'structures which are independently rushing into the arms markets often without taking proper account of security interests, secrecy or even maintaining adequate prices'(Kozyrev,1993:12-20).

The defence industry plants themselves complained that state weapons orders did not benefit them, as payment was in rubles, so that there were problems paying wages. Bureaucratic procedures in approving mili-tary exports were slow and cumbersome, and required as many as nine different signatures from the relevant ministries, including the Ministry of Security and the SVR, which apparently could take between eight and 15 months to collect. In view of this state of affairs, defence industry directors stated their intention to trade independently in arms produced over and above state orders. (Glebova, 1993:12-21).

The drive to compete with the West increased as Russia came into conflict with theUnited States over arms sales to countries such as Malaysia, Iraq and Cyprus. Thus, Shokhin declared Russia's intention to continue to denounce the 'dishonest competition methods' used by the United States in the world arms markets, quoting US opposition to Malaysia's purchase of MiG-29 fighter planes. (*SWB,* SU/1682 C2/1, 7 May 1993).

Meanwhile, the head of 'Oboroneksport', Sergei Karaoglanov, was accused in 1993 of 'allowing Russia's positions to weaken'. Meeting with the Chinese Chief of General Staff in August that year, Grachev stressed that relations with the PRC were 'one of the priorities of Russia's military policy'. He specifically emphasised the fact that determining China's military–technical requirements would make it possible to 'plan the load on the Russian Federation defence industry and to a certain extent to maintain a number of enterprises in China's interests'.(ITAR-TASS World Service, 17 August, *SWB,* SU/1773 C1/1, 21 August 1993).

The debate over whether defence plants should be allowed to take responsibility for exporting their own products was conducted by a myriad of interested parties. Vice-President Aleksandr Rutskoi accused Kozyrev of actively blocking 'advantageous deals' to sell Su-27s. According to the director of one defence plant, Kozyrev was to blame for losing a major deal with Libya, which subsequently bought instead from the United States, as well as ruining negotiations with Taiwan for the purchase of 150 Su-27s. When Kozyrev coun-tered that the latter deal could not go ahead because the Russian Federation did not recognise Taiwan as a sovereign state, Rutskoi retorted: 'Such considerations are not of great importance for the Americans: they have sold their F-16 aircraft to Taiwan.' Finally, Rutskoi concluded that Russia had lost US$15 billion in failed deals over the previous year, which was 'several times greater than $2.5 billion which the G-7 countries promised to grant Russia during the Tokyo summit' (*SWB,* SU/1774 C2/2, 23 August 1993).

The most controversial aspect of the Russo-Chinese military relationship was the sale to China of a licence for production of Su-27 fighter planes. In April 1996, Yeltsin apparently agreed to transfer a third batch of 18 S-27s and in principle to begin producing the aircraft under licence in China. (Sergounin and Subbotin,2000,:194-216) This brought the total number of aircraft sold to China to 72. According to one Russian analyst however this does not square with the facts – there was no confirmation of a third batch. The same analyst noted too that the sale of the production license was not as big a coup as had been claimed: the licence entitled China to produce 200 aircraft and no more, without the right of re-export to a third country.

In fact, the programme for the production deal was in two stages, the first being local assembly from kits produced in Russia, and the second being full local production with the licence covering production of between 90 and 100 aircraft, but according to Aleksandr Sergounin and Sergey Subbotin, 'most observers say production will probably be half that, beginning at a rate of ten to twenty per year'. (Sergounin and Subbotin, 2000:123-145). In any case, some argued, Russia was moving to a new generation of fighter plane, which it had refused to sell to China. There were those who argued that selling the production licences would mean a loss of hard currency for the defence industry, depriving them of serial production and future revenue. Others, including Yeltsin and Grachev, were sanguine that China would not use these weapons against Russia.

Further deals with China included the sale of four Kilo class submarines, con-cluded in late 1994, two being delivered in 1995 and two in 1997, but estimates of the price paid by the Chinese vary. Bates and Kim cite a figure of $250 million each, but others reckon the price to have been only $90 million per unit, while Germany had apparently sold equivalent submarines for more then $200 million each. It was also not clear what the final number of submarines would be. Western estimates often state that China has purchased higher numbers – one analyst maintained that China was due to purchase an additional 12 submarines by the end of the century (Starr,1996:104).

Further naval equipment was purchased by the Chinese in early 1997; two Sovremenny class destroyers were sold to China, apparently at below market prices. According to an anonymous Russian government source, the Chinese 'groundlessly lower prices and refuse to co-ordinate pricing methods', resulting in the difference between the buyer and seller price for the destroyers adding up to as much as $100 per ship. The substantial decline in Russo-Chinese trade turnover in 1997 was blamed on the slowdown in arms sales (*SWB*, SU/3074 S1/3, 12 November 1997).

As to the strategic implications of these sales, it is certain that the Kilo class submarines and the destroyers will add to China's naval projection capabilities. The submarines are apparently the best of this type in the world, their main advantage consisting in their extraordinarily quiet acoustics, making them extremely difficult to detect. The destroyers, while not the newest type, are a significant purchase due to the fact that they normally carry up to eight 'Moskit' surface-to-surface missiles as their main armament. According to one report the Chinese have requested 24 launchers on each ship. The purchases in the naval sphere have not been large but it should be noted that China has major ship-building capabilities of its own, so much so that one Russian naval officer asserted that despite the small volume of naval technology purchased, China could eventually 'rearm those submarines with cruise missiles and missile torpedoes' of their own design.(Blank,1997:65-98). However, most analysts are in agreement that for China to upgrade from a brown coastal to a blue water navy will take a considerable period of time: 'The Chinese navy will remain until and beyond 2015– an antiquated coastal navy' (Shambaugh, 1997:7-29).

In sum, although Chinese imports of Russian weapons began to decline after 1997, China remained Russia's largest client: thus, in 1991 China's share of Russian arms exports was only 3 per cent, compared to India's 29 per cent, but by 1992 China's share had already shot up to 37 per cent, against India with 35 per cent. However, there were no arms deliveries to China at all in 1994 and in 1995 its share was only 11 per cent, while India's was 21 per cent. 1996 was a bumper year for Russian arms sales to China, a massive 40 per cent of all Russian arms exports.[120] Nevertheless, despite the fact that Russia maintained second place in the world rankings of the 30 major suppliers of conventional weapons, the volume remained small compared to the world's leading supplier, the United States. In 1996 for example, a good year for Russian arms exports, the figure was still only $3.90 billion against $9.26 billion US sales. The aggregate figures for 1993–97 show that the United States sold $53.13 billion dollars worth with Russia trailing behind with $15.25 billion (SIPRI Yearbook,1998:124-130).

In 1998–99 China obtained the licence to manufacture Su-27SK Flanker B aircraft, and discussions began on the licence for Su-30K fighter jets. Russia was still cautious, however, and held back on the Su-30MKI licence, which was obtained by India in late 1999. The mercantilist motives behind Russian arms sales were questioned by Kokoshin in his new capacity as head of the Presidential Security Council, who declared that the choice of countries to which the Russian Federation exports arms should be dictated not by commercial, but rather by national security interests. Despite the large volumes of sales, one should not necessarily assume that Russia was making a significant contribution to China's conventional armory – according to Kon-stantin Makienko, these imports from Russia accounted for only about 1–2 per cent of the overall arms in the Chinese Armed Forces. Moreover, in terms of a threat to the Russian Far East, the types of weapons China was purchasing were strategic rather than tactical, i.e. more suitable for an attack on Taiwan and the South China Seas. Makienko, like many others, believed Russia's nuclear arsenal remains its main deterrent. Nevertheless, the words of one Russian analyst showed that arms exports were still perceived as a reliable instrument of foreign policy: 'Conquering the vast Asia-Pacific armaments markets can be of considerable economic and geopolitical significance to Russia' (Petrovsky, 1997:20-38).

By autumn 1995, it had become clear that the West intended to proceed with the eastward expansion of NATO and there were calls for Russia to respond by finding 'new allies'. In propaganda terms, it was more than ever vital to portray the relationship with China in a positive light. As the China expert Andrei Voskresenskii observed, the MID was pushing the 'soft variant' of friendly relations with China. A wide-ranging consensus emerged that saw the proposed expansion of NATO as a threat to Russian security, and essentially as a betrayal by the West. Lukin, although a moderate centrist, spoke of a possible Russian response that could include the 'formation of a strategic union between Russia and China and other eastern countries (SWB, SU /2811/ B/6 8th June, 1995).

This has been a period of reassertion of Russian foreign policy. Putin showed sign of cooperation with the US and the west during 9/11 after which there was a full scale cooperation in the war on terror. However disagreements arose with the expansion of NATO to eastward i.e. adding former Soviet Union republics to the NATO fold, on ABM treaty and on Iraq war. But Putin not allow the disagreement to grow to a rivalry and accommodated such behavior.

The main objective of this period was to give a predictable and pragmatic look to Russian Foreign Policy. This was evident in the foreign policy concept of 2000, which says, The Russian Federation is pursuing an independent and constructive foreign policy. It is based on consistency and predictability on mutually advantageous pragmatization. This policy is maximally transparent, it taken into account the legitimate interact states and is aimed at seeking joint decisions. Russia is a reliable partner in international relations.

Foreign policy service 2000 is marked by non-confrontationist approach. It took a flexible attitude towards NATO. Rhetoric was replaced by realism during this period. The introduction of new foreign policy concept in July 10, 2000 based on realistic assessment of the world situations was the first step. The concept itself acknowledges that, "A successful foreign policy of Russia on Federation must be based on maintaining observance of a reasonable balance between its objectives and possibilities of attaining these objectives. Concentration of politico-diplomatic military, economic, financial and other means on resolving foreign political tasks must be commensurate with their real significance for Russia's national interests, while the scope of participation in international affairs must be adequate to the actual contribution to strengthening the countries positions.

In his New Year speech of 2001, Putin emphasized acquisition of new friends and the regaining old ones as priority, "we can now say today that we choose the direction of our advance correctly and calculated our strength correctly also. Our achievement includes political and economic stability, economic growth, and prosperity for the people, strengthened statehood, law and order. They also include an open foreign policy, the acquisition of new friends and the regaining the old ones". He acknowledged that Russian Far East is rich in natural resources, but it is scarcely populated and underdeveloped. Involvement of China and Japan can contribute to the development of the region. The Russo-Chinese partnership has allowed the almost complete resolution of old disputes such as the border disputes, an increase in bilateral trade (US $ 8 billion in 2000 and $ 10 billion in 2001 set against $ 1 billion in 1990), in particular in arms sales of China, (over $ 4 billion in 2001) and the development of a few regional joint projects (People's Daily, 5th January, 2002, P-7). The establishment in 1995 of 'Sanghai Five' a group of countries comprising China, Russia and three central Asian Republics (Kazakhstan, Kyrgyzstan and Tajikistan) aimed at enhancing the economic development, stability and security of this region (the group is now known as 'Sanghai Cooperation Organization' following the admission of Uzbekistan in 2001). Even before September 11, the major goal of the group had moved from the establishment of confidence building measures (reduction of troops along borders) to the common fight against separatism, expansion and terrorism.

At first summit between Putin and Jiang Zemin in Beijing (18 July 2001), the two leaders signed a joint declaration and statement on ABM (Anti-Ballistic missiles) that criticized the US plan to develop NMD) system, strongly denouncing it as Washington's desire to seek unilateral military and security advantages. The US was warned of the most grave adverse consequences of it proceeded with the plan and that any damage to ABM treaty until triggers a new arms race. The incorporation of Taiwan into any foreign TMD (Theater Missile Defence) system was also declared as 'unacceptable' by both chiefs of state, while Russia stated that it faithfully' adhered to 'one China policy of Chinese communist party. The treaty concluded in Moscow a year later refigured their ideas and also incorporated a common wish to see the emergence of a multi-polar world.

In December 1991, the Soviet Union disintegrated into 15 independent republics and Russia succeeded it as a permanent member of the UN Security council. Russo-China relations thus face a new test. Would the two countries maintain normal relations regardless of their different social system and ideologies, or would their relations deteriorate even to a state of hostility? This was not only concern to the two neighbouring countries but also to many others, especially the US, Japan and other Northern East Asian and European nations. Fortunately, the leaders of both China and Russia handled the transition in the relationship carefully and skillfully.

On 27 December 1991, Chinese Foreign Minister Qian Qichen sent letters to new republics, including Russia, informing them that China recognized their independence and was preparing to establish diplomatic relations with them. Two days later, the Chinese and Russian deputy foreign ministers signed a protocol expressing the mutual desire to develop a "goodneighbourly" friendly relationship on the basis of the Five Principles of peaceful coexistence or Panchasheel (i.e., mutual respect for sovereignty and territorial integrity; mutual non aggression, non-interference in each-other's internal affair, equality and mutual benefits; and peaceful co-existence), and China expressed its support for Russia as successor of State to the USSR in the UN. Thus two nations made a first key step towards the normalization of their relations (Ditmer, 2001, pp- 399-401).

Since then the Sino-Russian relations have developed in a smooth and healthy direction. There have been three stages in the development of relationship:

1. In December 1992 Russian President Yeltsin visited China and met Chinese President Yang Shang Kin. This was the first summit meeting between Russia and China. The two singed a joint statement on the foundation of mutual relations, stipulating that they would establish a good neighbourly relationship on the basis of five principles of peaceful coexistence. The document set the tone of friendships and cooperation. They signed a further 24 agreements on cooperation in various field. (Donaldson & Nogee, 1948, p. 96)
2. In September 1994, Chinese President Jiang Zemin visited Russia for a summit meet with Yeltsin. This produced a second joint statement deepening the bilateral relationship as a "constructive partnership oriented towards the 21st Century", and a statement affirming the two countries commitment to no use of nuclear weapons and not to target nuclear armed missiles against each other. The two leaders also signed an agreement delineating the 55 km. western sector of Russo-China border. This second summit could be termed as stage of 'constructive partnership'. In May 1995 Jiang Zemin visited Russia to attend the 50th ceremony commemorating victory in World War II. During his visit Russia confirmed its support

for 'one China principle' and its opposition to Taiwan joining the UN; (Donaldson & Nogee, 1999, p. 96)

3. In April 1996 the third Russo-China summit meeting was held in Beijing. Jiang and Yeltsin signed a new joint statement proclaiming the forging of a 'strategic partnership of equality and trust oriented towards the 21st century'. The Chinese Leadership supported Russian position against eastward expansion of NATO. On 26 April, 1997 the heads of state of China, Kazakhstan, Kyrgyzstan, Russia and Tajikistan met in Shanghai and signed an agreement on the confidence building in the border area. Since then, Russo-Chinese relations, developed beyond a bilateral relationship, with greater cooperation in the international arena. This indicates that the relationship This indicates that the relationship has a stage of strategic partnership. (Qimao, 1999, pp. 288-290)

Russian leaders in the initial days of post-Soviet period entertained hopes of becoming a part of the Western world and bring about a systematic change from the communist political and economic system to western type liberal democracy and market economic with the help of Western political support and large scale economic and technological assistance. The then Russian foreign minister Andrei Kozyrev who was staunch supporter of "Pro-West approach" and followed Atlanticist foreign policy in the hope of Russia's political and economic integration into the West. In his talk with German foreign minister Heinrich Geuschev in January, 1992 Andrei Kozyrev called for the establishment of a 'single security space from Vancouver to Vladivostok'. The threat of eastward orientation of NATO was still not on the horizon and Moscow at this time had a benign and favourable view of the west. Kozyrev was fond of saying that democracies do not wage wars and he was keen that Russia joined the "civilized democracies" (Bakshi, 2004, pp. 24-26).

As regards the USA in particular, it was even hoped that partnership between two nuclear powers the USA and Russia - would provide strategic stability to the post-cold war world. Such a policy would be exact opposite of their global rivalry and deterrence of mutual annihilation during the Soviet era. The

Russian Ambassador to the USA called for 'special kind' of relations between the USA and Russia. Andrei Kozyrev said in February 1992 that the Russian US interaction could become one 'decisive factor in international security today". Lt. General Vladimir Manrikov proposed a "grand US-Russian geopolitical partnership." (Bakshi, 2004, pp. 27).

Thus, in the initial Russian order of priorities China was given a place behind the USA, Western Europe, Japan and Republic of Korea. The Russian foreign ministry even asserted that China was only of secondary importance in the Russia's foreign policy. Pro-Western proponents defended the idea of strong ideological, economic and even military alliance with the West. Former Russian Prime Minister Yegor Gaidar for example, recommended "cementing a military alliance with the West and switching our deterrence potential to the Far East. (Bakshi, 2004, pp. 27-28).

Honeymoon with the West ended very soon and disenchantment and differences started surfacing. Russia had expected and called for the unfolding of a new "Marshall Aid Plan" by the western countries in its aid. The failure of the reforms, also led to the growth of anti-Western sentiment in the country. While in the initial period of the westerners or the Atlanticists led by the foreign minister Andrei Kozyrev and his foreign policy establishment were more assertive, now the 'geopolitics' the 'Eurasists, the 'nationalists', and advocates of great power status for Russia became more assertive and began to criticize pro- Western policy of Kozyrev as the policy of "yes" and making one sided concessions to the west (Bakshi. 2004. pp. 28-29).

Following the dissolution of parliament in autumn of 1993 and the election of new bicameral parliament and adoption of new constitution in December 1993, a more workable relationship has developed between the parliament and presidency. The relationship has shifted from being strictly confrontational to one that includes more compromise and consensus building. As a consequence the foreign minister Andrei Kozyrev was forced to modify his pro- Western stance. One is able to recognize this shift in policy orientation in several areas. First, formal statements by the foreign minister Kozyrev were by then less cooperative in nature towards the west than was previously the case. Second, Russia stressed its role as a major factor in the world and asserted its position on such issues as the Balkan conflict. Finally there was a renewed emphasis placed on relations with the "Near Abroad" (Kavet & Kzhemiatin, 1997, p. 195).

There were shifts in emphasis and priorities, but no sharp turns in the policy. Moscow was neither in the position, nor willing to confront the West in the old Soviet style. But Russia began to pay greater attention to its neighbours in Asia. Ties with great Asian countries India and China - were consolidated through Presidential visits in January 1993 and December 1992 respectively. These visits were projected as imparting a greater balance to Russian foreign policy between the West and East.

As Yeltsin stated at a press conference on December 18, 1992 in Beijing "We want balanced relations in Europe and Asia alike". Similarly Chinese were feeling increasingly isolated in the world as tensions grew with great Britain over Hong Kong, and the USA and France concluded arms deals with Taiwan. For this reason, the Chinese leaders shelved their political differences with the Yeltsin Govt. and welcomed the opportunity to enhance cooperation with Russia. (Wishnick, 2001, p. 123).

In 1995, despite continued controversy on border trade and growing opposition in the border regions to any territorial concessions to Beijing as a part of the border demarcation process, high level meeting between Russia and China addressed many issues. Kozyrey's trip to Beijing in March led the groundwork for the year's bilateral contracts, including Li Peng's visit to Moscow to mark the 50th anniversary of the end of World War II', and the third Sino-Russian summit held in Beijing in 1995. In another sign of the continuing progress in Russo-China bilateral relations, President Jaing Zemin represented China at May 1995 ceremonies in Moscow marking the 50th anniversary of the victory against Nazi Germany.

It is broadly agreed that relationship between Russia and China in the post-cold war period can be classified into three stages. The period from 1992-94 is regarded as one of "Good Neighbourliness, the second phase from 1994-1996 as one of "constructive partnership" and third phase from 1996 onwards is regarded as one of "strategic partnership" directed towards 21st century. (Wishnick, 2001, pp. 124-125).

In 1997 "Joint declarations on a multipolar world and the formation of new world order", by then Russian President Boris Yeltsin and his Chinese counterpart Jiang Zemin announced their commitment to develop a 'partnership for the purpose of strategic interaction in the 21st century.' The statement was widely seen not only as a challenge to American "hegemonism" but also a confirmation of the qualitatively new relationship that had emerged between Moscow and Beijing after the end of the Cold War" (Sherman, 2000, p-10).

Moscow and Beijing also share many security interest and threat perceptions, from an attachment to geopolitical concepts such as spheres of influence and balance of power for international security agenda. Beijing has publicly backed Moscow on issue of handling Chechen conflict, while Russia reciprocated Chinese efforts to suppress separations in Xinjiang and supported 'one China' policy towards Taiwan. Both have a major stake in ensuring peace and stability in the Korean peninsula.

Both Russia and China have also developed a strategic relationship directed towards 21st century in the post-cold war era. At the summit which took place on April 24-26, 1996 both Yeltsin and Jiang affirmed that two countries "were entering into a new stage of partnership, based on equality and trust." Given continued attempt by certain states to apply pressure and engage in block politics, by cooperating in matters of strategy Russia and China would be able to work towards a multipolar world. During this summit meeting, it became apparent that Russia and China saw their bilateral relationship as a way of relieving perceived pressures from the West. Thus Chinese side expressed its understanding for the Russian position on NATO expansion, while Yeltsin affirmed Russia's support for the People's Republic of China's position on Taiwan. (Wishnick, 2001, pp. 128-130).

In Central Asia both Russia and China have their claims for energy security and in this region the interest of both countries seems to be on odds. After the disintegration of USSR, China acquired three new neighbours - Kazakhstan Kyrgyzstan and Tajikistan. Trade between Central Asia and China has been low with many of the same problems afflicting Russo-China regional trade. Like the Russian. Far East, Kazakhstan and Kyrgyzstan have also complained about unscrupulous Chinese traders and illegal migrants streaming across their borders. The governments of Kazakhstan and Kyrgyzstan, for example were vocal in their protests against Chinese nuclear testing, which took place near their border at Lop Nor in China's Xinjiang province. In May 1996 Xinjiang complained that Kazakhstan had shipped radioactive scrap metal to the region (Xing, 1996, pp. 58-60).

Beijing have some significant stakes in the Central Asian region. First, Central Asia neighbours the troubled Xinjiang Uighur Autonomous Region (XUAR), where a segment of Uighur Muslim population is striving for independence which is posing grave threat to Peoples Republic of China. Secondly, China is today a energy hungry country and a net importer of oil and wants access to Central Asia's vast petroleum resources. Thirdly, China's manufacturing sector is on the boom and need the market to sell its finished products, Central Asia is the ideal place for this purpose (Xing, 1996, pp. 58-62).

In 1994 Kazakhstan and Kyrgyzstan were among four Central Asian states to join NATO's Partnership for Peace programme and in beginning of 1997, a series of military exercises have been taken place in Kazakhstan. Chinese analysts have paid close atten1ion to growing military ties between Central Asian states and NATO, especially in the aftermath of the Kosovo crisis in the spring of 1999.

Due to their history of relation with Moscow and their geographic position at the crossroads of Europe, Asia and the

Middle East, the Central Asian states have tried to maximize their freedom to maneuver. Nazerbayev has called the "preservation of independence" the most important aim for Kazakhstan. While president Akaev of Kyrgyzstan has outlined a "Silk Road diplomacy" fostering relations with East and the West alike. As these leaders develop their own approaches to foreign, policy, differing from perspective in both Beijing and Moscow, Russian and China face an increasingly complex strategic environment in Central Asia (Xing, 1996, pp. 58-64).

The most serious potential flashpoints in relations between China and Central Asia, however, concerns ethnic relations. Central Asia and Xinxiang are linked by overlapping ethnic populations more than one million Kazakhs and 375,000 Kyrgyz live in Xinxiang, while 262000 Uighurs live in Kazakhstan and Kyrgyzstan. Another potential source of friction concerns the possibility of Russo-China rivalry for influence in Central Asia. For example in 1995 Nazarbaev signed in accord with China granting Kazakhstan the right to use China's pacific port at Liangyugang in Jiangsu Province. The agreement improved Kazakhstan's access to trading in Pacific rim by shorting the distance to Pacific it is only 3500km from Kazakhstan to Liangyugang less than half the distance needed to reach Russian Far East ports (Harris, 1993, pp. 112-115).

In the field of military cooperation China emerged as the Russia's most promising client in the 1990s. In fact, from 1992-94 China purchased 97 per cent of its weapons from Russia. In 1992 China spent $ 1.8 billion on Russian weapons, including 26 SU-27 fighter aircraft. The SU-27s were supposed to be the first installment of a total purchase of 72 planes. China also purchased missile - guidance and rocket technology, rocket engines and surface to air missiles including SS-300 air defence missile system, similar to Patriot. (Hallooway and Bicker, 1997, p. 20)

The show down between China and the USA's Seventh Fleet in the Taiwan Strait in March 1996 demonstrated to the Chinese the importance of modernizing their sea power. According to military analysts this motivated the Chinese to purchase of two Soveremenyi class destroyers equipped with advanced missiles including Sunburn ship-to-ship missiles, SA-N-17 surface to air missiles, and SS-N-22 cruise missiles. In addition, China had contracted for four advanced kilo class submarines. To improve rapid reaction capability China has purchased 14 IL-47 transport aircrafts. In August 1999, Russia agreed to sell China forty to sixty of the Su-30 MKK fighters for $2 billion. Chinese officials had expressed their interests in this top of the line aircraft ever since India purchased similar planes (SU 30 MKI) in 1997. In 2000 Russia provided the Chinese with several dozen SU-27 UBK fighters at a price tag of $1 billion in partial payment of Soviet debt to China (FBIS, Nov. 20, 2000, p. 20).

To conclude, the first half of 1990s, the improvement of relationship with China gave substance to Yeltsin's attempt to reorient Russian foreign policy away from a pro-Westerns focus and appealed to all political spectrums. Moreover Russian hostility to NATO expansion gave new impetus to rhetoric supporting a Russo-China partnership as counterbalance. Despite changes in the strategic environment leading to close cooperation between Russia and China in the short-term lagging Sino-Russian economic relations, the growing potential for Russo-China competition in Central Asia and continuing distrust of China in the Russia's border regions all sets for a more fluid Russo-China relationship in the new millennium.

Russia and China share common view on many national and international issues such as, joint fight against terrorism, opposition to the US led unilateralism and supporting multilateralism just international world order, strengthening the UNO; non-interference in the internal matters etc. Both countries are the permanent members of the UNSC. All these and many more political issues of divergence and convergence interests have been discussed in the next chapter.

2

Political Relations between Russia and China

By the early 1980s, leaders in Soviet Union realized that friendly relations with China was key that would help it to reduce its military expenditure and exploit its vast Far Eastern resources. Relationship between Russia and China took a new turn with appointment of Gorbachev as General Secretary of CPSU in 1985. Gorbachev had begun the process of over hauling the Soviet foreign policy immediately after he took over the leadership of the country. His new thinking in international relations certainly sought to add some new dimensions to the framework of Soviet foreign policy by novel ideas and concepts. However, its aim appealed to be mid course correction and adjustment rather than replacement of the traditional framework of Soviet foreign policy. By his new thinking, Gorbachev wanted to update it, and in this process, he put Soviet foreign policy on a new course (Imam, 1991, pp. 156-157).

As a consequence of new thinking in international relations, Soviet policy in Asia had logically moved to acquire a new look during the second half of eighties. It marked the activation of Soviet policy in Asia Pacific region. Improvement of relations with China was included in Gorbachev's speech to Central Committee on March 1985, who wanted to establish a rejuvenated socialist grouping on the basis of new type of Soviet-Chinese relationship. The creation of new socialist community, in which, due respect towards other viewpoints could be assured was one of Gorbachev's initial aims. The Soviet Union also sought China's cooperation against US military strategy in the Asia Pacific region in the name of socialist grouping (Imam, 1991, 56-57).

Gorbachev who took a major initiative towards improving relations with China, declaired in his famous Vladivostok speech on 28 July 1986:

> The USSR is prepared, at any time and at any level, to discuss with China the question of additional measures for creating an atmosphere of good neighborliness. We hope that the border dividing (I would prefer to say linking) us will become a line of peace and friendship in near future ... we do not want to view Amur river as a 'water obstacle: let the basin of this mighty river unite the efforts of Chinese and Soviet people in using for mutual benefit - the rich resources available there and for building water management projects. An intergovernmental agreement on this account is being jointly worked out and the official border might run along the main shipping channel. (FBIS-Sov-. July 29, 1986, p. 20)

Thus, the sign of improvement in the Soviet-China relation was clearly visible after Gorbachev took the charge as General Secretary of CPSU in 1985. Later Boris Yeltsin first president of newly independent Russia indicated inclination to further strengthen the relationship with China. Russia under the leadership of Boris Yeltsin reaffirmed its commitment to all the positive achievements of Russo-China relations. Russia further pledged to continue implementation of obligations of the treaties and agreements signed by Soviet Union and China in May 1989 and May 1991. On 15 September 1992 President Yeltsin signed the "order of Russian Federation's relations with China" and reaffirmed that:

a) there is only one China;
b) the PRC government is the sole legal representative of China;
c) Taiwan is the part of China; and
d) Russia will never establish official relation with Taiwan.(Chufrin, 1999, pp. 292-96).

Russia and China shared views on increasing numbers of international issues in the light of the challenge from the USA and its allies. In the first year after the collapse of Soviet Union, Russia adopted a pro-western foreign policy, hoping for economic aid from the west and for recognition as a strong power and an equal partner of the USA. Soon, however, Russia was deeply disappointed by the level of western aid. Moreover, it faced fierce competition from the west over the sphere of influence in the newly independent states. These realities forced Russia to switch to an 'omni-directional' or 'two headed eagle' (Russia's national emblem) policy, pursuing relations with countries of both the East and the West. Especially after 1995, under heavy pressure from NATO's eastward expansion led by the USA, Russia attached greater importance to its relations with China, India and other Asian countries. Russia termed Asian countries as 'natural allies', among which China got the top priority. Despite odd relationship in the past both countries evolved consensus on various national and international issues.

Areas of Common Concern

On the question of separatism, religious extremism and terrorism both countries share common view today. In March 1995, Chinese president Jiang Zemin visited Moscow to participate in the celebration of 50th anniversary of victory over Fascism. In an agreement between the two, Russia reiterated its support to China on Taiwan issue and on its part, China extended its full support to Russia in dealing with the Chechnya problem. (Chufrin 1999, pp. 292-296).

Both Russia and China are opposed to US hegemonic policies and favour a multi-polar world order with different power centres. In April 1997 Chinese president Zemin paid another visit to Moscow on April 23 and the two countries issued a joint statement on the multipolarisation of the world and establishment of new international order. The statement rejected hegemony and power politics, and stated that 'Cold War' mentality must also be abandoned and bloc politics opposed. They called for preservation of the Anti Ballistic Missile (ABM) Treaty of 1972 between Soviet Union and USA and they supported lifting the UN Security Council sanctions against Saddam Hussain regime in Iraq.

On 24 November 1998, when Jiang Zemin paid another crucial visit to Russia, the Russian side reaffirmed its "four nos" position. The basic thrust of which was - no support for any conception of 'Taiwan's independence; no acceptance of the position of 'two Chinas' or 'one China and one Taiwan'; no support for Taiwan's participation in the UNO or other international organizations in which only sovereign states participated; and no sales of weapon to Taiwan (Jingjie, p. 528).

NATO bombing on Yugoslavia from March end to mid June 1999 without getting any authorization from the UN Security Council sent shock waves in both Russia and China and tended to bring together the two in joint opposition of NATO action. NATO's intervention on 'humanitarian ground' was an ominous development. Being multi-ethnic and multi-religious states, both Russia and China have their own separatist movements, Russia in Chechnya and China in Taiwan, Tibet and Xinjiang province. Being a Slav country, Yugoslavia was traditionally friend of Russia and attack on it, aroused Russian sentiments in the form of massive protests in Moscow (Saiget, 2000:11-18).

a) NATO Eastward Expansion

With the end of cold war, Warsaw Pact ceased to exist. However its western counterpart, North Atlantic Treaty Organization (NATO) kept on expanding and adopted a new strategic concept in 1999, which permits out of area operations.

Thus, NATO forces entered in Asian territory for the first time in Afghanistan in 2001 during US lead war on terrorism. Both Russia and China are concerned about the unilateral actions of NATO by passing UNSC. Further it has started inducting erstwhile USSR republics like Poland and Czech Republic thus coming very close to the Russian borders.

NATO works on the principle of collective security under which attack against one member is considered as attack against all. The way NATO forces attacked Yugoslavia, Iraq has raised apprehensions in the minds of Russian and Chinese strategists.

Russia and China apposed the expansion plan of NATO and the US plan of unilaterally withdrawing from Anti-Ballistic Treaty of 1972. NATO bombing on Yugoslavia in 1999 without UN approval and adoption of a new strategic concept permitting out of area operations were apposed by Russia and China, which brought their convergence of interests further. Russia felt that a number of states are stepping up efforts to weaken Russia politically, economically, militarily and other ways.

Both Russia and China felt that they are under western pressure. Russia apposed of NATOs eastward expansion (without prior constrainty on further expansion and with consideration of explicit inclusion of the Baltic States). Western pressures on Chechnya issue and more generally because of perceived broader US design on former Soviet republics, including central Asia and the Caspian Sea region. Whereas China is experiencing pressure on the human rights issue and feel threatened by the US arms sale to Taiwan and more generally, an East Asian security policy which moves towards greater role of Japan in balancing China.

The NATO bombardment on Yugoslavia was the most glaring violation of international laws by the US led forces. With the war in Yugoslavia (before which the world had witnessed three US bombardment of sovereign states-Afghanistan, Iraq and Sudan), it appeared once more that the world was left with one single super power, the European powers being unable to act as an independent actors.

With the NATOs bombing campaign against Yugoslavia, the conviction grew that US was now overemphasizing the use of force. This experience Moscow watched an alliance that westerners had traditionally characterized as purely defensive, made into a domestic conflict, China watched a US B-2 bomber reduce its embassy to the Yugoslav Capital to rubble.

Russia and China also felt the need to maintain their strategic autonomy and independence vis-à-vis the west that has financial resources. China is determined to define its four modernization model "based on socialism with Chinese characteristics" and perceives the US use of human rights and democracy as excuses to interfere in China's internal affairs to permanent instability. China treats Taiwan as its internal part and seeks to bring about Taiwan's return at the earliest possible date, while Washington is perceived as trying its level best to prevent this move. The strengthening of Japan-US alliance established during the cold war period is perceived as anti-Chinese as well as the US willingness to develop a regional anti-ballistic missile system.

Similar contradiction exists between Russia and US where the US is perceived as doing its best to hinder Russia's integration with the other CIS countries in order to prevent the restoration of a Russian empire, whereas Russia favours establishing an all European security system which each country of Europe participates equally. US favours a system dominated by a US led NATO. Finally the US is perceived as trying to upset the existing nuclear balance formed by itself and the USSR during cold war, through missile defence system.

However, there are some specificities as well as a certain degree of ambiguity in the relationship of each of the two countries with the US. This ambiguity is largely due to the degree of mutual economic dependence between China, Russia and USA. As already said that good relations with the sole superpower are beneficial for all but both Russia and China can generate the same interest from Washington whose attitudes and policies are determining factors.

The US policy vis-à-vis China during the Bush and Clinton administration and so far, despite initial tension even the Bush administration for example has been neither punchy of engagement, nor of containment but constrained elements of both. On engagement side, it has been sucking normal trade relations by granting China most favoured nation for trade relation facilitating Chinese entry in WTO, allowing Chinese companies to operate in the US and reducing the number of goods and technologies covered by export control.

Politically, both Clinton and Bush administrations have tried to bring China into various multilateral regimes, whether on arms controls, weapons of mass destruction etc. while militarily, they enhanced military to military contacts, thus trying to avoid conflicts with China but promoting its participation in regional organizations such as ASEAN Regional Forum. The two countries are bound together through extensive commercial ties.

Sino-Russian strategic cooperation culminated in the increasing close condition of their response to the NATO attacks against Yugoslavia in the spring of 1999. In the protest against air strikes, Primakov, who had been on the way to Washington on March 25, the day the bombing began, ordered his plane to turn back to Moscow. From the very beginning of Kosovo war, Russia and China had the similar view that UNO should be respected and not substituted by NATO. However, China became more furious after NATO mistakenly bombed Chinese embassy resulting in three deaths and numerous injuries. Washington regretted the incident and agreed to compensate Beijing with $28 million for the destruction. (Wishnick, 2001, pp. 146-150).

The problem of the NATO enlargement that Russia faced in full complexity in the middle of the 1990s posed a serious challenge to the Russian foreign policy thinking and practice. Moscow faced the necessity to find a new role as an actor of world politics after the "cold war", to draw the distinction between its real and imaginary foreign policy capabilities, to re-consider the motivation and political values of the key players of the international system. This process was taking place in the context of violent domestic struggle, with the variety of ideologically biased perceptions of the world scene. Given such conditions, the practical recommendations of various political factions were contradicting to each other.

With the heat of discussions on the NATO enlargement becoming higher, the proponents of the "the China card" became more and more active. In the opinion of the pro-China pundits, this "card" was the "irresistible" anti-NATO measure of Russia. With different nuances in understanding, in general, the notion of the "China card" was perceived as the close military and strategic ties with Beijing, close to, or even "beyond" the distinction line of the military alliance. Such sentiments in Moscow grew stronger since 1996 as the result of the two groups of factors. First of them was directly related to the new Minister of Foreign Affairs of Russia E. Primakov. He was known as the tough negotiator, with the "centrist approach" in understanding and upholding of national interests of Russia, having personal experience in "oriental" countries. The second group of factors was related to the positive by that time dynamics of the Russian-Chinese relations, which created the perception - adequate or imaginary - about the big future of ties between Russia and China. Many analysts viewed considerably big volume of Russia's arms sales to China, progress in settling the territorial problem, progress in achieving the military detente between Moscow and Beijing as the grounds for such optimism. The results of the Russian-Chinese summits, with the formulas of "confidential strategic partnership, facing the 21st century" were fueling such optimism.

One can distinguish three basic trends in Russian political science in analyzing the foreign policy problems of Russia in general, and relations between Russia and China in particular.

1. "Leftist" or "propatriotic".
2. "Rightist" or "pro-western"
3. "Centrist" The essence of political and intellectual disagreements among these three trends ascends to different systems of political-ideological beliefs, to different understanding of the basic problems and contradictions of the modern international relations. In compliance with this, the political analysts differently understand the balance of power in the modern world, disagree on the question: who are the basic international allies and contenders of Russia.

At the level of practical policy, the key moment, in which the proponents of the different views disagree, is the orientation of Russia either towards the US or towards China.

The "leftist" analysts view the modern international relations through the concept of the contradictions of the "poor" and "rich" states of the world, as the demonstration of aspiration of NATO, led by the US, to fix and to cement their victory in the cold war. Those analysts view NATO and the US as trying to transform the international relations in order to guarantee their prevailing and dominant role and to control natural, financial and human resources of other world. According to the "leftist" views, China, as the growing Asian power, which has not abandoned the communist ideology, is the only country capable to constrain "hegemonist" ambitions of the US. Hence, China is perceived as the obvious ally of Russia, and their "confidential strategic partnership" is recommended as the long-term Russia's policy, aimed to limit the domination of the Western powers in the world (Yakovlev, 1997: 136-137).

The apologetic, noncritical approach to China's domestic political reality, to the practice and results of Chinese economic reforms, questionable comparisons of political and economic transformations in Russia and China, are the characteristics of this trend.

The policy recommendations of the proponents of the "leftist" trend are based on strong anti-American sentiments. They stress the symptoms of growing domination of the USA and NATO in the world, that was clearly visible during the Kosovo events. These analysts argue for broad military cooperation with China for the sake of curbing the "hegemonism" of the US and NATO. They give recommendations of the similar type to the Russian policy in other directions - in Asia, in relation with Japan, on the Korean peninsular.

Accessing the reality of the modern world, political analysts, belonging to the second – "rightist" or "pro-western" – trend, are building their recommendations on the other hand at disputable premise. According to this premise, both global and regional foreign policy interests of Russia could be most successfully realized in close cooperation with the United States. The publications of this trend being pretty visible in Russian media three–four years ago are very rare now.

The alarmist attitude to China's policy, both foreign and domestic, strong criticism of Chinese authoritarianism, focusing on the traditional issues of the Western media – human rights, Tibet – are the characteristics of this approach. Consequently, the authors of this trend are critical to the long-term strategic partnership of Russia with China. They consider close military ties and the arms sales to China as detrimental to the Russian interests in Asia (Chudoduv, 1998: 15).

The analysts of the "centrist" trend in the similar negative way -though not in such strong formulations, as the "leftists" - assess an offensive pressure of the US in building the monopolar world. The centrists also pay the due tribute to successes of the Chinese modernization and point out the obvious parallelism of foreign policy interests of China and Russia. This parallelism, in their opinion, stems from the fact, that both populous societies are now being in the process of large-scale pro-market reforms. Notwithstanding the obvious difference of starting conditions, strategy and tactics of socio-economic transformations, Russia and China share the same future in the sense, that both are transforming itself into market societies with the "nonwestern" structure of ideological, social and political values. Facing the competitive pressure of the outside market world, China and Russia are inevitably bound to interact with each other, including the cooperation in security sphere. (Chudoduv, 1998: 20-32).

At the same time, the "centrists" do not exclude the probability, that in the process of increasing of its economic power, the military and geopolitical ambitions of China will grow too. These ambitions could be visible not only in the southern and southeast geopolitical direction – where as the basic financial, transport and economic flows to China are coming from now - but also in the northern direction, in the direction of Russia. Taking into account the demographic problem in China, geopolitical projection of densely populated northeast provinces of China on the poorly managed and deserted territories of Russia's Siberia region and the Far East, weakened connections of these regions with the central part of Russia, the "centrists" are sober in seeing the obvious risks of development of the Russian-Chinese relations in the mid-term and long-term future.

The "centrists" argue that in parallel with development of comprehensive economic and limited military-political cooperation with China, Russia should fix a line of "soft restraint" of China. Russia's strategy, both regional and global, according to the "centrists", should avoid excessive pro-Chinese tilt.

Some Russian analysts, belonging to the centrist trend, believe that the interests of Russia in the long-term perspective would be mostly favored, if being related to the "US-centered" security structure in Asia Pacific. It is necessary for Russia to be insured from a quite probable aggravation of the geopolitical contradictions with China in the future and to have an opportunity to counterbalance this threat. (Bogaturov, 1997: 44)

b) Dynamics of the Russia-China Security Dialogue in 1996-1998.

Political and security relations between Russia and China has been steadily progressing from 1992 - the actual starting point of Russian independent diplomacy. The main stimuli of this progress were the relevant similarity of the phases of pro-market social and economic reforming of the two countries, shared security interests and the benefits of close economic cooperation. However, till 1996 China was, obviously, a supplementary, than dominant foreign policy priority for Russia. The inadequate understanding of the Russian status and interests in the post-cold war international relations together with ideologically biased domestic motivations resulted in obviously "pro-western" orientation of Moscow's diplomacy. This diplomacy was closely associated to the name of Russia's then Foreign Minister Andrei Kozyrev.

Primakov's coming to the Foreign Ministry, was the result of the growing frictions that Russia was experiencing in its relations with the West as well as the obvious evolution of the Russian political elite from the "anti-communist" towards more "centrist" values. Increasing importance of China in Russia's foreign policy became the benchmark of Moscow's new course.

In 1996, China and Russia reached an agreement to arrange summit talks on the regular basis: once a year on the level of Presidents and twice a year on the level of Premiers. The same year the "hotline" telephone channel between two Presidents was arranged to demonstrate the growing need for policy coordination. Noteworthy that the Chinese Premier Li Peng was the first foreign visitor that was, received by Yeltsin in December 1996 after the Russian President started his second term and recovered from illness.(Blank, 1997:121-134).

Almost simultaneously the contacts of the Russian and Chinese Defense Ministers have been intensified. These contacts now were arranged on the regular basis. Such meetings were mainly focused on the demilitarization and confidence building measures on the border, the growing arms transfers and security situation in Asia Pacific.

The exchanges between the Head of the Parliaments, as well as the key economic, financial and "power" ministries (internal affairs, intelligence, border guards troops, etc.) took place in 1996-1997. Many bilateral agreements were signed during this period, thus laying the legal basis for cooperation in different spheres. These were the agreements on peaceful use of nuclear energy and nuclear security, energy, intellectual property rights, antitrust legislation, space research, foreign currency control, control of the quality of exported goods. (Rakhmanin, 1999: 166-173).

The third Russian-Chinese summit (since 1992) - the first one after Primakov held the office of the Foreign Ministry - took place in April 1996. This summit was held in the situation of the growing strain of bilateral relations of both Russia and China with the United States.

In Russia's case this deterioration was caused by the evolution in the issue of NATO expansion. Moscow considered this evolution as jeopardizing its previous accords with the US. At the US Russian summit in October 1995 in New York, President Clinton and Yeltsin reportedly agreed that Russian cooperation in Bosnia with the NATO forces would delay NATO enlargement decisions. However in January 1996 the US Congress passed Public Law 104-107 endorsing the principle of NATO enlargement, though not identifying candidates and deadlines for admission. Reacting to these developments, Russia demonstrated the growing toughness in Moscow's approach. In February 29 Primakov declared: "We are not against speedy NATO expansion, we are against expansion" (Salmon, 1998: 156).

In China's case, the deterioration of relations with the US were related to the growing tension at the Taiwan strait and the chronic frictions between Beijing and Washington on Tibet and the human rights issues. These difficulties were exacerbated by the visible internal struggle in Beijing on the eve of Deng's passing away. The imperatives of this struggle was orienting Jiang Zeming, as Deng's successor to firmness and "ideological purity" in his relations with the West.

This Russian-Chinese summit of 1996 took place shortly after the G-7 meeting in Vancouver with Russia's participation in this meeting as an associated guest. For the first time in Russian-Chinese official dialogue, Moscow claimed for mutual firm stand against "one dominating power" – code word for the United States. The inclination of the both parties to start the new phase of "equal and confidential partnership aimed at the strategic cooperation in the 21st century" – the expression initiated by President Yeltsin - was included in the Joint Declaration of this summit. However the direct naming of any states as the sources of domination was avoided in the text of the Declaration. The NATO expansion issue was also omitted from the text of the Declaration, but was mentioned in the final Communiqué. "China understands Russia's position aimed against the expanding of NATO eastward", Communiqué said. At the same time Russia confirmed its solidarity with the Chinese stand on Tibet and Taiwan problem (Solomon, 1998: 156-158).

Agreement on the confidence building measures (CBM-1) among China, Russia, Kazakhstan, Kyrgyzstan and Tajikistan - the one that was signed by the leaders of the five states in Shanghai - was another practical result of the 1996 summit. However, at that time these five states failed to agree on the key item of negotiations - on the reduction of troops and armaments in the regions along the borderline of the former Soviet Union with China. In 1996, this reduction was being negotiated already for six years. Moscow and Beijing hasn't reached the compromise on the limits for deployment of the troops in the border areas. (Blank,1997:123-134).

At this summit the Chinese side confirmed its decision to join the Treaty on Complete Banning of the Nuclear Tests (CBNT) till the end of 1996. Russian President B.Yeltsin acted as a broker in this issue between China and the West after he suggested to take this role during the G-7 meeting in Vancouver. China – the only nuclear state that abstained from the Treaty at that moment - kept his promise to Russia and the world community.

The next summit meeting between Russia and China took place in the April 1997 in Moscow. The deepening of the contradictions between Russia and NATO - notwithstanding the formally compromising the Russia-NATO Founding Act, prepared for signing in May – formed the background for the new summit on the Russian side. The Chinese position was strongly influenced by the death of Deng Xiaoping in February 1997. His successor Jiang Zemin entered the critical period of consolidation of power. His diplomacy towards Russia was considered domestically as one of the strong points of his leadership and statecraft. The new wave of hostilities on the Taiwan Strait made the Chinese-American relations even tenser.

Given this background, it was not a surprise that the Russians during this summit were more actively and rather successfully exploiting the "anti-hegemonist" sentiments of Moscow and Beijing. The military and security component of their relations has become more vivid.

The central document of the 1997 summit was the "Declaration on the Multipolar World and the Formatting of the New International Order". This document stressed that nobody should seek hegemony, pursue the policy based on force and trying to monopolize the international relations. Both sides showed their firm support of the UN; they stressed that nobody should curb the authority of the UN Security Council UNSC, including the rights of the UNSC Constant Members for veto.(SWB, SU/2811 B/6,January 8,1997).

Notwithstanding the agreed text its noteworthy, how differently both leaders assessed the signing of the Declaration. B.Yeltsin praised the document highly, saying that "for the first time in thirty years Russia and China make a joint assessment of the world affairs...We have not signed the similar document with anyone else" (Solomon 1998: 157).

Jiang Zemin was more cautious in his comments. Speaking at the State Duma, he only stressed the "necessity to establish the relations of confidential partnership in different spheres as the basis of the strategic cooperation in the 21st century." He hasn't made the slightest reference to NATO in his public speeches in Moscow, though he is reported to criticize the NATO expansion behind the closed doors.

The Chinese leader probably was closer to reality in assessing the practical importance of this Declaration than its Russian counterparts. This document couldn't be even compared to the Russian-Chinese Treaty on Friendship, Alliance and Mutual Assistance signed at 1950. However the Declaration manifested the visible intention of both parties to transform the "equal partnership" in their relations to the model of "strategic partnership" in the 21st century.

During this summit of 1997 the multilateral agreement among China, Russia, Kazakhstan, Kyrgyzstan and Tajikistan 'On Confidence Building in the military field in the Border Area' (CBM-2) was eventually reached. The agreement set the limits for ground troops, air force and air defense planes in the 100 km zone on the both sides of the border line between the former USSR and China. Notwithstanding the fact that the specifications of the agreement were kept close to public, Russian analysts were discussing it and they were not unanimous in their comments.

The analysts of the pro-western orientation argued that this agreement is weakening Russia's military posture at the Far East since Russian ground troops should be reduced on the greater scale than the Chinese ground troops. The main bulk of the Chinese ground forces deployed on the Chinese-Russian border, were deployed beyond the 100-km zone, in the depth of the Chinese territory.

The analysts of the "leftist" orientation were not sharing this view. According to CBM-2 agreement, they argue, strategic missiles, air defense missiles, long range air force and fleet were not scheduled for reduction. Therefore, the overall military balance between Russia and China at the Far East remained favorable to the Russians.

The evolution of the negotiations on the CBM-2 agreement shows that Russia, evidently, paid the higher price for it, than the Chinese. The breakthrough in the negotiations that was being held for more than 7 years was done only in December 1996 during Li Peng's visit to Moscow. Russia's effort to speed up the process and gain this important security commitment from China was evidently related to the mounting pressure that Moscow was facing from NATO. On September the 6th 1996, the US Secretary of State W.Christopher stated at Stutgart, that a 1997 NATO summit "should" invite "several" partners to begin accession negotiations. Later this year on October 22, President Clinton proposed 1999 as a deadline for admitting the first group of new NATO members (SWB, SU/1753 B/1,October 24,1999).

In parallel with development of security dialogue the settlement of territorial problems between Russia and China was equally important element of detente.

Given the complexity of territorial delineation between Russia and China starting from the end of the 21st century, China was always reluctant to acknowledge the full legitimacy of Russia's rights for vast territories of Siberia and Far East Region. The scale of this claims has reached its peak during Sino-Soviet rift, especially in the mid-sixties, when the Chinese side actually claimed territories up to 1.5 million square kilometers. Border negotiations, started in 1964, and being held for nearly three decades, were fruitless during the period of confrontation.

Only at the Gorbachev era, in the situation of political detente between two countries, the breakthroughs at the border negotiations became possible. At 1991 and 1994 Moscow and Beijing signed two border agreements fixing the border line on the two main parts of the Russian-Chinese border: eastern part, from Korea to Mongolia (4200 km) and western part (55 km).

However almost all the governors in the Russian Far East (governors of Primorski and Khabarovski krai, Amurskaya and Chitinskaya oblast) have expressed their dissatisfaction with the agreements. They argue that these agreements were not reflecting the interests of their regions and making too many concessions to the Chinese side. The process of demarcation of the border according to the Agreements of 1991 and 1994 was slowed down and partially blocked by the regional authorities' regulations.

Only after 1996, due to the effort of the central government, the demarcation process was resumed. For the first time in bilateral history the territorial belonging of a plenty of islands on the frontier rivers was defined. 1163 islands were defined to belong to Russia, 1281 - to China. Besides that, Russia and China still have two sites, negotiation on which was postponed "up to the future generations". One of them is located in the region of Khabarovsk, another - on the river Argun. At the present moment the status quo is kept: the disputed islands remain with Russia (Godwin,1998:171-193).

On November 1998 Presidents Yeltsin and Jiang Zemin stated during their first informal meeting that the demarcation process on the border according to the Agreements of 1991 and 1994 is completed. At the press conference Yeltsin stated that the border problem between Russia and China is "solved forever".

In the process of evolution of the Russian-Chinese relations in the 1990-s the policy-makers were facing the necessity to formulate Russian interests in the various spheres of these relations. One of these spheres appeared to be the most delicate and controversial - arms sales to China. Realizing this necessity, we would like to set up our vision of the Russian interests in this issue.

c) Arms Sales to China: Motives and Risks

The negotiations on the arms sales to China have started as early as 1990 under Gorbachev government. Arms sales, the concrete parameters of military cooperation between any countries, for obvious reasons, are confidential topics. The details of the arms purchases for the several past years - types of weapons, and amount - are little-known to the public. Inevitably, there are distortions and "phantom" fears in Russian and world press, relating to the deals, that the military and political leaders has really made behind the closed doors. China's military modernization requires substantial improvements in its air force, command control and communications, naval power projection, and space technology capabilities. Russia has accommodated or appears willing to accommodate China in all these areas. It has sold China a range of electronics, air-to-air and surface to air missiles and air defense systems, armored fighting vehicles and T-72 tanks, and SU-27 fighters (including the license to manufacture this aircraft, provided in 1996). China is reported to place the orders for several "Kilo" class submarines. There are also reports that China is trying to acquire other types of advanced technology, such as the TU-22m bomber ("Backfire") cruise missile technology, missile guidance and satellite systems, and nuclear weapons related technology. (Pierre & Trerrain 1997: 19-20).

The arms sales between the two are the sign of the certain trust between them, especially if they are close neighbors. Russia has obvious grounds for such trustful reasoning, taking into consideration the visible rapprochement between the two countries during the last decade and the absence of any serious contradictions at the present moment. Such situation is stemming from close interdependence of security interests of Russia and China. Maintaining, as the minimum, the nonconfrontational atmosphere on the demilitarized border and, as the maximum, the high level of economic interdependence and the goodneighborly ties along more than 4200 km-long Russian-Chinese border – is the sign of political wisdom for any government, whether it be in Moscow or in Beijing. (Godwin,1998:171-193).

Speaking about Russia, without the stable and deep partnership relations with China, including partnership in the military area, it is impossible to guarantee necessary stability on Russia's eastern borders. This is especially true in the situation of mounting pressure on her western borders and direct contiguity of the NATO borders to Russia as the result of the enlargement of the block.

Without decent relations with China it is impossible to solve such a critical problem for Russia as reverting the backwardness and preventing the centrifugal tendencies of the regions of Siberia and Russian Far East.

However, it is necessary to distinguish several possible levels or stages of military interaction:

1) Arms trade;
2) Military cooperation;
3) Political-military partnership;
4) Military alliance. Speaking about the Russian-Chinese military ties, we believe, that only the first stage of such interaction (arms sales) with some elements of the second stage (military cooperation) could be favoring Russia's interest at present.

The logic – both strategic and commercial – suggests that at observance of the certain obvious criteria – rational limits, proper bureaucratic control (done both within the related governmental agencies and on the inter-agency level) control on the part of the legislative branch (with strict observance of the state secrets) such cooperation with China is reasonable. The selective and portioned arms export to China is undoubtedly favorable to Russia and does not jeopardize the interests of her security.

Firstly, the technological superiority of the Russian army in comparison with the PLA creates a situation, in which delivery of separate types of the Russian weapon, in particular, fighters, antiaircraft missile systems, submarines – at the scale that are taking place now, could not undermine this superiority.

Secondly, most part of the world arms market now is being controlled by the West. China - one of the few segments of this market, that is accessible by Russia.

Thirdly, the Chinese orders are very profitable for Russian defense industry. Many Russian plants are standing idle because of the ill rationalized policy of conversion. At the same time the market price of one Russian fighter varies between $ 30-50 million.

At last, fourthly, any deliveries of high technology arms and, furthermore,–licensing of its production, leads to the certain "binding" of the exporting country to the importer. This can be useful in the context of long-term development of the Russian-Chinese relations (Paramonov and Strokov, 2007:3).

However the rational limits - how many, what type of weapon and on what conditions to sell to China - remain the main problem. The optimum choices could be made while analyzing the three sets of criteria – related to military, commercial and foreign policy. This is the only possible way to arrive to the decision, that is dictated not by the corporate motives but by long-term interests of Russian security.

In the military sense, the decision-makers, should, at minimum, know the answers on the following set of questions:

- How big is the qualitative, technological gap between Russian and Chinese military capabilities, especially, with relation to the types of weapon, that Russia delivers to China; how this gap changes after the acquisition of the Russian arms;

- What is the evolution of the military balance between Russia and China at the frontier zone, in particular as a result of the CBM agreements of 1996 and 1997;
- To what extent the obvious advantages of Russia in firepower and offensive weapon are being compensated by the superiority of the Chinese army in manpower, by quantitative superiority in the certain types of armaments (in particular, in military aircraft), in the situation of remoteness of the Russian Far East theater from the core part of Russia and vulnerability of the long stretched line of the Russian communications.

Also Russia should be sure that its arms deliveries to China will not violate the general military balance between China and its regional neighbors, including Japan, otherwise leading to the new wave of arms race at the Asia Pacific and striking with a boomerang on Russia. Similarly important to take into account the opinion of Russia's CIS partners - Kazakhstan, Kyrgyzstan and Tajikistan, other Central Asian countries, whose interests are indirectly involved in the Russian arms sales to China.

Speaking about commercial issues, the competent marketing of the Russian military technology, reasonable price policy, optimum schemes of payments are necessary. Last but not least, in view of uniqueness and high profitability of the arms deals, Russia needs strict control over Chinese re-export of Russian-made Russian-licensed weapon. The Russian public and legislative branch has all the rights to be informed, who, how legitimately and how competently is dealing with the export of such delicate production to such a delicate buyer. The corruption and shadow lobbying in this matter can bring unprecedented damage to Russia's security interests (Kuhrt, 2007:121-145).

The foreign policy problems, related to export of arms to China, can be even more difficult, than military and commercial considerations. It's difficult to forecast medium and long-term international consequences of Russian arms sales to China.

Among risk factors in this sense – the uncertainty of political future of China. This uncertainty stems from two main reasons.

First of them relates to the character of the political regime of China. Due to the weakness of the representative power and the dominance of the military high command, the role of the individual leader or the narrow group of leaders in China's foreign and domestic policy is extremely high. The process of formulation, coordination and implementation of China's foreign policy is not well institutionalized. It is not grounded upon wide social base.

The other source of instability - complexity of a present stage of economic reforms related to conversion of the large state-owned enterprises. The problems of the huge manpower surplus, economic frictions between center and the provinces, uneven development of the rich maritime provinces and considerably poor internal regions remain to be serious.(Kuhrt,2007:235-243).

Taking into account this knot of political and economic problems, one cannot exclude the possibility of the crisis of a present regime in China. If such crisis occur, drastic shifts of the basic vectors of China's military strategy and foreign policy are highly probable.

The development of military cooperation between Russia and China, undoubtedly, relate to the relations of Russia with the USA and the West as a whole. Russia being unilaterally oriented on increasing of its arms sales to China, is facing the risk of eventual confrontation with the United States, Japan, Taiwan, South Korea and the ASEAN countries, which are feeling anxious about Chinese military might. It is also a foreign policy risk factor, which Russia should take into consideration while developing military ties with China.

It is noteworthy, that the USA, having an extensive foreign market for US-made weapon, has never delivered this weapon to the states even hypothetically capable to pose a threat to the US. On this background, Russia's policy is contrasting. The key buyer of Russia's military production is the state that both, historically and potentially, could not be excluded from the list of Russia's military competitors.

To be fair, it is necessary to note, that presently known volumes of contracted deliveries of the American weapon, for example, to Taiwan essentially surpass present Russian sales to China. (Jacks, 1997: 132). In this sense it is unfair, to blame Russia as a state that is destabilizing the military balance in Northeast Asia.

But, first, Taiwan at any circumstances can not pose danger directly to the U.S. Secondly, it is necessary to take into account psychological anxiety with which Washington perceives the current trends of the Russian-Chinese ties. China is considered by the US as its basic global competitor in the next century. The fears concerning the Russian fighter aircraft at the Chinese airfields raise the probability of inadequate reaction of the US on the Russian-Chinese arms deals.

There is a reasonable question: should the psychological complexes of the US be considered as the factor limiting Russia's military deliveries to China? The answer, to this, we believe, should be "yes", but qualified "yes". This qualification pertains to the argument, that the fact that matters is not the ephemeral and unsteady "psychological complexes" of the third side (i.e. US) but quite firm and pragmatic reasoning of Russian interest. (SWB,SU/1472,A1/1 August 29,1992).

This reasoning should be based on her solid national priorities - socially balanced pro-market reform, openness to the external world, constructive co-operation both with the West, and with the East, including to the East the non-Chinese part it too.(Japan, Korea, ASEAN). The one-sided bias in Russia's military-commercial policy, exceeding the rational limits of arms sales to China could damage and even ruin all these priorities.

Thus, we are not speaking about the extremist and, as a matter of fact, a "deadlock" scenario, sometimes offered by Russian analysts. In this script the present sale of the weapon is considered as an intermediate phase towards to closer political-military partnership or even to military alliance with China. This is considered to be a "strong" Russian counterplay against the West.

(Jenks 1997: 137). Such scenario is an obvious foreign policy trap for Russia, leading to the new global confrontation and, besides that, the confrontation on the "etnical-civilizational" basis.

It is not necessary to idealize the West and to neglect its contradictions with Russia on many points, that resulted, first of all, in NATO enlargement, in crisis around Kosovo, in the US policy within the the CIS. It is necessary to bargain with the West and to press back Russian interests everywhere, where it is possible. Nevertheless, in conditions of present deteriorating relations with the West after Kosovo, Russia should use positive foreign policy experience of China itself. During recent two decades China, on the one side, managed to cooperate rather efficiently with the USA ,within the framework of the "open door" policy, and, on the other side, to keep independence and evenhandedness of its external strategy, thus being not overwhelmed by the nationalist ambitions and confrontational mentality. (Anderson,1997:121-133).

d) China's Approach to the NATO Expansion: Compatibility with the Russian Interests.

Up to the middle1980s Europe and NATO was the peripheral sphere of China's foreign policy interests. China was not linked to Europe neither through its own security interests, nor through active trade and large investments. The volume of China's trade with the countries of EU in mid 1980-s did not exceed 15 % of China's total trade. Consequently, China's approaches to the military balance and the problems of security of this region were bearing the imprint of "secondary" priorities: Beijing was viewing Europe only as a sphere of rivalry between China's key competitors - USSR and USA - and was interested in Europe only from the point of view how the balance of power between Moscow and Washington was changing.

Approximately since the first half of the 1990s China's approach to the European realities started to change, China's European diplomacy became more active and "nuanced". This evolution was stimulated by the obvious globalization of foreign policy interests of China, the rapid growth of its external economic activity as the outcome of the successful course of economic reforms inside the country. The drastic reshuffle of the entire system of international relations was the other incentive for such change: with the dissolving of the Soviet Union the status of China, as the potential contender to the United States has raised considerably.

Almost simultaneously, with the news on NATO enlargement became public, the negative attitude of China to this process became explicit. The NATO enlargement was unequivocally assessed by Beijing as strengthening of the American control over Europe. The alternative scenario, leading to the "Europesation" of NATO, strengthening of Europe as the independent center of power, was considered in China as less probable. The main argument of the Chinese analysts, supporting this view, was that only US was capable to provide the overwhelming security to the European allies and to face any military challenges, including those coming from Russia. Only Washington, they argued, is capable to carry the basic financial and technological burden of admitting the new member-states to NATO. (Rearming of the new members, standardization of military arms equipment, reorganization of the structure of management). According to Beijing's view, such developments in Europe actually would block the tendency to global "multipolarity", that is more beneficial to Chinese interests than the monopolar international system under the control of the US. (ITAR-TASS, and SWB, SU/1707 A1/5, June 5, 1999).

To add to this strongest anxiety, the Chinese were also concerned, that the US could extrapolate the European mode of behavior to the Asia Pacific. While the European members of NATO consider the fear of Russia and destabilization of this country as the basic reason for the block's enlargement, China was afraid of being treated in the same capacity as Russia in Asia, by Beijing's regional neighbors–Japan, Korea and the ASEAN member-states. The Chinese were not excluding the developing of its relations with the regional neighbors according to the worst possible scenario: deteriorating of Beijing's security and economical relations with Washington and consolidating the latter's strategic and political links with Japan and Korea for the purposes of containment of China.

Therefore China was seriously anxious about the "new guidelines" on military cooperation between Tokyo and Washington, that was signed in the autumn of 1997 on the basis of the existing US-Japanese Security Treaty. The new arrangements, which in 1999 were approved by the Japanese parliament, actually provide the further enlargement of the military role of Tokyo in vaguely defined "surrounding zone" of the northeast part of the Pacific ocean, that was considered to be the "zone of responsibility" of Japan (ITAR-TASS Oct 14, 1999).

One more factor relating to the NATO enlargement and to the strengthening of the American influence in this block, also irritated the Chinese. The NATO enlargement was posing the additional political obstacles to Chinese penetration to the trade markets of Europe. Such prospects were even more painful for China, given the permanent trade frictions with the US, difficulties of China's admission to the WTO and deteriorated situation of the global trade market as the result of the world financial crisis of 1997. Under these negative circumstances, expanding trade with the countries of EU would be rather desirable compensating factor for China. Its notable that, starting from 1992, the volume of trade of the EU countries with the Asian countries of Asia Pacific has exceeded volume of trade of the Europeans with the USA ($ 249 and $ 206 bn.) And the volume of direct investments of the countries of the EU in Asia Pacific has reached the level of the US investments in the region. The volume of trade of the majority of the countries of the Asia Pacific now in comparable parts are distributed on three equally important parts - trade with the US, with Europe and within the Asia Pacific region (John, 1998: 27).

One more quite probable consequence of NATO enlargement that could have a far-reaching negative impact on China. With consolidation of this block under the leading military role of the

USA, Beijing practically loses hope for the alternative to Russia donors of modern weapons. Previously, under certain circumstances, China could have expected to acquire considerably sophisticated weapon, for example from Czech Republic or Poland or even, possibly, France. Under current tendency of the growing of the US role in NATO, and facing the high probability of developing of the Chinese-American relations according to the worst – "deteriorating" scenario (that has proved to be true recently) - such prospects for China actually disappear. The outcome of this - becoming the "hostage" of Russia in delivery of modern arms, with all the inevitable political linkages, is very unfavorable to Beijing.

At last, one more essential motive of China's negative perception of the NATO enlargement. The situation when the military structure of NATO will eventually move close to the borders of Russia, (especially if the Baltic states are, eventually, admitted), will inevitably stimulate Moscow's effort for the utmost political-military consolidation of the CIS countries under Russia's leading role. Notwithstanding all the obstacles for such consolidation, Moscow still possesses a set of political-military levers to invigorate this process. To name first, the threats from Islamic fundamentalism to the southern states of CIS (Tajikistan, Uzbekistan), "detonating" role of Russian community in Kazakhstan, ethnic conflicts inside the Transcaucasian states (Azerbaijan, Armenia) are giving such levers to Moscow's hands. (Ziegler,1999:537-543).

China has little interest in consolidation of the CIS under Moscow leadership. The more friable and unconsolidated CIS will be, the less problems for Chinese security in the future. Besides, China itself is willing to penetrate into the economic space of the CIS, especially in Kazakhstan and some Central Asian states. Beijing is very interested in raw, and energy resources of these countries, while facing the necessity to expand the resource base of its actively growing economy. Thus, it is possible to see the whole array of negative consequences that China is facing as the result of the NATO enlargement.

These were the reasons that caused growing solidarity of Beijing with Moscow during the summits of the 1996-1997. It reached its peak in first half of 1997, when the clauses about "understanding" of the Moscow's concerns of NATO enlargement began to appear in the text of joint statements.

At the same time it was clear, that the approach of China and Russia to the NATO enlargement, though obviously parallel in many principal characteristics, was not identical or coinciding. More than that, many facets of Russia's behavior towards NATO, especially in 1997- 1998, in the period before events in Kosovo, was viewed with suspicion by the Chinese counterparts.

For Russia the most important problem is the growing proximity of the military infrastructure of NATO to its borders, the dramatic decreasing of "buffer" geopolitical space between Russia and the West. For China, to whom this infrastructure directly does not threaten, the main problem is the development of cooperation and interaction between Russia and the Western alliance. In opinion of China's analysts, if this cooperation will be unfairly close and leading to Moscow's loosing its independence in military planning and security strategy, the Chinese interests will be seriously damaged.(SWB,SU/3077 B/ 10,November 1997).

From the very beginning of the bargaining process between Russia and NATO on the problem of enlargement, Beijing was watching very attentively the evolution of negotiations, being mainly focused on evaluation of the tendencies "of struggle and cooperation" between Moscow and NATO.

The signing of the Russia–NATO Founding Act in May 1997 was met in Beijing with obvious coolness. Judging by the tone of the some Chinese published commentaries, it was possible to make conclusion, that Beijing was mainly disappointed by a complaisance of Moscow, which has signed the Founding Act on such unfavorable terms. Official Chinese press was pretty ambivalent in assessing the Founding Act. On the one hand, it was stressing the historic importance of this agreement, comparing it with the Versailles and Yalta Treaties and noting, that Russia and NATO opened the "critically new phase" in bilateral ties. On the other hand, Chinese official media pointedly stressed the fact that Russia failed to sign the really effective and legally solid document with NATO. Thus, it was argued, the Founding Act could not prevent the serious contradictions and frictions of the partners in the future. "Time alone could evaluate the political effectiveness of this Document" - was the dominating tune of the official comments (China Daily, 28 May, 1997).

Many Chinese political analysts shared the evaluation of the Founding Act as the amorphous document, unable to prevent the future pressure of NATO on Moscow's vital military interests. According to the view of the expert from the Chinese Institute of Modern International Relations Feng Yujun, this pressure will be especially detrimental for Moscow in three basic directions:

1. In the problems of the intra- European security, where the Joint Committee of Russia–NATO doomed to only decorative, and not a meaningful role.
2. In the problems within CIS, where Russia will most probably be separated from its traditional allies.
3. In negotiations on arms control on both global and regional levels. Moscow's inability to achieve the firm promise on the side of NATO not to place the nuclear weapons on the territory of Poland, Hungary and Czech Republic was considered to be the weakest point in the Russian position. (John, 1998: 15-16).

Shortly after signing of the Founding Act in 1997 President of China Jiang Zemin paid his first official visit to the US. (October, 1997) During this visit the Chinese and American presidents have stated the mutual inclination to develop "constructive strategic partnership" (Ribao 1997: 230). Both in essence and in phrasing, this inclination resembled the similar approach to "confidential strategic partnership" with Russia and indirectly devaluated the importance of the latter formula. Such devaluation could possibly be linked to the Chinese dissatisfaction with the Russian arrangements with NATO.

In June 1998 the next summit between Jiang Zemin and Clinton took place in Beijing and the Chinese-American dialogue has advanced further. During this summit the new agreements were achieved, some of them being similar in essence to those in the Russian-Chinese relations. The US and China have agreed not to orient their nuclear weapons on each other (the similar agreement between China and Russia was concluded in 1994.) Clinton made important statement on Taiwan (three "no" statement) which was evaluated as the compromising step towards Beijing. (Washington Post, 23rd June, 1998).

Noting the obvious elements of parallelism and concurrence in the approach of Russia and China to the NATO enlargement, it is quite reasonable to raise the question: does this parallelism mean Beijing's readiness and ability to take the definite practical actions of "strategic partnership" with Moscow?

The forms of "strategic partnership" vary. Such partnership can exist in the form of the full-fledged political-military agreements with the distinct clauses of mutual defense guarantees or in the form of tight military cooperation, including coordination of the military procurement and training policy and "unification" of the military doctrines. It could take the forms of deliveries of sophisticated types of weapons and close diplomatic interaction, including, as the example, the "diplomatic bloc" in the UN Security Council.

From this point of view, real "strategic partnership" between Russia and China, especially those in the tight military forms mentioned above, are unlikely. Such type of partnership would contradict the basic priorities of Chinese foreign policy.

China's central political priority at the present stage is to maintain open, flexible, evenhanded foreign policy that is not binded by any obligations of alliance and thus not leading to any international confrontation. Such strategy provides the maximum possibilities for China's foreign economic ties - active trade and inflow of the foreign investments into the country. At present China's security is not facing any challenges that could justify

Beijing's closer strategic tilt to Moscow, though this should not be interpreted as Beijing complete satisfaction over its strategic position now (Hasegawa,1999:318-337).

The obvious parallelism of the Chinese interests with the interests of Moscow towards NATO is not sufficient to be the basis of real political-military bloc of the two countries. This bloc could be destructive to Chinese interests in several ways.

Firstly, such bloc unequivocally would put China in confrontational, unfavorable or extremely burdened relations with the entire Western world and, first of all, with the US, thus excluding active economic interaction with the group of countries that China needs most.

Secondly, the alliance with Moscow, almost for certain, would result in the scenario of the international relations in Asia Pacific that is mentioned above the consolidation of political-military ties of the US with Japan, Republic of Korea with, most probably, supportive approach of the ASEAN countries towards such consolidation. It is exactly the situation that would create serious problems to China's security – the problems that Beijing is not experiencing now.

Thirdly, any forms of close partnership with Moscow and, consequently, developing confrontation with the US, would freeze the solution of the problem of Taiwan, since this solution is impossible without Washington role as a broker. (FBIS-EAS-97-010, October 1,1996).

The close partnership of Moscow and Beijing oriented against NATO or US is also inhibited by the set of both - explicit and hidden -"conflict zones" that are existing in bilateral Russian-Chinese relations.

To name such zones it is necessary to start from the geopolitical friction between the two countries. The striking contrast between deserted, ill-managed, and rich with mineral resources territories of Russia's Siberia and the Far East on the one side, and overpopulated, physically exhausted and highly polluted territories of China's north – east provinces is the obvious ground for such frictions.

Notwithstanding the rapprochement of the last years, arms sales and serious breakthrough agreements in security, the friction zones based on the geopolitical contrasts has not vanished. Moreover, due to the different pace and results of the economic reforming in China and Russia, strengthening of the centrifugal tendencies at the Russian Far East, exacerbated by the financial decay of the Russia's center, these contrasts became more visible.

Such view is not contradicting to significant progress in settlement of border disputes that was mentioned earlier. The fact of the bilateral legal registration of the line of border in the recent border agreements, though confirm the present status-quo in territorial control, is not drawing the final line in the geopolitical competition of the two neighboring states for "living space". China repeatedly claimed its rights for extensive territories of Siberia and Far East in the past. Symptomatically, that in 1991, already after the main basic border agreement between Russia and China was signed, the Chinese official press, nevertheless, declared again, that "imperial Russia teared away almost 1.55 million square kilometers of China's territory" (China Daily, Nov. 11, 1997).

The forms of competition for concrete geopolitical space are definitely not limited to negotiating the border delimitation. Such competition includes various methods of penetration – legal and illegal emigration, economic projection, support of the separatist movements. Thus, the territorial delimitation, though important, should be viewed only as a phase, but not the last phase, in geopolitical competition.

Besides, even within the framework of the present border agreements of 1991 and 1994, Moscow and Beijing failed to reach an agreement in two dispute areas, having left the decision of these disputes "to the future generations" and having accepted the compromising formula of "joint economic usage" of these areas. Despite the insignificant size, such "blank spots" can be the pretext for the future arguments of "incompleteness" of border delimitation between the two countries. (ITAR-TASS,and FBIS-SOV-94-194,October 6,1994).

Another friction zone of the bilateral relations could be designated as the factor of "immanent threat". At any present level of cordiality of the bilateral relations and demilitarization of the border, the fact of physical proximity of military machines of Russia and China, different in capabilities, but posing potential danger to each other, hasn't ceased to play a role in the calculus of both governments. The decision makers of both capitals has always been closely watching the evolution of the military possibilities of their counterpart. Very often in the past military and strategic orientation of both Moscow and Beijing was assessed with bias and suspicion. Prevailing nuclear capabilities of Russia, including all components of its nuclear triad, potential ability of the Russian armored troops pose a threat of the brisk offensive operation aimed directly at Beijing, on the one side, no less than obvious superiority of the Chinese PLA in manpower, exacerbated by strategic vulnerability and remoteness of the Russian Far East from the center, on the other side, continue to be taken in full consideration in military planning of Moscow and Beijing. (FBIS-SOV-94-197, October12,1994).

Naming the conflict zones, existing between Russia and China, it is necessary to point out, that during the 1990-s these negative factors exerted incomparably smaller influence on dynamics of the bilateral relations, than the motives of mutual gravitation and détente. The relative influence of these latter factors could be explained, besides all other things, by high economic cost of geopolitical confrontation, obvious benefits of economic interaction, similar processes of pro-market reforms obviously inducing many shared values of both political elites.

By virtue of these motives, the recent period was marked by the obvious evolution from irrational and ideology biased confrontation to normal good-neighborly state of relations. During this evolution the motivation for political rapprochement and military detente prevailed over all other motives.

e) NATO's Involvement in Kosovo and its Impact on Russia-China Relations

The crisis over Kosovo marked by itself a critical stage in the international development after the end of the cold war. It has the visible impact not only on the foreign policy motivation of the countries, directly involved in it, but also on all participants of international relations. Since the main events of the Kosovo crisis are well-known, bearing in mind the topic of our research, we would mainly focus on the impact of these events on the development of bilateral partnership of Russia and China, on analyzing these two countries' motives of conduct in this crisis, the new developments in Russian-Chinese tandem in the aftermath of the crisis.

The main conclusion, which the two capitals - Moscow and Beijing - have arrived to in the course of this crisis is the following: the events that they were fearing most and were trying to prevent, eventually happened. The global "superpower" – United States - has used the powerful military machine of NATO for resolving the urgent international problem according to its own consideration, without the sanction of the world community, represented by the United Nations, using almost exclusively the methods of military force, having achieved rather doubtful results. While doing this, NATO actually violated the sovereignty of the independent state of Yugoslavia and created the extremely dangerous precedent in jeopardizing basic values and principles of the international stability - the national sovereignty, non-interference in internal affairs, international legal regulation of the conflicts, prerogative of the United Nations and its Security Council.

This is against such type of events both sides - Russia and China - have joint their forces earlier, while signing the Declaration on the multipolar world and formation of the new international order (1997), that became the important codification of principles for bilateral relations. As a result of events in Kosovo, it became explicit, that the world is far from moving towards multipolarity, it is actually moving towards dictate of one most powerful power-USA. To counteract this tendency, Russia and China appear to be "doomed" on the further rapprochement and coordination of their policies. Moscow and Beijing arrived to the obvious conclusion, that for the sake of higher priorities of opposing the unilateral dictate in international relations, both countries have to increase effort at all directions of Russian-Chinese cooperation, including the military sphere, and to downgrade the priority of the existing or potential frictions on the bilateral level. (ITAR-TASS and SWB, SU/3065 N 14,November,1997).

The positions held by Russia and China during the Kosovo crisis were similar in many respects. Both sides claimed for resolving the crises through political and diplomatic effort, both were opposing the use of the military force without the approval of the UN Security Council, both were striving for the immediate ceasing of NATO bombings as the necessary precondition for political settlement. The differences between their positions were as follows. Till the end of hostilities China was constantly supporting the prerogatives of the UN Security Council, claiming that only UNSC, and not NATO has the legitimate right for regulating and using the military instruments in Kosovo crisis.29 Russia while supporting China's activity in Security Council, eventually joined the NATO peacekeeping forces but on its own conditions.

To make it clear, the positions that Russia and China held during the crisis did not mean that Moscow as well as Beijing, were showing full support and understanding of the policy of the President of Yugoslavia Milosevic. Both Moscow and Beijing disagree with many of his actions, though they didn't qualify them as the "ethnic cleansing". Russia and China never doubted the legitimacy of Milosevic as the President of Yugoslavia and were against interference in internal affairs of this country (ITAR- TASS, May 2, 1999).

Moscow and Beijing's approach to the conflict in Kosovo was motivated by the set of various circumstances.

First, not sharing completely the policy and actions of Milosevic, they considered methods of the USA and NATO for resolving this international crisis more dangerous to the maintenance of international peace.

Secondly, being multi-national states, and having ethnic problems, similar or resembling those of Yugoslavia, Russia and China were gravely concerned, that the precedent for "resolving" such a crisis, demonstrated by the actions of the USA and NATO, will pose it direct threat to their own sovereignty and security in future.

Thirdly, Russia and China had no other choice, but to insist on respect of a role and prerogatives of the United Nations. The opposite would mean moving of the international relations to "superpower oligarchy", but not to "multipolarity" (SWB FE/3623 E/1, August 26,1999).

As the result of the Kosovo crisis both China and Russia arrived to one more important conclusion. Their worst fears of the new role of the expanded NATO as the key element of the European security after the cold war have come true. During Kosovo events, the NATO acted not as the structure, that was synthesizing multipartite interests and oriented on evolutionary, political resolving of complex problems of Europe, sometimes deep rooted in history. NATO actually acted as the military machine, obviously dominated by the interests and perceptions of the US, and thus trying to resolve this European problems mainly in a unilateral and biased manner (ITAR-TASS May, 5, 1999).

It's pretty clear, that besides the obvious humanitarian motives for the USA and NATO actions in Kosovo, the pragmatic and power interests of the NATO allies in this operation was very visible. With all the possible criticism of the Yugoslavian leader's actions, Yugoslavia is the sovereign state and Milosevic is the legitimate president of this state. In contemporary Europe, to the west of borders of the former USSR, Yugoslavia remains the only state that is not oriented on the NATO – centered structure of military security of the continent. All other NATO non-members, either, being neutral, actually are still oriented and protected by the NATO security "umbrella" (Austria, Switzerland, Sweden, Finland), or aspiring to enter this block -Bulgaria, Romania, Baltic states (ITAR-TASS and FBIS-SOV-2001-0527).

Speaking about the "policy message" which Russia and China has received as the result of the Kosovo crisis, let us quote how President Clinton himself formulated this message in one of his interviews in June 1999:

"We can't stop every fight like the fight between Eritrea and Ethiopia and the struggles in Chechnya. But where we can, at an acceptable cost; that is without risking nuclear war or some other terrible thing, we ought to prevent the slaughter of innocent civilians and the wholesale uprooting of them because of their race, their ethnic background or the way they worship God" (Clinton on ABC Network, June 12, 1999).

What message Moscow or Beijing could get from this? Speaking logically, the implications of such a formula for them could be pretty obvious: since these two countries cannot be guaranteed, that one of its internal ethnical "problem zones", either Chechnya or Tibet or Xinjiang, could at one point, using the very biased, politicized criteria and the double standards approach, be qualified as the "humanitarian disaster", the only way to avoid the humiliation for Moscow and Beijing is to increase the price tag for NATO to do that.

The obvious reaction of the Russians and the Chinese on that was the visible intensification of effort in defense, creation of the new systems of weapons, including "smart weapons , which has played a special role during the bombing of Yugoslavia. This is the effort, that is being undertaken individually by each country as well as within the framework of military-technical cooperation between them.

As to the individual effort, Russia in a course of the Kosovo conflict has announced putting into operation of the new missile system "Topol-M". Its successful tests were conducted earlier of this year. In June - September, 1999 a series of sessions of the

Security Council of the Russian Federation were held. The sessions that were presided by the President Yeltsin were focused on the broad range of questions relating the reform of armed forces, revision of the concept of national security of Russia in the aftermath of the Yugoslavian crisis, additional financial allocations to the defense ministry for the state funded contracts on new military procurement. The Council made the decision to raise defense expenditures in the budget of 2000 by substantial margin (the specific figure to be fixed in accordance with government financial situation). These last decision is unanimously supported by all factions of the State Duma, despite of serious differences among them practically on all other parameters of the budget of Russia (ITAR-TASS and FBIS-SOV-2001-0328,May 27,2001).

Speaking about China, Beijing in July 1999 has announced that China has the "know-how" of a neutron bomb and miniaturization of nuclear explosives. It for the first time was stated by the Director of Information Department of the State Council Zhao Qizheng. This Chinese official resolutely denied allegations of China's stealing of nuclear secrets from the USA (ITAR-TASS, July 15, 1999).

In the short aftermath of the events in Kosovo, the Russian and Chinese representatives has repeatedly stated their inclination to progress to the new, more advanced stage "of strategic partnership" between the two countries. This advance should take place both in political, and military-technical sphere. The Russian foreign minister I. Ivanov, while communicating with his Chinese counterpart Tan Jiaqiuan (they met thrice within June and August 1999), has stated, that the importance of interaction of Russia and China in Asia Pacific" is growing in the wake of potential danger of downgrading of regional stability. According to I. Ivanov, "the further extending of military-technical cooperation and gradually increasing coordination in the field of conversion of the enterprises of a defense industry is the vivid sign of confidentiality of the relations of the strategic partnership" (ITAR-TASS, July 26, 1999).

From his side, the vice-premier of China's State Council Qian Qichen while characterizing the state of bilateral relations in the period after Kosovo has stated, that now they experience "the best times in a history".

Discussing the consequences of the Kosovo events, it is necessary to stress, that internal political climate and the correlation of forces in discussion about "pluses" and "minuses" of bilateral strategic partnership has changed strikingly in both countries. If earlier, foreign policy elites in both Russia and China had serious reservations to the thesis «of strategic partnership» and different understanding of this partnership, now, the necessity to develop such partnership for countering "hegemonism" and "military dictate" of NATO outweighs all other arguments. To illustrate this the recent decision of the State Duma to ratify the CBM-2 Agreement between Russia, Kazakhstan, Kyrgyzstan, Tajikistan and China should be mentioned. The results of the ballot are indicative: "yes" - 321 vote, "no" – 1, abstained – "1". As we mentioned earlier in this report, the assessment of this agreement was far more critical, especially, among the right-wing oriented politicians shortly after the signing of this agreement in April 1997. Now, notwithstanding its party or faction affiliations, the members of Duma unanimously supported the document, that is strengthening the level of military trust with China. The Chinese side Parliament has ratified this agreement earlier (ITAR-TASS, June 26, 1999).

As the obvious consequence of the Kosovo events one should consider China's evidently growing anxiety over the potential advance of the NATO to Chinese borders in Central Asian direction.

It is known, that majority of the Central Asian countries (those being the former republics USSR) are the participants of the NATO's Partnership For Peace program (PFP), and some of them, Azerbaijan in particular, have already shown its strong desire to become the full member of the block. China is seriously concerned over the possibility, in addition to deteriorating military relations with the USA, eventually, to deal with the element of the military mechanism of NATO in close proximity to its western borders.

To counteract such tendency, China recently demonstrated its stressed interest to developing relations with the members of the so called "Shanghai Five states" - participants of the CBM agreements of 1996 and 1997, the first of which was signed in Shanghai. Three Central Asian members of this group - Kazakhstan, and Tajikistan – by virtue of their individual political circumstances do not gravitate to the NATO and keep close comprehensive ties with Russia.

In August, 1999 in Bishkek (Kyrgyzstan) the summit of the leaders of the "Shanghai Five", was held, with both Russian and Chinese Presidents taking part in it. Both of them stressed their presence at this meeting. In the process of the meeting, Russia showed it's inclination to institutionalize the interaction of these five countries. The Russian president has offered to conduct regular separate meetings of ministers of foreign affairs and ministers of defense, to create working groups of experts, and by 2000 to conduct the meeting of the Premiers of the "Shanghai Five" countries (Garnett, 2001:324-345).

During bilateral meeting of Yeltsin and Jiang Zemin the Chinese President was briefed on the recent Russian-American consultations on START and ABM Treaty. " We consider the ABM Agreement to be the basis of strategic stability and we have complete mutual understanding with our Chinese counterparts on this issue" – the Russians has stated.

During their private meeting Yeltsin and Jiang Zemin highly evaluated the negotiation on military-technical cooperation between Russia and China, which were in parallel conducted in Beijing. The head of the Russian delegation at this negotiation, vice-premier I.Klebanov confirmed Russia's intention to sell the Su-30 fighters to China (ITAR-TASS, Oct. 25th May, 1999).

It is necessary to note that the events in Kosovo, took place on the background of gradually deteriorating of the Chinese-American bilateral ties in the first half of 1999. Such deterioration was related to the charges of espionage in the field of military technology, put forward against China, failure of negotiation on the China's admission to WTO during the visit of the Chinese Premier Zhu Rongji in the USA in April, 1999. The culmination of this negative development was the bombing of the Chinese embassy in Belgrade, which despite of explanations of the American side, was qualified in Beijing as the deliberately planned "action of intimidation". Responding to it, China took several countermeasures concerning the USA and countries of NATO. The American-Chinese consultations on human rights and nonproliferation of military technologies were suspended. The visit of American military ships to Hongkong was cancelled. The visits of the US Minister of Defense to Beijing and the Commander of China's Navy to London were postponed (ITAR-TASS Oct. 22, 1999).

In July, 1999 the President of Taiwan Lee Deng-hui has stated that the relations between Taiwan and China should be treated as "the special relations between two peoples". This statement of the Taiwan leader was qualified in Beijing as the deviation from the principle "of one China" and the policy aimed at stimulation of separatism and tension. The relations between China and Taiwan were deteriorated seriously.

It looks like the timing of this Taiwan President's statement was not occasional. President Lee most obviously take an opportunity of the present international situation. Due to events of Kosovo and other reasons - the relations of Beijing with the USA and NATO were at the lowest point for the last few years. Thus, for China the Kosovo events and deterioration of the situation in the Taiwan Strait was obviously linked to each other.

The deterioration of the situation in the Taiwan Strait indirectly increases the importance of Beijing's ties with Moscow. During the whole history of its ties with China, Moscow consistently kept loyal to the principle of "one China" and never hesitated in its support of China's sovereignty over Taiwan. Under current circumstances, in conditions of the strained relations with the US, such support is extremely valuable in Beijing's eyes. Its value has both diplomatic and military-strategic dimension. The latter is based on the Russia's ability to render reliable military and strategic "rear" in the north of China in case of an unpredictable aggravation of a situation in the Taiwan Strait and possible military conflict.

In August 1999, reacting to the new stage of tension in the Taiwan Strait, Russian foreign minister once again confirmed Russian firm standing on this issue.

The crisis in Kosovo stimulated the new round of Moscow's effort to initiate the coordination of foreign policy actions and joint counteraction to "hegemonism" on the part of three large states - Russia, China and India. This idea for the first time was stated in January 1999 by E.Primakov during his visit to India. That time it had not received the active response on the part of the Chinese and Indian colleagues. This theme was raised again, now on the military level, after events in Yugoslavia. In June 1999 in Vladivostok the working meeting of the military delegations of China and Russia was held. The delegations were leaded by Russian deputy minister of defense N.Mikhailov and deputy chairman of the Central military council of China Zhang Wangyan. At this meeting the Russian counterpart has stated, that"the strategic cooperation of Russia with China and India in a near future will ascend on a qualitatively new level". It is also notable, that the idea, that in the aftermath of Kosovo, China have to reconsider its criticism of India's and Pakistan's acquisition of the nuclear weapon, is being actively discussed in China's influential academic circles (FBIS-CHI-2000-0717, July 2000).

The current state of relations between Russia and China reflects their basic foreign policy interests and perceptions, with the shared distrust of NATO strategy, especially after Kosovo, being the vital part of these perceptions. Therefore no big negative changes in the Russian-Chinese bilateral ties are likely in the nearest future. The opposite trend is possible in case of drastic internal shifts in the elites of the both countries, leading to the cardinal reassessments of the basic orientations of foreign and domestic politics. The probability of such internal changes is very low in the short-term future.

Both sides have achieved quite a stable level of security in relations with each other. That is extremely vital for Russia with her situation of protracted socio-economic crises, deficit of financial resources for the defense needs and the deterioration of its strategic posture on the western borders after the expansion of NATO. It is also beneficial for China given her priority of active economic growth and considerably vulnerable situation at the East, South-East and South geopolitical directions (US-Japanese axis, Taiwan, Korea, South China Sea).

Military détente between Russia and China, settling the territory disputes and the demilitarization of the border were achieved without any serious jeopardizing of interests of any one of the parties. The compromises are quite reasonable and stable. All these interim results of the progress of bilateral relations of the recent years are obviously valuable to both Moscow and Beijing and none of them would put at risk this status-quo.

The same tendency to preserve status-quo would be most probably manifested by both capitals in economic sphere and trade. During last years both partners occupied the natural niches in each other's necessities and capabilities. Both sides are interested to keep these niches for the future.

It's difficult to foresee in details how the military co-operation and arms sales between Russia and China will develop in the coming years. Though stimuli of the international origin – like Kosovo syndrome – will continue to have effect on the flow of weapons through the Russian-Chinese border, the volume of the arms trade will depend more on the financial limitations of the buyer and security considerations of the seller.

The most reasonable forecast will be that the volumes of arms trade will grow, but not very substantial. The nomenclature of arms export will not change substantially and not many new sophisticated types of weapon will be sold. It looks like Russia and China has neared the rational threshold in arms trade. Russia has no reason to sell to China new types of weapons that would substantially expand the range of Beijing's military capabilities, and it will not be reasonable for the Chinese to purchase the types of weapon that would not increase greatly that range of capabilities.

From the point of view of Russia's internal political scene it's hard to foresee any drastic shifts that could destabilize the current flow of Russian-Chinese relations. During the coming presidential election in Russia, Moscow's China policy will hardly be the object of discussion and dispute. It would be risky and unreasonable for any presidential candidate, notwithstanding his political affiliation, to put into question the key milestones of Russia's China policy, including the CBM agreements, border treaties and bilateral cooperation vis-a-vis the US and NATO.

The arms sales and military co-operation issues could be, within certain limits, be variable of the outcome of the Presidential election. The left-oriented candidate, being ideologically more sympathetic to China, will probably be more inclined to closer military ties with China. More active military ties, however, could be seriously inhibited by the left-wing candidate's special sensivity to the electorate in Siberia and Russia's Far East with strong anti-China sentiments. In general, notwithstanding his possible sympathies to China's ideology, the left-wing candidate, if being elected, will hardly exceed the limits of rationality and wise sufficiency in military ties with China.

The other sound factor in Russia's future China policy is the growing interest of the Russian business community, especially the energy companies (like "Gazprom" or "Yukos") to the long-term projects with China. The ability of these companies to lobby successfully the necessary decisions of Russia's China policy, including the basic geopolitical orientations of their partnership vis-a-vis the West, will be visible in the nearest future.

The Russian and Chinese Presidents met in Bishkek at the fourth meeting of Shanghai Cooperation Organization. President

Yeltsin told the reporters at the airport that he was ready for a battle "especially with the westerners". Bishkek Summit declaration underscored the commonality of Russian and Chinese opposition to NMD and TMD projects and their insistence that 1972 ABM Treaty must be respected as the basis for maintaining strategic stability in the world (Wishnick, 201, pp. 146-156).

Both Russia-China condemned strongly the NATO's bombing on Chinese embassy building in Yugoslavia. Moscow and Beijing demonstratively came together and registered strong protest against unilateralism of USA. Both countries also issued joint statement that "plans by some countries to build power bloc against others" should not be accepted. Jiang Zemin repeatedly declared that "hegemonism and power politics" are the main source of threat to world peace and stability" and as well as China's interests (SWB. Aug.26, 1999, p. 21).

Both Russia and China are also opposed to USA's National Missile Defence Programme and fear that it will disturb the balance of power and hence start a new arms race. It is also proposed that US will transfer Theatre Missile Defence (TMD) system to countries like Japan and Taiwan which would greatly undermine the peace and security in the Asia-Pacific region. The US withdrawal from ABM Treaty of 1972 added more suspicion among the strategists of Russia and China about the real intension of USA (Pillsbur, 2000, pp. 10-15).

Both Russia and China agree on the proposal of restructuring of UNO. Both call for strict adherence to UN rules and regulations especially in the context of developments in Yugoslavia 2nd Iraq crisis in which NATO and US forces greatly undermined the UN authority. Both countries want greater representation from developing world but they differ on the issue of members of their choice.

In Central Asia Russo-Chinese interests converge on the issues such as Islamic extremism, drug trafficking, arms smuggling etc. It is in the larger interest of the two countries to maintain stability in the region which is prone to Islamic extremism due to its relative backwardness. Being, the region's largest neighbours and trading partners, the two countries have huge stake in the region. Also by promoting economic cooperation together, Russia and China could partially alleviate the fear psychosis among the Central Asian states that one or other will dominate the region (Bilal and Olarreaga, 1998. pp. 153-166).

In post-September 11, world scenario both Beijing and Moscow view with considerable concern and consternation the presence of US troops in the Central Asian Republics, which is strategically situated very close to their borders. US military bases in Uzbekistan and Kyrgyzstan have provided the former an opportunity to monitor some of the sensitive strategic facilities that Soviet Union had on the territories of these countries. The presence of US troops at Manas airbase in Kyrgyzstan. just 200 km. from the Chinese border have provided USA unique opportunity to keep on the eye on the Chinese territory from there (Ruisheng, 2002, pp. 331-335).

Russia-China and the Multipolar World Order

Since the late 1990s, the concept of multipolarity has gained prominence around the globe. Russia and China, in particular, have repeatedly agreed on this ill-defined term and subsequently have included it or alluded to it in nearly all of their joint declarations, statements, and treaties dating from the mid-1990s to the present. At a time when American hege- mony is declining and speculation abounds as to which among the world's burgeoning nations will rise to power, it is important to examine the renewed Sino-Russian relationship and one of its foundational pillars—the promotion of multipolarity. This article deconstructs the definition of multipolarity as it applies uniquely to Russia and China in an effort to determine the depth of the two countries' agreement. Though the two may agree upon the same "solution" to the next world order, China and Russia employ very different strategies to achieve it.

Nearly two decades ago, Charles Krauthammer prophesized that "multipolarity will come in time ... in perhaps another generation or so there will be great powers coequal with the United States, and the world will, in structure, resemble the pre-World War I era" (Krauthamer, 1990 pp. 23-33). Since the beginning of the 21st century, and especially within the past couple years, the seeming actualization of Krauthammer's prediction has caused many to believe that the world now stands on the precipice of a multipolar order. China and Russia have long been in the forefront of nations advocating for this order and have included multipolarity as a joint cause in many of their statements, declarations, and treaties. Despite their frequent use of the term, however, China and Russia have failed to elaborate upon how they believe multipolarity is best achieved (Hass; 208, p. 46).

Considering the power of these two countries and their tumultuous pasts (vis-à-vis one another and the rest of the world), it is crucial to examine the depth of their supposed agree- ments. As such, this article examines Russia and China's joint campaign for a multipolar world order in the 21st century and the dangerous potential for similar rhetoric to disguise dissimilar methods and objectives. The first part will examine the joint statements, declarations, and treaties of China and Russia advocating multipolarity, the second will analyze their separate discourse on the subject, and the third part will study their separate foreign policies and actions in order to illustrate the different means each country has chosen to achieve the same end multipolarity.

a) A Shared Perspective

Due to China's and the Soviet Union's prominent roles in the bipolar world order, the end of the cold war and the exclusion of both countries in the subsequent unipolar world left leaders in both countries feeling disillusioned. China, in particular, experienced what Dong Yuan describes as an "identity crisis", because it no longer had leverage in the "superpower balancing game". (Yuan, 1998: 56).

Instead, China, like the rest of the world, was subject to one "policing" superpower—one with the self-proclaimed authority to encroach upon the domestic affairs of other states. China first experienced the ramifications of this in the aftermath of the Tiananmen Square massacre, when the U.S. Congress suspended arms sales to China and attempted to make China's most favoured nation (MFN) status contingent upon the improvement of its human rights record. Although China's MFN status was renewed, Bush incorporated Congress's concerns in his "constructive engagement" policy toward China in 1991. China's foreign minister, Qian Qichen, declared the following year that "The USA's hegemonic stance and its attempts to interfere in the internal affairs of other states pose the greatest danger to socialist China," and suggested that in order to "weaken pressure from Washington, China must broaden relations with Japan, Russia, South Korea, and other neighboring countries." Two years later, China turned to Russia—a country with its own qualms with U.S. ascendance (Levin, 2008, p. 98).

Compared to China, Russia's "identity crisis" in the post- cold war era was more severe and took the form of an acute (and prolonged) case of schizophrenia, with its foreign policy oscillating between allying with the West and allying with the East. Russia's first inclination after the cold war was to reconcile its relations with the United States and join it in world dominance. Unfortunately for Russia, however, the U.S. government did not share this ideal, but seemed to undermine Russian power by providing fewer post-war funds than Russia wanted and by keeping the North Atlantic Treaty Organization (NATO) intact despite Russian objections. Primakov also believed that the United States was directly responsible for the International Monetary Fund's stringency in extending loans to Russia for bridge construction. These events caused many of Russia's political elite to agree with the conclusion of the Izvestiya Politklub that Russia was "too big and too Russian for the West" (Levin, 2008: 98-100).

It was in the context of their "identity crisis" that China and Russia established a "constructive partnership" in September 1994. In 1996, the word "strategic" replaced "constructive" in defining the two countries' partnership and Evgeny Primakov replaced the pro-Western Andrei Kozyrev as the new foreign minister of Russia. These two exchanges indicated not only the advancement of Sino-Russian relations in general, but also the direction their relationship was heading—away from the West. (Noorling, 2007, pp. 33-36) Thereafter, the official rhetoric of the two countries oscillated between promoting a multipolar world order and denouncing the current unipolar system. An example of the latter appeared in a 1996 statement by Primakov to the Kremlin News Broadcast:

> Russia in her transition from the bipolar world to the multipolar one should play the role of a counterweight to the negative trends that are appearing in international affairs. In the course of this transition not all power centers, determining this multipolarity, have yet formed. And somebody wants to dominate in this situation. (Ambrosio, 2005, p. 86).

The 1997 "Joint Russian-Chinese Declaration about a Multipolar World and the Formation of a New World Order" reiterated Primakov's sentiment (albeit more diplomatically), and was first among a string of statements emphasizing multipolarity and denouncing U.S. hegemony. The negative trends alluded to in Primakov's statement in 1996 and in the first 1997 declaration materialized in 1999 in the U.S. invasion of Kosovo and the "accidental" bombing of the Chinese Embassy in Belgrade. In response, China and Russia issued another joint statement on December 10, 1999 outlining their continued joint commitment to combat the "negative momentum" that had been developing in the international arena over the past year, particularly the intrusive U.S. actions in Kosovo, its consideration of a National Missile Defense (NMD) system, and its refusal to sign the Comprehensive Nuclear Test Ban Treaty (Xinhua, Dec. 10, 1999).

In 2001, China and Russia formalized their relationship by cosigning the Sino-Russian Treaty on Good-Neighborliness, Friendship, and Cooperation, a twenty-year renewable treaty outlining their joint resolve to promote "a just and fair new world order".

Although the treaty does not elaborate upon the necessary conditions of a "fair and just" society, the Joint Statement signed the following clarifies that both governments believe that such a society can only be the consequence of a multipolar world order.

The call for multipolarity was silenced a few months later with the terrorist attacks against America on September 11, 2001, which brought international terrorism to the forefront of the international agenda and was followed by the multilateral backing of the U.S. war in Afghanistan in March 2001. This international solidarity was shaken, however, in 2002 when the United States petitioned the United Nations to invade Iraq and was shattered in 2003 when it did so without UN sanction. To many, the Iraq war demonstrated the peril of an unchecked superpower a peril that China and Russia had continuously tried to highlight in their promotion of multipolarity.

China's and Russia's cooperation over the past decade and their joint opposition to U.S. unipolarity has caused some westerners to predict an impending clash between a Sino-Russian alliance and the United States. Others, however, discern several discrepancies between Chinese and Russian motives in the propagation of multipolarity, and thus question the durability of such an "alliance". (Wishnick, 2001, : 797). The next section of my analysis addresses this question more deeply by delving into the separate rhetoric of China and Russia's vis-à-vis multipolarity in order to identify if, in fact, the two countries have the same or separate agendas for constructing a new multipolar world order.

Perusing the plethora of summits, statements, declarations, and exchanges that have occurred between China and Russia over the past decade, it seems the two countries have established a successful and solid friendship founded on a shared world perspective. Analyzing the sub-text, however, tells a very different story. First, one must not forget the context in which China and Russia first turned toward one another—the end of the cold war. As mentioned, after the dissolution of the Soviet Union, Russia had initially wanted to cooperate with the United States. Only after Russia's stint of attempting to court the West did Russia turn its aspirations eastward. Seven summits were held with China between 1992 and 1999, during which the Treaty of Good-Neighbourliness and Friendly Cooperation was signed in 2001 (Noling, 2007, p. 35).

Russia again tried to join forces with the United States immediately after September 11 (this time against international terrorism), but to little avail. So fervent was Moscow in its attempt to gain Washington's favor that the Russian Foreign Policy Council actually advised Putin to drop the "multipolarity emphasis" in foreign policy altogether and acquiesce to the U.S. position on missile defense. Balancing American power, the council concluded, would be "too costly and unpragmatic" for Russia. Latent in Russia's switch in position was the hope that a U.S.-Russia alliance, or at least Russia's inclusion in a broader coalition against international terrorism, might allow for alleviation of some of its Soviet-era debts and provide it with the necessary leverage to join NATO, which the council believed would then "grow into a universal organization of European and international security and shed its destabilizing features".

Despite Russia's internal debate, China maintained its position on the benefits of multipolarity in ensuring world peace and stability and promoted multilateralism as the primary means for fighting terrorism. In 2002, Russia reverted back to its previous position and once again jumped on the multipolarity bandwagon, with President Putin claiming that "Russia and China have always stood for the establishment of a multi-polar world and the strengthening of the role of the UN." (Xinhua, Nov. 25, 2001).

Putin exemplified his renewed dedication to multipolarity with his vehement opposition to the U.S. invasion of Iraq the following year. To China and Russia (and much of the international community), the invasion of Iraq was nearly paralleled to its actions in Kosovo. To this end, Russian rhetoric did not extend any leniency to the United States. At a trilateral summit of Russia, Germany, and France in April 2003, for example, when Putin was asked at a Russian press conference about the possibility of relinquishing Russian servicemen to fight in Iraq, he retorted: "Find idiots elsewhere" (ITAR-TASS, Nov. 10, 2003).

Fortunately for the United States, there were "idiots" aplenty willing to join forces, including the new members of NATO—Estonia, Latvia, and Slovenia—and several of Russia's newly democratic neighbors. As the United States continued to occupy Iraq well after 2003, the military and political support of these and other countries significantly waned. While the UnitedStates justified its presence by reiterating the importance and difficulty in establishing a democratic government in the Middle East, Russia increasingly questioned U.S. motives and called for a withdrawal date.

Even in the midst of such tensions, however, the rhetoric of the United States and Russia remained tame. That is, until February 2007, when President Putin spoke at the 43rd Munich Conference on Security Policy. At the start, Putin promised to avoid "excessive politeness." A few minutes later, he explained the danger he believed was latent in the current unipolar world system and lambasted the United States explicitly for defying international law and "overstep[ing] its national borders in every way". Additionally, Putin emphasized that a world ruled by one power is definitively undemocratic—regardless of rhetoric to the contrary. Just as he promised, he avoided diplomatic necessities.

b) Chinese Perspective

China responded to Putin's impassioned comments with calculated equanimity, making sure to reiterate the importance of peace and prosperity for all. This common refrain has caused several American analysts to suspect that beneath China's rhetoric of a "harmonious world" and its "peaceful rise" lies a hegemonic agenda. (Ikenberry, 2008, p. 30). Is there a foundation for such speculation? Rhetoric alone indicates not.

Unlike Russia, China had great success in establishing a rapport with America after the cold war. As such, China has justifiably exerted extreme caution in propagating the cause of multipolarity and directly criticizing U.S. hegemony. Furthermore (and also in contrast to Russia), China has exemplified a general regression of its overall use of anti-hegemony and unipolarity rhetoric. Although Deng Xiaoping was the first to formally express China's view on multipolarity, his successor, Jiang Zemin, officially incorporated the concept of duoji shijie (multipolar world) into Chinese foreign policy in 1992 at the 14th Party Congress. During Jiang's presidency, China's foreign ministry asserted its strongest position on the issue of multipolarity and the dangers of unipolarity, stating:

> [Multipolarity] helps weaken and curb hegemonism and power politics, serves to bring about a just and equitable order and contributes to world peace and development. . . . At present, by virtue of its economic, technological and military advantages, an individual country is pursuing a new "gunboat policy" in contravention of the United Nations Charter and the universally acknowledged principles governing international relations in an attempt to establish a unipolar world under its guidance. (Britingham, 2007, p. 99)

After 2003, and with the appointment of Hu Jintao, China's multipolar position subtly changed to include the disclaimer that it was not "targeted at any particular country, nor ... aimed at re-staging the old play of contention for hegemony in history," but should be viewed as a means to ensure "world peace, stability, and development".

These positions were later clarified in an article by a leading policy adviser, Zheng Bijian. Writing in Foreign Affairs, he emphasized China's conciliatory emergence onto the world stage as a prominent economic and political power (and served as a formal rebuttal to foreign allegations of a "China threat"). Zheng explained that unlike Nazi Germany or Imperial Japan, China does not harbor an ideological agenda or vie for global dominance, but instead seeks "a new international political and economic order ... achieved through incremental reforms and the democratization of international relations." (Bijian, 2005 18-24). Within the year, China's "peaceful rise" became a part of its official political discourse, with Hu and other senior officials incorporating the phrase into their domestic and international dialogues (Men, 2007, p. 47).

Even buffered by disclaimers, however, the term "rise" made many Americans uneasy, especially as it supplemented China's growing strategic partnerships around the globe. In response, China soon substituted "peaceful development" for "peaceful rise" so as to less blatantly assert China's ascendance as a future pole of power. Today, with China's GDP projected to surpass that of the United States, and with its dramatic increases in military expenditures, Beijing has even more reason to retain its cautious rhetoric. It has also shifted from solely promoting multipolarity to actively defending itself against those who might claim that its strengthening political, economic, and military circum- stances are indicative of hegemonic interests.

Although Russia and China both seemingly share the critique of hegemony and agree on the justice, peace, and stability inherent in a multipolar world order, the individual tone of each country's leaders in doing so indicates a discrepancy in the means by which they might want to achieve this order. As exemplified in the previous analysis, linguistic oscillation persists between advocating multipolarity and denouncing unipolarity and hegemonism. Still, neither China nor Russia is quick to define these terms strategically. Instead, the pursuit of a multi- polar world order (without mention as to how to achieve it) has become a ready-referenced point of agreement between the two countries in joint statements, treaties, and declarations. Another indicator of a discrepancy in China and Russia's perception of multipolarity is the actions each country has taken since first adopting the term. In the next section, I will explore their actions in three areas: arms acquisitions and sales, regional alliances, and the U.S. invasion of Iraq. I will also explore the implications of Russia's recent invasion of Georgia and China's response, as this event illustrates a dramatic rift in the two countries' positions on sovereignty—a formerly agreed upon principle incorporated into their mutual definition of multipolarity.

c) Arms Factor

Although the 2001 Sino-Russian Treaty on Friendship and Cooperation did not establish a formal alliance between China and Russia, it did include rhetoric indicating the anticipated military cooperation of the two countries. Article 7 of the treaty states that each signatory should look after its nation's security by "maintaining reasonable and adequate weapons and armed forces." Additionally, both countries should "consolidate each other's security" by pursuing "confidence building measures in the military field." The last clause of that article attempts to assuage any suspicion of ill intent, explaining that neither of these two objectives is aimed at a third party. This disclaimer, however, did not ease the anxiety of the United States, which classified both China and Russia as "global peer competitors" in the Pentagon's 2001 defense report (US Dept. of Defence, 2001 at www.srwolf.com/reports/qdr2001).

Not long after the ink dried on the Sino-Russian Friendship Treaty in August 2001, China procured forty Su-30MKK jetfighters from Russia's primary arms export company, Rosoboronexport. Also within the year, China imported 168 Russian missiles and missile launchers, including $400 million in S-300PMU-2s (missile systems with long-range anti-aircraft capabilities). The following year, China purchased two Project 956EM destroyers and eight Project 636 vessels. In 2003, China procured twenty- four additional Su-30MKKs. Overall, according to the UN Register of Conventional Arms, Russian exports to China between 2001 and 2007 totaled 3,857 missiles and missile launchers, nine warships, and 120 aircraft (UN Office of Disarmament Affair-www.disarmament.un.org/UN_Register.ns)

Although many question such liberal arms exports to China, President Putin has repeatedly emphasized the importance of China's defense capabilities in establishing a multipolar world order. China has also defended its military modernization, saying it is only attempting to "catch up" to the "international military evolution", and that despite its increased expenditures, China's military arsenal pales in comparison with that of other major countries.

Perusing comparative data on military expenditures and capabilities, one finds that China's claim is correct, especially when one compares China to the United States. According to a 2005 study conducted by the RAND Corporation, the maximum amount China will be able to spend on researching, developing, and procuring weaponry between 2003 and 2025 is $490 billion dollars. This amount, while substantial, is only half of what it would take for China to develop or acquire weaponry as sophisticated as the current arsenal of the United States (Crane, Cliff and Overholt, 2005: 235-236).

This particular approximation also assumes China's continued economic growth, which is no longer a safe assumption due to the dramatic effect of the American financial crisis on Chinese exports. Additionally, due to China's over-employment in the military sector and the lack of financial incentives it offers for military innovation, its military evolvement relies predominantly on Russian intelligence and technology rather than on indigenous production. Any serious prediction of China's "catching up" to developed nations, or any serious claim of a Chinese military threat, must thus include an explanation of how China will overcome its weapons dependence and how it will substantially increase its military budget. Russia has a considerable head start on China in military modernization due to the prominent role of the Soviet Union in World War II, its "Chief Designer" program in the 1960s, and its arms race with the United States during the cold war. Russia's consequent acquisition of human and material resources propelled it to the fore of the arms industry, and today, although Russia's own (aging) military is not seen as a direct threat to the United States, its role as the world's primary arms dealer allows it a leading role in building up militarized powers that can collectively rival the United States. It also allows Russia the authority to say which among those powers gets what. Russia's weapons allocation is telling. Though China and Russia may be "friends" inthe strategic sense, and Russia sells most of its arms to China, its most advanced weapons actually go to India, China's global competitor, exemplifying Russia's own "check" on Chinese power (Buszynski, 2004, pp. 158-167).

Alliance Politics-Sanghai Co-operation Organization (SCO)

Prior to their agreement to a strategic partnership in 2001, China and Russia were already cooperating in the context of the "Shanghai Five," a group comprised of China, Russia, Kazakhstan, Kyrgyzstan, and Tajikistan that focused on regional security and border disarmament. The grouping also stood against the international "tendency" to unipolarity and subsequently to balancing the U.S. presence in Central Asia. With the expansion of NATO and the U.S. led invasion of Serbia in 1999, the group signed the Bishkek Declaration, emphasizing a regional commitment to continued political and military cooperation in the context of a "general trend" of the world toward multipolarity. Although the declaration included diplomatic rhetoric, Russian President Boris Yeltsin, who was less keen on euphemistic language, stated bluntly that he was "ready to fight, especially with the Westerners." Yeltsin employed milder rhetoric in his joint statement with Jiang subsequent to the summit, stating: "The two sides agree to work together with the rest of the world to oppose the tendencies currently preventing the establishment of a just multipolar structure for international relations".

On June 7, 2001, Uzbekistan became the sixth member of the Shanghai Five, and the Shanghai Cooperation Organization (SCO) was established. The SCO posited its objectives against the backdrop of multipolarization, but it remained ambiguous as to the full extent of the military cooperation and economic cooperation the members thought necessary to achieve multipolarity. The organization's charter, signed in 2002, was similarly vague, stating in its preface that the SCO's purpose was "to jointly contribute to the strengthening of peace and ensuring of security and stability in the region in the environment of developing political multi-polarity and economic and information globalization".

Agreeing to "develop multipolarity" leaves much up for debate—including how a multipolar world order would best be achieved. Perhaps beneath the diplomatic rhetoric lies a fuller explanation as to each country's definition of multipolarity—and thus, whether or not there should be concern about the undefined. The SCO exemplifies China's and Russia's commitment to the concept, as well as their first joint-effort to breach the rhetorical; but agreeing on a vehicle to balance unipolarity is still not synonymous with defining the means by which to do so. And even if the SCO's charter and declaration seemingly outline the agreed-upon means, evidence indicates that the prioritization of these means very much differs as between China and Russia.

Mark Katz has identified the discrepancy between the Chinese and Russian perspectives on SCO by saying: "Instead of seeing the SCO as developing into a politico-military alliance [as does Moscow], Beijing views it more as an economic cooperation zone." (Katz, 2007 p. 15). The chasm Katz highlights in the Sino-Russian perspective is exemplified by distinctive Chinese and Russian rhetoric regarding the SCO and also in the separate regional "alliances" they have chosen to participate in over the past decade.

Of course the term "alliance" in and of itself is a much contested term in the international community, especially when it suggests a counter to the West's NATO. This is also the reasoning behind Beijing's and Moscow's continual protestations that the SCO is not an exclusive military bloc. The Russian presidential envoy for SCO affairs, Vitaly Vorobyov, emphasized this point in 2006, stating: "All the SCO's founding documents are open. I do not think you can find any signs of a military-political bloc in them, even with a microscope." (Interfax, June, 2006) Still, despite the professed openness (or ambiguity) of the SCO's founding documents, Vorobyoy admitted that its activities have a prominent "political component" that "logically" leads to "cooperation between the member-states' defense and other security agencies ...." (*Ibid*). Examples of such military cooperation include the China- Kyrgyzstan antiterrorist exercises in October

2002, the five-state exercises in August 2003, and the comprehensive military exercise dubbed "Peace Mission 2007" in July 2007. This last exercise was the most organized SCO operation to date; not surprisingly, Russia and China took the lead.

"Peace Mission 2007" was also the largest of the joint-military operations conducted by the SCO. It involved over 4,000 soldiers from all six member-states, including 2,000 from Russia and 1,600 from China. Along with infantry, much of China's Russian-procured arms accompanied China back into Russia for the operation. Despite the size of the affair, China was quick to assert that there was no intention of forming an alliance. An article written shortly after the exercise in Jiefang junbao, the Chinese People's Liberation Army newspaper, explained: "China has conducted more than 17 joint military exercises with ten-plus countries. Does it mean to say that China is entering into military alliance with any of these countries? The answer is certainly negative." (PLA Daily, July 20, 2007). China similarly dismissed the notion that the SCO would ally or collaborate with other regional security mechanisms in the affair, and rejected the proposal of General Yuriy Baluyevskiy for the involvement of the Collective Security Treaty Organization (CSTO).

The CSTO emerged out of the Commonwealth of Independent States' (CIS) Collective Security Treaty in 1992; it includes Russia, Belarus, Armenia, Kazakhstan, Kyrgyzstan, and Tajikistan. The organization's intent, as posited by the then-CIS duma committee chairman, is to become "a functioning security organization with its own secretariat and rapid deployment force." The role of this force is, in part, to quell international terrorism. Russia's role in particular, as the largest and militarily strongest signatory, is to protect the other CSTO member states—and thus counteract the continued military presence of the United States in Central Asia. At its embryonic stage, the CSTO's rapid deployment force consisted of a Russian military base in Kant, equipped with 15 SU-25s and SU-27s and 500 soldiers supplementing the Tajikistan force. In 2003, the CSTO requested to join forces with NATO, the justification being that while "NATO and the CSTO might be in different weight categories . . . in essence they are similar organizations because they include military components, political components, and components that deal with today's challenges." Despite the supposed benefits of NATO-CSTO cooperation, however, NATO remained reluctant to cooperate with the CSTO. (Bhadrakumar, Asia Times March 6, 2006). The CSTO continued on without NATO's endorsement, determined to become its own regional alliance. General Baluyevsky further explained that the CSTO was in response to "NATO's attempts to involve CIS states in the bloc's activity and to weaken their relations with Russia".

In 2006, Russia announced that it planned to double both its infantry and military arsenal at Tajikistan. In July 2006, Russia and Tajikistan held a joint military exercise on the coast of the Caspian Sea, followed by a similar Russo-Kyrgyzstan exercise in October. In 2007, "Peaceful Mission Rubezh-2007" was held, in which Russia test-launched several of its missiles and the organization declared its intent to develop a more extensive military force—including four or five of the CSTO states. In 2008, Russo-Armenian forces participated in "Rubezh-2008" command war games, and Russia proposed that Article Four of the Cooperation Security Treaty be revised to encompass nuclear weapons, so as to further protect CIS states (Ria Novosti, Dec. 3, 2007).

While the SCO and CSTO might seem to have similar aims, and did sign an agreement of mutual cooperation at the CIS summit in 2007, the discrepancies between the two are telling, and reflect differences between Chinese and Russian strategy when it comes to multipolarity and security. First, the intended scope of the CSTO is much broader than that of the SCO, as exemplified by its ambitions to mimic NATO. Second, the CSTO was established as more of a military alliance than the SCO, whose charter only gives cursory mention of the military implications of the organization. What one might argue is that despite these differences, Russia and China share the view that multipolarity means respect for a state's sovereignty. After all, both the SCO and the CSTO emerged, in part, as a response to perceived U.S. encroachment on Central Asian territory. But do they truly hold the same view of sovereignty?

The internal rhetoric of Russia and China surrounding the SCO's military operations seems to indicate that the two countries might attach different meanings to sovereignty. As Michael Levin notes: "While some PRC commentators went as far as to suggest that the terrain of the exercise areas was similar to Tai- wan's coast, the Russian media toyed with the idea of a joint occupation of North Korea, if necessary." (Levin, 2008: 101). In contrast to the China-Taiwan situation, North Korea is well outside the territorial jurisdiction of the Russian Federation. Thus, Russia's allusion to the occupation of another country shifts the definition of sovereignty away from the territorial (and objective) into the realm of the moral (and subjective). But is this application universal? To answer this, I next examine China's and Russia's conceptions of sovereignty in the context of the U.S. invasion of Iraq, Russia's relations with post-Soviet states, and China's relations with Taiwan.

In September 2002, the United States proposed a resolution in the UN Security Council (UNSC) accusing Iraq of illegally concealing weapons of mass destruction (WMD) and threatening military action if the weapons were not surrendered. Russia, France, and China agreed that this was a rash decision and proposed that the United States await the conclusions of UN weapons inspectors in Iraq. Consequently, an amended resolution was proposed and passed the UNSC in November 2002. When the United States continued to press the necessity of invasion even after the Security Council's chief weapons inspector issued his report questioning the U.S. claims, both China and Russia expressed concern. Russia went so far as to join Germany and France in issuing a joint statement and later a memorandum to the UNSC requiring that the United States give the UN more time to assess the situation.

Despite Russian, French, and German opposition, Britain and Spain joined the United States in invading Iraq on March

16, 2003. China adhered to its position on the importance of multipolarity and the danger inherent in unilateral action, but did not choose to align itself with either the Germany-Russia-France or the U.S.-Britain-Spain coalitions. Kishore Mahbubani explains China's silence in relation to its broader understanding of the United States: "[China] bent over backward to accommodate U.S. hegemony, bearing in mind the wisdom of an ancient Chinese proverb, in moments of weakness, swallow your bitter humiliation, and focus on growing stronger." (Men, 2007: 52) While China was biting its tongue, Russia was less reserved: "[if] we allow international law to be replaced by might of the fist, according to which the stronger side is always right," stated Putin, "then a key principle of international law, that of the sanctity of sovereignty of all states, comes into question" (Ambrosio, 2005: 52).

The sincerity of Putin's words is suspect considering Russia's invasion of Georgia on August 10, 2008. Perhaps it is this action of the Russian Federation that best exemplifies Russia's inconsistent rhetoric and the significant rift between the Chinese and Russian views vis-à-vis multipolarity. Immediately after Russia's invasion, President George W. Bush warned that "only Russia can decide whether it will now put itself back on the path of responsible nations, or continue to pursue a policy that promises only confrontation and isolation." The President's statement indicates that Russia had to choose between two paths. But, did the Russian decision to invade Georgia represent a country blazing a new path, or was it only a stark example of a path already chosen? As mentioned, Russia has not taken well to the democratic revolutions of the former Soviet states or their incorporation into NATO—and Georgia is no exception. Since the Rose Revolution of 2003 and the election of President Mikhail Saakashvili, Georgia has positioned NATO membership among its top foreign-policy priorities. Furthermore, after the dissolution of the Soviet Union, the international community formally recognized the contested areas of South Ossetia and Abkhazia as part of Georgian territory. According to Putin (now prime minister), Russia had every "moral right" to acquire these territories after Kosovo independence, but instead agreed to a 1994 UN peacekeeping mandate to protect the citizens of these breakaway areas (most of whom were Russian). Consequently, Putin justified his 2008 attack against Georgia as a response to the Georgian government's acts of genocide—against Georgian and Russian citizens.

Critical analysis, however, indicates that Russia's actions were premeditated and were the culmination of a series of provocative Russian actions against the Georgian government dating back to 2006. A recent study of the conflict published by the Central-Asia Caucus Institute concludes that contrary to Putin's claims, Russia's invasion of Georgia was not a response to human-rights abuses in South Ossetia, but was a calculated Russian decision to punish Georgia for seeking collaboration with the West and to demonstrate to the West Russia's renewed primacy over the post-Soviet space.

The West, in concert, disapproved of Russia's action. Still, on August 10, 2008, Russia declared the independence of South Ossetia and Abkhazia, in opposition to the opinion of the other states in the G-8 economic group. Russia's recognition of Abkhazia and South Ossetia also contravened the SCO's commitment to respect sovereignty and territorial integrity as outlined in Article Five of its founding charter. Moreover, it violated Article One of the organization's 2001 document, the Shanghai Convention on Combating Terrorism, Separatism, and Extremism, which prohibits member-states from instigating or abetting separatism. Consequently, although Russia wanted the SCO to issue a communique endorsing its actions, the other members refused to do so. Instead, they issued the Dushanbe Declaration, which diplomatically reiterates the SCO's commitment to thwarting separatism and adhering to international law and asks in Article Three that the parties involved in the South Ossetian issue reconcile their differences through peaceful dialogue.

Among the SCO member-states, China in particular was placed in an extremely difficult position. Although China had established a rapport with Russia promoting a multipolar world, it could not openly endorse Russia's invasion of Georgia and its acknowledgment of the independence of Abkhazia and South Ossetia. Nor could China agree to Russia's later request for a Sino-Russian "joint action on security and prevention issues" without simultaneously appearing to encourage separatism in Tibet, Xinjiang, and Taiwan (Ching-wei, Sept. 11, 2008).

The tension between China and Russia in this regard demonstrates a significant rift between the Chinese and Russian perspectives on state sovereignty. Although China and Russia may seem similarly situated as aspiring regional hegemons in a multipolar world order, China's means of aggrandizing power is by promoting the unification of its country and defending its sovereignty against foreign and separatist threats, foregoing peace if necessary. Russia, on the other hand, with its recent invasion of Georgia, exemplifies a willingness to forego peace in order to violate a state's sovereignty and demonstrate its military prowess to surrounding states and the world. As such, China's position (and even its military preparation for a conflict with Taiwan) is more clearly in line with Article Four of the Sino-Russian Friendship Treaty, in which both sides agree to support each other in "defending the national unity and territorial integrity," and Article Five, which explicitly mentions both countries' commitment to defending Taiwan. Russia's recent actions, in addition to contravening the SCO charter, also violate Article Twenty of the Sino-Russian Friendship Treaty, expressing their joint commitment to "cracking down on .... splittists."

China's 11th Five Year Plan states: "The trend toward multi-polarity in international politics is developing amid twists and turns, and voices for multilateralism are growing in the international community, imposing effective constraints on hegemonism and power politics and making it possible for China to manage big power relations, oppose foreign interference, and defend the national interests." (People's Daily, Jan 19, 2006). Undoubtedly, many twists and turns have occurred over the past decade, to which China's promotion of multipolarity has remained a consistent subplot. Russia, in contrast, with its bellicose demeanor and dramatic policy shifts, has emerged a quite different champion of multipolarity—one content with directly challenging the hegemony of the United States and perhaps even making it possible for China to ascend peacefully.

As the second half of this article illustrates, China and Russia do not merely have differences of tone when addressing multipolarity. They also appear to differ fundamentally in their approach to it. Elizabeth Wishnick initially explained the Sino-Russian partnership by saying that "Russia, a declining great power, aims to recover its lost status, while China, a rising power, resists efforts to constrain its emerging global role". Wishnick acknowledged that China and Russia had different motives in regard to their partnership. Time has eroded these ambitions. Now, the same motives that propelled Russia and China toward partnership and agreement on multipolarity have since driven them toward different means to reach these ends and caused them to employ a different definition of multipolarity altogether. Considering the lessons learned in regard to the recent past and the unexpected Sino-Soviet split, we might not want to overlook the danger in the undefined.

Decades old border dispute was another area which the two states have successfully tackled though some misunderstandings and suspicion among the populations of the both sides persists. Under the agreement on the eastern border signed in 1991 an area of 15 km in Russia's Primorski Karai (Maritime Province) including some small piece of islands in the Amur and Ussuri rivers and small piece of land along the Tumen River was to be transferred to China. However, some local officials in Primorski Karai denounced the agreement alleging that land to be handed over would include two strategic section of Tumen river that would provide direct access to the sea of Japan and 'that Chinese were expected to build a seaport in the area that could compete with existing Russian Far East ports. (Ruisheng, 2002, pp-331-335). Now the border dispute has been resolved with the help of Shanghai Cooperation Organization (SCO). Nevertheless, some

Russians still fear that China will claim territory from Russia in the future.

Problem Areas between Russia and China

A Russo-China border issues of considerable sensitivity concerns the extensive Chinese migration much of it illegal in to Russian territory. The demographic imbalance along the border with 150 million Chinese crowded in the North Eastern part of China and only 7 million Russians in the vast bordering territories of Siberia and the Far East has been a source of concern for Soviet and Russian citizens, officials and journalists for many years. As the border tensions eased at the beginnings of the 1990s, the scale of illegal immigration increased rising three fold between 1992 and 1993. This prompted Russia to conclude an agreement with Beijing in 1994 to establishing formal border crossing posts and tighten visa restrictions. The immediate impact was the sharp reduction in Sino-Russian trade much of which "concentrated across the border by Chinese traders. The Russian press continued to provide sensational accounts of illegal immigration (termed in one account as an "invasion of Huns"), prompting to an advisor to Yeltsin, Emil Plain, to write an article in the government's newspaper stating that "claims about dangerous level of Chinese immigration and related real threat to national sovereignty in Russian Far East are not supported by the actual facts." By his calculation the "Chinese Diaspora" in Russian Far East accounted for less than 3% of the region's population - about half as many as resided there after World War II. Pain pointed out that trade with China is a "life preserver" for the Far East and he blamed local authorities for whipping up anti-Chinese fears. (Donaldson & Nogee 1998. pp. 233-245).

The reduction in shuttle trade used the level of Sino-Russian trade, which had reached $7.8 billion in 1993 (second only to the level of Russia's trade with Germany), to fall to $ 5 billion the following year. It recovered somewhat in 1995, reaching at $ 5.5 billion and rose to $6.8 billion in 1996 with the Russians enjoying a $ 3 billion trade surplus. YeItsin-Jiang set a target of $20 billion by 2000. (Donalson & Nogee, 1998, 233-254).

a) The Issues of Chinese Emigration to the Russian Far East

The emigration of Chinese into Russia has never been a primary issue in the meetings and discussions between Chinese and Russian government officials. The in/outflow of Chinese has been documented, effectively obviating the need to discuss Chinese emigration at the official level. The issue that the Russian government seems to be reluctant to speak about is what the Russian media bring up repeatedly. Although more than ten years have passed since the disintegration of the USSR, along with the communist system, the Russian people seem to think that Russia may once more fall under communism, this time under China. The Russian mass media, especially in the Russian Far East, have reported widely exaggerated numbers of Chinese in Russia. They seem to think that the emigration from China has been arranged and is being conducted by the Chinese government, which supposedly wants to obtain that which cannot be obtained with force - the expansion of territory. That Russia will change and become Chinese and that Russia will become a province of China (Zhinzni, 2002: 10) are two of the major themes the Russian media are propagating among the Russian people. It should be pointed out that there are more objective viewpoints based on investigation and research conducted by Russian scholars. However, these viewpoints do not appear to be widely supported by the public because only a small number of scholars hold those viewpoints.

It may be obvious that the Chinese government has never in the past planned and is not currently planning emigration to any specific country in the world. On the contrary, the Chinese government has gradually strengthened its control of illegal emigration from China. In fact, there are no massive migrations from China to Russia. Therefore, there can be no massive illegal migrations either. But the negative propaganda in Russia continues to have a very damaging effect on bilateral trade and people exchanges between China and Russia.

Prior to the 1980s, China's national policy on the exit and entry of its citizens and foreign citizens was very strict. Since then China has reformed its policy towards a more open stance. Accordingly, the number of Chinese citizens traveling out of the country and the number of foreign citizens coming to China has increased rapidly. In response China's legislature has had to gradually strengthen the laws in this area.

In November 1985, the Standing Committee of China's National People's Congress approved the Law on the Entry and Exit of Foreign Citizens and the Law on the Entry and Exit of Chinese Citizens. In July1995, China's State Council approved the Act on Frontier Checking of the Entry and Exit and promulgated the act in September of the same year. The act contained regulations about the entry, exit, transit, length of stay, and travel of foreign citizens in China. It also contained regulations regarding the entry, exit, private travel, and punishment of violations for Chinese citizens. At present, the main purposes of foreign travel that are considered appropriate for Chinese citizens are to visit relatives and friends, to take care of settlements in foreign countries, to study in foreign countries, and to maintain professional duties. After receiving a passport, Chinese citizens are allowed to go to foreign embassies and consulates and apply for a visa. They may then travel abroad with their valid passport and visa.

In March of 1994, the Standing Committee of China's National People's Congress approved the Additional Stipulations on Chastising Crime of Illegally Organizing and Transporting Persons across the National Frontier. These articles were added to the Criminal Law of the People's Republic of China (PRC), which had been revised in March of 1997. Clearly, strong authority from the legislature has supported the efforts against illegal emigration from China.

In May 2000, China's Ministry of Public Security issued the Act of Frontier Management on Ships along the Coasts. This act was dutifully incorporated into the provinces and autonomous regions of coastal China, effectively ending the previous system of different rules for different provinces. This act has also played an extremely important role in protecting China from the illegal entry of foreign citizens and controlling illegal emigration of Chinese citizens.

Without a doubt, China has accomplished much in the last 20 years, especially in the areas of legislative and federal power. China's political situation has stabilized, the protection for the public has improved, and the living standards of the population, especially in several regions, have risen considerably. Yet China's economic development lags behind developed countries, and this results in illegal immigration of foreign nationals and illegal emigration of Chinese citizens. The majority of illegal emigrants are peasants from the coastal regions of China. International criminal groups collude to offer illegal travel to Chinese peasants who are eager to go abroad in search of a better life. Because peasants often have little knowledge of the national laws regarding exiting China, criminal organizations have no trouble tempting them away from China. However, illegal emigration from China exceeds the norms only in a few regions and is very small in absolute terms or as a proportion of the total number of illegal migrants in the world.

Illegal Chinese emigration has been located to certain processes. First, an individual may choose a country from which it is relatively easy to obtain a visa, travel to that country with a valid visa, and then slip through to a Western European or North American country. Second, Chinese citizens may travel abroad with false documents. The Chinese in this group will alter their passport by putting in a different identification photo or otherwise altering the passport. Third, some individuals hide in shipping containers or in other places on ships to escape from the routine customs and border inspections. Fourth and finally, Chinese citizens slip through weak points in the federally enforced check points either on land or on the seas. In response to the knowledge that Chinese citizens have been misusing their passports, the Chinese government has strengthened the operation of its passport offices.

The government has increased its vigilance at every stage of passport procedures, including application, approval, frontier check points, and patrols along the coasts.

The judicial department of China has taken a strong stance against illegal emigration, especially against the illegal organization and transportation of Chinese citizens across Chinese boundaries and forgery, alteration, and sale of immigration documents. In June 2000, the twelfth edition of the Chinese passport was issued. This edition was produced with a high level of technical expertise, which should make it more difficult to forge or alter passports. In addition, the regional departments of China have been using television monitori systems in governmental offices on land and on the ships which began patrolling the Chinese seas in 1998. All of these measures have enhanced the Chinese government's ability to control illegal emigration and immigration.

While the judicial branch has been strengthening its enforcement of laws and punishments, the Chinese government has also been increasing its cooperation with the countries that share its borders in order to improve the exchange of information and technology against illegal immigration. Illegal Chinese emigrants in foreign countries have been repatriated in shiploads when their Chinese citizenship has been confirmed. International cooperation in repatriation has played an important and active role in the effort against illegal emigration.

According to China's Ministry of Public Security, Chinese governmental offices along the nation's border handled 315 cases of illegal emigration between 1999 and 2001. These offices reported seizing 2,057 illegal emigrants passing to and from China in the frontier areas. In 2001, Chinese authorities on the seas dealt with 540 cases of illegal emigrants and apprehended 2,480 illegal emigrants. In 2002, the numbers decreased by 22 percent and 54 percent, respectively. These figures demonstrate that illegal emigration of Chinese citizens by sea has been dealt with effectively. In addition, Chinese officials arrested 2,715 organizers and transporters of illegal emigrants, 511 of them being convicted as felons (China's Ministry of Public Security, 2002).

In summary, the various efforts of the Chinese government over the course of the past decade in the customs offices, over land, and on the sea have reduced the scale of illegal emigration of Chinese citizens.

In the early 1990s, the flow of Chinese nationals across the Chinese-Russian border increased due to the expansion of trade between the two countries, especially between the Chinese and Russian frontiers. In 1982 the two governments signed an agreement to restore the validity of a 1958 trade agreement. The earlier agreement put a stop to the flow of Chinese and Russians over the Chinese-Russian border in the 1960s and 1970s. At that time, travel cooperation was worked out between Heihe City, China and Blagoveshchensk, USSR whereby each side limited the number of tourists traveling to the other side to a maximum of 100 per day. Because of Soviet regulations, the "tourists" were not allowed to sell the goods that they might have brought with them. They were allowed to buy only a few local goods and bring them back to their country. On the eve of the disintegration of the USSR, trade between the border provinces of China and Russia stood at one hundred million Swiss francs, and there were more than 10,000 Chinese citizens in the Russian Far East working under labor contracts under a bilateral agreement (Guozeng, 2000: 708).

On December 27, 1991, the Chinese government recognized the independence of the Russian Federation and the two countries agreed that the diplomatic relationship that had existed between China and the USSR would continue. New bilateral trade links were established quickly. In early March 1992, the two sides concluded the Agreement on Trade Relations between China and Russia. The agreement provided for the building of zones for cooperative development on the Russian side of the Sino-Russian border. In May of the same year, the construction of a zone for mutual trade between Manchuria City, China and Zabaykalsk City, Russia began. In August 1992, Deputy Prime Minister Tian Jiyun's visit to Moscow resulted in the signing of the Agreement on Principles of Sending and Accepting Chinese Citizens in

Russian Enterprises, Joint Companies, and Departments. These agreements promoted the frontier trade and mutual visits of citizens of the two countries, and Chinese citizens going to the Russian Far East increased rapidly. During the first visit of President Boris Yeltsin to China in December 1992, the leaders of the two countries signed a joint statement, which pointed out, "Both sides should create beneficial conditions for the trade links within the framework of the agreements and protocols between the countries, including the trade links between the regions along the frontier and on the basis of direct contacts between enterprises, organizations, and entrepreneurs". (People's Daily, Dec. 19, 1992).

It should be noted that a bilateral agreement from the Soviet era stipulated that Chinese and Soviet visas must be remitted for the citizens from either country who carried diplomatic, public, and ordinary passports. For the first two years after the disintegration of the USSR, this requirement was still valid and provided the convenience for mutual visits of the citizens of China and Russia.

On December 9, 1993, at the request of Russia, the Chinese and Russian governments signed the new Agreement on the Remittance of Visas for Persons with Diplomatic and Public Passports and the Agreement on the Visas for the Citizens Coming and Going. The two agreements became effective on January 28, 1994, just 30 days after signing. The first agreement stipulated that the regulation of visa remittance was changed to the regulation of visa requirement for all Chinese citizens with either an ordinary public passport or a diplomatic passport. The new visa regulations did not play a positive role in bilateral trade. On the contrary, these measures drastically reduced the number of Chinese citizens going to Russia, especially in the frontier regions of Russia and, consequently, cut the volume of trade and other forms of economic cooperation in the frontier regions (Chinese Diplomatic Year Book, 1999: 254).

Meanwhile, the Chinese government has taken steps to simplify the procedures for the entry of Russian citizens into

China to promote exchange between the two countries. In February 1998, the Chinese Ministry of Foreign Affairs sent the Russian Ministry of Foreign Affairs a note concerning the Agreement for Building Sino-Russian Mutual Trade Zones and Simplifying Visa Procedures for the Entry of Russian Citizens. The note stated, "in order to further consolidate Sino-Russian trade relations and promote economic prosperity in the frontier areas, China and Russia agreed to simplify the procedures for the entry of Russian citizens into the trade complexes in Manchuria City, Heihe City, and Suifenhe City, China in the frontier areas. Russian citizens with a valid passport are allowed into the above trade complexes under the visa remittance after checking with the departments of customs and frontier defense, but they are forbidden in other areas than the trade complexes". (Li & Takalev, 2001: 50).

Early in the new century, at the suggestion of the Russian government, China and Russia continued to strengthen the management of their respective citizens' travel between the two countries. On February 29, 2000, the two sides concluded the Agreement on Citizens Coming and Going. The new agreement became effective on May 25, 2001 and invalidated the previous agreements (the Agreement on the Remittance of Visas for Persons with Diplomatic and Public Passports and the Agreement on the Visas for the Citizens Coming and Going). The new agreement stipulated that after May 25, 2001, citizens of each country, except diplomats and employees in land, sea, and air transportation, were required to obtain a valid visa to visit the other country. On November 1, 2002, the Russian government published the Law on the Status of Foreigners in the Russian Federation, which provided that all foreign residents, regardless of nationality and occupation, must obtain a migrant card.

In order to prove their status and occupation, all foreign residents were asked to show to the local police their migrant card together with their passport, visa, and a document that shows they were permitted to reside in the Russian Federation. According to the regulations of the Migration Department of the Russian

Federation, the deadline for obtaining the migrant card was February 15, 2003. However, as of early February, only a small number of foreign migrants had obtained a migrant card. For example, in Moscow alone, only 30,000 out the estimated 800,000 foreign residents or more in the city had obtained their migrant card. At present, Chinese citizens in Russia are mainly permanent personnel working in official agencies, students, businesspersons, and laborers in Russian companies. Among these groups, the businesspersons and laborers have the greatest difficulty in obtaining the required migrant card (Chinese Diplomatic Year Book, 2003: 272).

Since 2002, the Russian government has continually published several laws and decrees. Based on the new regulations, Russian companies are required to provide documentation on their tax situation and financial standing to the relevant governmental department as a precondition for receiving a permit to employ foreign workers. Because of this paperwork, many companies have lost and will continue to lose their eligibility to invite foreign workers. A great many Chinese laborers and businesspersons are anxious that they may have to return to China on account of expired documents.

These Russian restrictions began early in the new century. For the last two years, Chinese citizens with a valid visa issued by the Russian embassy often failed to go through customs at Moscow airports. Most of the Chinese citizens that were denied exit or entry in Moscow were laborers and businesspersons who were unfamiliar with Russian laws and language. After paying many fines, they typically had to return to China. Russian customs officials explained that the Russian companies that had invited these Chinese citizens to work for them had lost their standing with respect to foreign employment.

Under these circumstances, many Chinese citizens face difficulties in entering and exiting Russia. The application process for Russian work permits has been suspended since August of 2002 and this has forced some Chinese citizens to return to China, while others have been waiting a very long time for approval of the applications they had already submitted. The Russian media reported that the number of Chinese citizens who work as laborers or businesspersons in Russia would decrease by roughly 50 percent by 2003 (Songline, 2003: 42).

In summary, the number of Chinese citizens in Russia has been drastically reduced due to the Russian regulations. As a result, Sino-Russian trade has not increased as fast or as much as it could have during this period. For example, due to the new visa regulation that became effective in early 1994, the overall volume of foreign trade in the Russian Far East decreased by 30 percent from the previous year and trade between Russia and China specifically dropped by 79 percent. In Khabarovsky Krai, trade decreased by 83 percent; in Amur Oblast, by 80 percent; and in Chita Oblast, by 83 percent during the same period. In addition, the share of Sino-Russian trade in China's total trade fell from 2 percent in the second half of the 1990s to less than 2 percent in 2002.

The Controversy over the Number of Chinese Migrants in the Russian Far East since the 1990s, Chinese government agencies and academic institutions have not conducted any systematic investigations or surveys about Chinese migrants in Russia, including the Russian Far East. In the strict sense of the word, "migrant" means the populations who migrate across a border with the aim of long-term or permanent settlement in the destination country. Therefore, it is doubtful that the information that Russian scholars have obtained through local surveys reflects accurate information on Chinese "migrants" in Russia. The real number of Chinese migrants in Russia is very small. As for the Chinese government and academic institutions, they have not recognized that there has ever been a massive wave of Chinese migrants to Russia. It follows logically that, in their view, neither could there be a massive wave of Chinese migrants to the Russian Far East.

It is quite possible that when conducting the surveys, Russian scholars thought that "Chinese migrants" meant those Chinese who permanently live and/or routinely conduct business in

Russia. Under this definition, Westerners, Japanese, or Koreans who do business in Russia should also be seen as migrants. In the opinion of one Russian scholar, however, Westerners, Japanese, and Koreans are not considered "migrants" because they "leave the country when their contracts expire." According to the scholar's own logic, Chinese citizens who periodically travel between China and Russia should be seen as a case similar to a Westerner, Japanese, or Korean who does the same. As this demonstrates, there are inconsistencies in the popular beliefs of the Russian people, which are also apparent at the scientific level. The crux of the issue is that if these Chinese who often leave and return to Russia are not seen as migrants, then it would make no sense to discuss "massive waves" of Chinese migrants in the Russian Far East.

Furthermore, according to Dr. Larin, "not more than 30,000 Chinese were simultaneously in the Russian Far East" in 1999, and the number was not significantly different in 2002. (Gelbrass, 2003: 197). If the Chinese who live in the Russian Far East for more than four years are seen as migrants, their share of the total number in 2002, shown in the above table, was roughly 10 percent, so they should have been about 3,000 in number. The Chinese prefer to live in Khabarovsk and Vladivostok because of the areas' climate and location, so the Chinese migrants in the rest of the Russian Far East should be lower than 10 percent of the total number, that is, far less than 3,000 persons.

Table: 2.1: Length of Chinese Respondents' Stay in Russia

	Khabarovsk			Vladivostok		
	1999	2001	2002	1999	2000	2002
Less than 1 year	24.6	17.6	51.4	23	46	65.3
1-4 years	21.2	45.6	37.9	51	26	23.5
Over 4 years	15.1	26.5	10.7	10	21	11.2
No answer	39.1	10.3	_	16	7	_

Source: Vilya Gelbars, "Chinese Migration to the Russian Far East," in Tsuneo Akaha, (ed.), Human Flows Across National Borders in Northeast Asia, United Nations University.

Since 1992, there have been a great many articles and reports in the Russian media that seem to believe that the Chinese government has organized and encouraged emigration of Chinese citizens to Russia, especially the Russian Far East. As with most reports on the number of Chinese citizens in Russia or the Russian Far East, this viewpoint is utterly groundless. President Jiang Zemin addressed this belief in September of 1994 and stated,

> In recent years, because of the situation of rapid expansion of bilateral exchanges, there has emerged some out-of-order phenomena in the fields of frontier trade and people coming-and-going. I want to point out that the disorder has occurred because of the actions of individuals, not because of any policy of the two governments. (People's Daily, Sept. 4, 1994).

In fact, even in 1992 and 1993, when the visa was remitted to Chinese citizens with ordinary public passports, the number of Chinese who went to the Russian Far East was limited, especially when compared with the vast population of China. According to Russian scholars, "the number of Chinese in the Far East in 1992-1993 did not exceed 50,000 to 80,000, including some 10,000 to 15,000 legal contract workers and 10,000 to 12,000 students." The head of the Primorye passport and visa service stated, "there were only 37 permanent Chinese residents registered in the Krai in 1999." (Larin & Rubtsova, 2001: 233). It needs to be stressed that the Chinese shuttle trader, who often leaves and returns to Russia for individual business and always brings money obtained in Russia back to China, does not intend to live in Russia for a long period of time.

An article published in Moscow in August of 2003 also discussed this problem and stated that "the surveys revealed an interesting trend. Chinese migrants in most countries want to leave the homeland permanently, but Russia generally cannot retain them. The majority of Chinese come here to do business only for one or two months, or, if they are contract workers, 10 months. Therefore, it may be only an illusion that Chinese laborers can reconstruct the Far East. Moreover, the survey shows us that our neighbors are so scared of the Russian departments at various levels that they need to offer bribery to all Russian personnel, including the staff in the frontier stations and in customs. All people recognize that Russian policemen can be avaricious and they are anxious that the 'bare-headed gang' is lawless" (Saronkov, The Times, Aug 3, 2003).

The popular and much discussed topic of the Russian media is that China aims to take back the territory it lost to Russia in earlier history. Even after the Sino-Russian Treaty of Good Neighborliness, Friendship, and Cooperation was signed in July 2001, Russia's viewpoint was that "the treaty of 2001 states PRC's official abandonment of any territorial claims against Russia. The fact is that the treaty is in force only for twenty years on behalf of the government, but the ordinary Chinese who arrive in Russia have their own understanding of who is the real owner of the land they want to settle. Often they directly say that the territory will be returned to China soon." (Gelbras, 2003: 134) This Russian contradicts himself when he points out in the same article that "one of the most important conclusions from the research was that the largest concentration of Chinese migrants in Russia are found not in the Russian Far East, but in European Russia." According to this logic, the Chinese go to European Russia because they think they are the real owner of territory there, including Moscow and Saint Petersburg, and that those two cities will be returned to China. Could that viewpoint be right?

In conclusion, international research about the issue of in/outflow of Chinese nationals in Northeast Asia has not only academic significance, but also real-world significance that can be used for clarifying the relevant problems in the mutual policies and mutual relations among the countries of the region. The Russian academic institutions conducting local surveys and opinion polls should be urged to provide only the facts, so that objective researchers can deduce logical conclusions about the issues from the data obtained. Those logical conclusions can be beneficial to the Chinese and Russian governments as they work to develop relevant policies for a practical solution.

In fact, this insecurity regarding illegal migration are not the result of Chinese actions and policies but a reflection of internal Russian problems. Russian concern that Chinese could become the lingua-franca of the Russian Far Eastern Region are directed at the failure of the Russian authorities Central and local - to regenerate the region. Possible remedies, such as incentives to encourage migration from European Russia and from ethnic Russians in the Baltic States and Central Asia have not been seriously attempted. In the meantime, local inhabitants are leaving in droves in response to living miserable conditions even by Russian standards. Unfortunately, in the absence of any early prospects of improvement (let alone a lasting solution) the Chinese serve as convenient scapegoat and bogeyman (Dmtri, 1989, p. 9).

Apart from migration problem, there is some concern that Russia could loose control of its most advanced military technology. The Russo-China trade relationship is a prime example of one in which armaments constitutes the single most important export accounting to at least one third of the $7 billion at the beginning of 1997. Combat aircrafts have been the chief components of Russian deliveries; China has purchased at least six dozen transcontinental SU27 fighters, which are capable of making Beijing-to-Moscow trip in two and half-hours with one mid air refueling. Other categories of purchases which have been concluded or which are being discussed include naval vessels (Soveremanyi-class destroyers equipped with Supersonic missiles, two kilo 636 diesel-powered submarines and less advanced Varshu-Vianka Submarines), S-300 surface-to-air missile sets, T-72 Tanks, Smerch multiple rocket launchers, and the technology for advanced gas centrifuges used in uranium enrichment and for MIRV missiles (Dmitri, 1999, pp. 9-11).

According to the Russian air force Chief of Staff, China concluded the largest military contract in Russia's history in 1995. The deal amounted to more than $ 2 billion for the technology and licenses to manufacture the SU-27 at a factory in Shenyang province. Production began in 1999. Russian press reported concern that China would thereby free itself of the need to purchase aircraft from Moscow in future, and that if China made minor modification to the plane's design, it might even become competitor in the export market. (Singh, 1996, pp. 180-182).

Another area of major concern between Russia and China is that by no means all the payment comes in the form of cash and defense factories often ended up relying on bartered products in order to realize their value. There has been such extreme cases as the case of the Chinese pigs which were traded for an arms shipment that was banned in Russia by the veterinary inspector, who suspected that they might spread hog plague in the country.

In another instance, the Chinese barted 15000 low-quality radio-cassette players for three MI-60 helicopters. However, whereas the barter method initially constituted about three fourth of Chinese payments, China's growing dollar trade surplus have enabled Russian negotiations to arrange for hard currency payment in recent year contracts.

A far more significant issue is whether Russia is endangering its own long-term security by selling to its giant neighbour its most advanced weapons and the know-how to produce them. Russian military sources have expressed envy that Beijing is receiving more modern equipments than their own units possess.

China is said to be a 'sleeping giant' who is fully devoted to its economic development today and does not want to be involved in any conflict to divert its attention from development. But one can not be sure whether its present state of mind will remain same in the future. Today, Russia is desperately selling its advanced weapon to earn foreign currency which its Soviet era defence industry badly requires for its survival. In the long run once the Chinese get to acquire the technological know how this could be dangerous for Russia's own security. The AK-47 is the best example. The Chinese acquired its technological knowhow and subsequently produced AK-56 with slight modification and now Russia has lost the control over AK-47 completely world over.

On their part, Russian dealers are outraged over blatant Chinese imitations of their weaponry, built from designs supplied on an explicit understanding that the weapons were to be purchased.

The overdue aircraft are from a deal signed in 2005, in which China agreed to buy 30 IL-76 transport aircraft and eight IL-78 aerial refuelling tankers from Russia. But the Tashkent Aircraft Plant, based in Uzbekistan"s capital, declared soon after the signing that it was unable to build the planes independently owing to financial and technical problems.

To resolve the problem, Russia gave three alternative proposals to the Chinese. The first was to co-produce the plane's parts in Tashkent, as well as at the Ulianovsk and/or Voronezh aviation factories in Russia, and assemble the aircraft in Voronezh. The second was to completely manufacture the aircraft in Russia. And, the third was to assemble the planes in Tashkent, with parts produced in Russia. But this meant Russia would have to add new equipment to the Ulianovsk and Voronezh aviation factories, so Rosoboronexport asked the Chinese to accept a higher price for the aircraft.

China"s response was swift and savage. It twice postponed an annual high-level conference on cooperation in defence technology. Beijing says that to restart the talks, Russia has to fulfil the aircraft contract. Russia counters that the present problem requires new discussions, without any conditions. US and Japanese negotiators know from beforehand the Chinese tendency to set stringent pre-conditions for political talks and other negotiations. Now, the Russians are feeling the heat.

b) China's Complaint regarding Quality of Goods from Russia

To press home its advantage, China also criticised the quality of its Russian weapons, especially about the short service-life of optical and electronic detection devices (IRST) fitted on the SU-27SK fighter. Russia says the problems are caused by improper use, and shows photos of the IRST being used for the Chinese air force's Su-27SK without protective coverings, even in bad weather.

To compound the problem, the Chinese air force (PLAAF) is one of Russia's biggest customers. It has bought 100 advanced Su-30MKK multipurpose fighters and 48 Su-27SK fighters. It also obtained license production rights for 200 Su-27SKs and started making them in 1996, but suspended production after 95 Chinese-made J11As were completed last year. Russia also backed out of the deal owing to technical reservations.

The Chinese navy has bought 12 kilo class 877/636 diesel submarines and four 956E/EM missile destroyers, new warships, as well as eight battalions each of S-300PMU/PMU-1 and S-300PMU-2 long range surface-to-air missiles, apart from other naval subsystems for Chinese carriers.

c) Russia Calls China as 'King of Copying'

Moscow is unhappy with China's massive production of copycat versions of Russian weapons. Russian arms manufacturers have been taken by surprise with the sheer speed and scale of China's copycat capabilities.

Often, Chinese dealers say they want to buy Russian arms, begin negotiations, and ask as many technical questions as possible. They then take photos and videos of the weapons, request all available documents, and repeatedly come back to the table to discuss technical issues.

After major document exchanges and extensive technical negotiations, the dealers disappear. Two or three years later, a Chinese copy of the weapon that was under discussion appears on the market.

The Chinese A100 multiple launch rocket system (MLRS), for example, is almost identical to the Russian SMERCH MLRS. Even the shape is the same! The Chinese PLZ05 155-mm self-propelled gun (SPG) howitzer system (like the Bofors gun) is a copy of the Russian 2S19M1 SPG.

In the mid-90s, China asked the Russian Phazotron Radar Design Bureau to help the PLAAF to upgrade the Chinese F8II fighters. China purchased two ZHUK-8II airborne radars from Phazotron, ostensibly to test their capabilities. The PLAAF gained access to many technical documents, as it had promised to buy at least 100 radars. But, the Chinese never came back. Two years ago, the new Chinese F8IIM fighter was launched, with new "indigenous" multi-function radar.

When the Chinese navy bought the Russian 956E/EM missile destroyer from Russia, it came with a number of subsystems including the Fregat M2EM 3D radar and the MR-90 tracking radar and sonar. China's domestic Type 054A missile frigate (FFG) now has an identical radar system. Russian designers from the Salyut factory that developed the radars say the speed at which they have been cloned is "unbelievable".

But Italy and France had almost identical experiences during their military hardware honeymoon with China in the '80s. China bought two sets of Sea Tiger onboard ship radars, two sets of Crotale air defense missiles, and two sets of Tavitac naval command and control systems from France. It also picked up a few sets of sonar and EW systems from Italy. Chinese versions of the above systems are now standard issue on Chinese navy warships.

In the year 2000 there were rumors that Putin had signed a secret decree suspending of transfer of sensitive arms technology and know how to China. Moscow was concerned that China was buying Russian military technology and know-how while avoiding the purchase of large ready-made stock of military hardware. (Times of India, March 13, 2000). In other words China was more keen for technology transfer. This would obviously help it to develop its own defence production capability while lessening its dependence on Moscow (Sakwa, 203, p. 186).

Most Russian analysts appear to believe that China's short term foreign policy ambitions are directed towards Taiwan and the South-China Sea, and that her interest in stability in Central Asia parallels those of Russia. Russian made equipments may indeed enable Beijing to obtain a regional advantage in force projection capability in future Taiwan crisis; the Soveremennyi destroyers cruise missiles have a combat range of three hundred miles, are reportedly resistant to US air defence system, and will allow China to test the naval superiority of US in the East China Sea. But expressing Russian government's view point, former defense minister Pevel Grachev declared in 1995 that "China posses no threat to Russian security now and will not in the near future" and he asserted that if Russia did not sell arms to China, some other country would (The Economist, April. 26, 1997, p. 19).

Another trouble spot in China's Xinjiang province, whose population is ethnically kin to that of the neighbouring post-Soviet states, is troubled by sporadic anti-Beijing rebellious that could potentially spark a cross-border "liberation war". From that perspective even with respect to the near future by closely associating with China and by selling it arms, Russia risks upsetting the delicate military balance in Asia and even being drawn into China's territorial disputes with Taiwan, Vietnam, Japan, and ultimately the U.S. (Moltz, 1995, p. 1995).

At a more generalized level, there exists a cultural divide that frequently obscures and undermines commonalities of interests. Many Russians who even advocate strategic partnerships, subscribe to the image of Russia as a "civilizational barrier" against the barbarian, 'East'. Although these days the principle danger is seen as Islamic radicalism emanating from the South, the very concept of Russian as a guardian of 'western' values inhibits rapprochement with China. It foster a superiority complex that many Chinese find unwarranted in a state they view as economically backward, militantly crippled and of diminishing international influence. (Menon & Ziegler, 2002, pp. 38-39).

The combination of historical fears and political/ civilizational stereotyping has reinforced to some extent West-centrism in both Russia and China. As a consequence, the strategic partnership carries the whiff of second class treatment, actual priorities being elsewhere. This is especially true in Moscow, where relations with America, Western Europe and former republics of the Soviet Union absorb considerable more attention and resources. Such relativism detracts from the bilateral relationship in two ways. In the first place, it sometimes translates into a careless attitude towards the strategic concerns of the other. For example, Putin administration made significant commitments in its external relations - notably endorsement of American military presence in Central Asia post 9/11 and strategic arms agreements with Washington after only minimal consultation with Beijing. Second China and Russia have to some extent become competitors for Western favours, whether in the form of foreign investment, political approbation or advantageous security arrangement (Menon & Ziegler 2002 pp. 38-39).

Over the next decade, radical changes in the thinking of both countries are unlikely. The ambiguities with strategic partnership will remain. On the plus side, a confluence of views on many international issues, common threat perceptions, expanding economic ties can be detected. In the minus column the burden of historical and civilizational prejudices, an increasingly dominant West-centrism in Moscow and Beijing and the Russian anxieties regarding China's rise as the next superpower continue. Within this overall dynamic, three issue areas will bear particular altention i.e.,

(i) Development over the Angarsk-Nakhodka oil pipeline;
(ii) Security management on the Korean peninsula; and
(iii) Strategic projections h former Soviet central Asia. (Lo, 2004. pp. 295-309).

Few issues highlight the dual nature of the Russian-Chinese dynamics so vividly as the pipeline debate. On the one hand collaboration on this project reflects the determination of both countries to take their relationship up to the next level. However, this symbolism is double-edged and has raised stakes all round, for ill as well as for good. Large scale energy and infrastructural projects represents the 'future' and most promising avenue for diversifying and enriching the bilateral relationship, yet they also enhance the potential for serious disagreements. In the event that Putin opts for Nakhodka route, as many believe he will, there will be political as well as economic ramifications. Beijing will not take only grave offence at the cancellation of prior intergovernmental undertakings but might also interpret the decision as signaling a fundamental reorientation in Putin's foreign policy away from geographical 'balance of multivectoralism' towards a clear strategic commitment to the West (Lo, 2004, pp. 295-309).

Moscow is also tying to restrain China discreetly from occupying too dominant a position in north-east Asian affairs, in the first instance on the Korean peninsula. To some extent Russ a sees China regionally as the analogue of the US globally i.e. as a country with an overtly hegemonic agenda. Paradoxically, Russia's position as the least influential of all the parties involved in the Korean question is to it:; advantage, since its weakness enables it, more or less plausibly to put itself forward as the disinterested facilitator of the peace process.

In Central Asia, Moscow is engaged in much more activist project i.e., reestablishing itself in the traditional sphere of influence. Here Russia sees itself as a regional hegemon, a position it is reluctant to cede. However, China's geographical proximity to Central Asia and considerable security and economic interests there mean that it will not simply 'go away'. For the moment this is not an issue, given Beijing's willingness to accept a secondary role and the existence of a Russian-Chinese security consensus against the threat of Islamic racialism. But there is no guarantee that this commonality of interest will remain the dominant reality. As Russia seeks to reassert its presence and influence in the region, and China attempts to maximize its economic stake Central Asia looms as perhaps the most likely theatre for renewed bilateral tensions (Shaumina, 2003, pp. 361-363).

In early June 1999, a joint statement by the foreign ministers of Russia and China insisted that neither of them intended to form a 'political-military alliance directed against any country or group of countries'. From 10 to 11

December 1999 President Yeltsin visited Moscow and issued a joint statement with Jiang Zemin on world affairs. They unilaterally opposed NATO action in Yugoslavia, the US targeting of Chinese embassy in Belgrade, and Western 'hysteria' against Russia's military action in Chechnya. Russian analysts linked the declaration closely to Yeltsin's blunt reminder to President Clinton not to forget "for a moment that Russia holds a full arsenal of nuclear weapons" and "would not allow the USA dictate to the entire world" (Black, 2004, pp. 297-305).

At present both Russia and China is using each other to counter balance Japanese or US regional dominance. Yet the emergence of China as a global super power may conflict with Russia s strategic interest, particularly if it succeeds in becoming an active and important partner with Asia-Pacific countries, which is also China's ultimate regional goal.

Russian and Chinese relations has collapsed and been restored many a time, and have also been interpreted differently in both countries. Each of the two states has complex relations with outside world. Both states were subject to aggression on the part of third countries and helped one another to struggle against foreign aggression. Taking on overview to the history of Russo-Chinese relations it is possible to make some generalizations.

1. Russia and China have always had controversies in their relations but generally managed to keep the peace, not entirely large scale military hostilities towards each other and never proclaiming war against each other;
2. Russia and China have always been exploring some form of alliance with each other;
3. Russia and China have several times tried to conclude treaties of friendship and union, but these treaties have been broken several times. (Voksresenski, 2003, pp- 207-208).

As Putin assumed office on December 31, 1999, he was determined to reassert control over the state apparatus (primarily in the energy sector), Russia's periphery such as in the Far East, and its "near abroad" in Central Asia and the Caucasus. (Wishnick, Moreover, the strong China-Russia relations developed under Yeltsin changed as a result of Putin's initially pro-Western policies. Russia's involvement in the war on terror together with Russia's agreement to a US military presence in Central Asia in 2001 did not go down well in Beijing either. Putin's domestic constituency, including the elite and the general population, found his reengagement with Washington equally awkward.

Convinced that things could not get much worse, Putin's acceptance of NATO's expansion into the Baltics, permission given to the US' withdrawal from the ABM-treaty, and quiet consent of American forces' presence in Georgia raised additional fears in the Duma, within Russian public opinion, and to some extent among the Chinese. These fears from the Chinese side were somewhat put to rest as Chinese president Jiang Zemin and Vladimir Putin signed the Treaty of Good-Neighbourliness and Friendly Cooperation on July 16, 2001 (China Report, 2001: 25).

The 20-year strategic and economic cooperation treaty was to be the most far-reaching one ever entered into since the time of Mao and Stalin. Yet only two days after, on July 18, Russian President Vladimir Putin seemed to demonstrate little intention of limiting himself to the sole China option. At a press-conference on the ABM-treaty he proposed that NATO should either be disbanded or that Russia should join it, and seemed to place little emphasis on the significance and the implications that this would have for Russia's China engagement.18 Especially since the Treaty signed with China two days earlier specified that: "The contracting parties shall not enter into any alliance or be a party to any bloc nor shall they embark on any such action, including the conclusion of such treaty with a third country which compromises the sovereignty, security, and territorial integrity of the other contracting party." Considering Putin's statements, China cannot have put much trust in the value of this agreement. The Chinese, however, continue to say that Sino-Russian ties are budding. This was not least seen with the publication of an article in the CCP's mouthpiece People's Daily in late November 2002 titled "China-Russia Relations Remain Better than Russian- US Ties." (Legando, 2001, 10).

d) The Siberian Pipeline Struggle

Besides seeking to engage with both the east and west, Vladimir Putin was also able to strengthen his control and presidential powers in the domains of foreign and security policy at the expense of the federal Duma (the parliament). This was particularly seen in Putin's foreign policy towards Japan and China, and especially with his decision to favor Japan in the Siberian pipeline project, something which was opposed by most Russian decision-makers at the time. This was in contradiction with the agreement signed in July 2001 specifying that the Siberian pipeline would be built from Nakhodka in Russia to the Chinese town of Daqing. The 2,400-kilometer pipeline was planned to carry up to 20 million tons of oil representing 12 percent of China's total oil consumption. In late May 2003, the deal was finally settled as the head of Yukos, Mikhail Khodorkovskiii, reached an agreement with Chinese state-owned oil company Chinese National Petroleum Company (CNPC). An agreement was also inked on expansion of oil exports in general where Yukos pledged to boost oil deliveries to 20 million tons annually from 2006-2010 to be increased to 30 million tons over the period 2011-2030. The deal was supported by most concerned domestic actors in Russia ranging from the Energy Ministry, to PM Mikhail Kasyanov, as well as the pro-China group within the Russian Foreign Ministry (Buszynski, 2006: 288).

Yet Putin opposed reducing the pipeline to the sole Chinese option and started advocating the stretch to Japan instead. To be fair, this was not solely for the reason of short-cutting China but also because of a generous Japanese counter-offer. This coincided with a crack-down on the oligarchs and private interests in the Russian energy industry, and, as is well known, the Yukos CEO Khodorkovskiii was arrested, Yukos assets were seized, and the pipeline to China was paused. In September 2004, in an effort to rescue the vital agreement signed with Yukos, Chinese PM Wen Jiabao paid an official visit to Moscow. He was unable to secure the construction of the pipeline but he managed to get the Russians to agree on an increase of oil exports. To ensure an uninterrupted supply of Russian oil, Chinese banks also provided Russia with a $6 billion loan for them to acquire Yukos' assetsin exchange for energy contracts. Finally, in October the same year, Putin eventually decided for the route to Japan but with a branch line extended to China. (Buszynski, 2006: 289-290). Since then Putin has shifted back to the Chinese option, yet refraining from giving any details whatsoever when the project could be realized. Although China has tended to smooth over this disappointment with diplomatic rhetoric there should not be any doubt that this has had a negative effect on bilateral relations.

Even though this indecisiveness from Moscow clearly worked against Chinese interests, Russian foreign policy started to change towards a less Western-oriented and more China-focused foreign policy overall around 2003–2004. Instead of band wagoning with the US the Kremlin chose to shift its attention to a Russo-Chinese balance. This coincided with the US launch of Operation Iraqi Freedom and intense opposition from China and Russia to this breach of Iraq's sovereignty. One of the manifestations of these deepening Sino-Russian ties was the further institutionalization of the Shanghai Cooperation Organization (China, Russia, Kyrgyzstan, Kazakhstan, Tajikistan, and Uzbekistan).

Besides the Iraq war, the primary factor accounting for this sudden strategic shift of Moscow's is most likely found in the simple fact that Russia perceived no tangible benefits from the deepened engagement with Washington that it had initiated after September 11, yet was forced to make numerous unbearable concessions. This relate perhaps primarily to the allowance of a US presence in Russia's vicinity. This ignored the benefits accruing to Russia from the US role in stabilizing Afghanistan, but nevertheless remains the perception in Moscow. This was highly unpopular among public opinion, the Duma, the Defense Ministry and other ministries where the Soviet nostalgia still lives.

The pressure exerted from these groups was one of the reasons Putin started to explore overlapping interests with China. The strengthening of the Russian Federation through increased oil and gas exports combined with a relatively high price-level may also have contributed to this.

Despite this strengthening of the Russian energy-incomes, Russia has been forced to attract foreign investors into its energy industry. This was primarily seen in 2004 when Chinese banks financed Rosneft's acquisition of the former Yukos asset Yuganskneftegaz with a $6 billion loan. Another similar deal was concluded between Chinese state oil-company Sinopec and its purchase of TNK-BP's 96.9 percent $3 billion share of Russian Udmurtneft in 2006. The precondition was that it would sell 51 percent of the shares to Rosneft once the deal was finalized. Although Beijing got 49 percent of the shares in the latter deal, and the deal represents the first time a Chinese company get direct access to Russian assets, the significance of this should not be overestimated. Both, because Russia isforced to give something to keep the strategic partnership from reversing, but also because Russia is in dire need of foreign investments to maintain energy infrastructure and explore new energy discoveries. As revealed in Russia's Energy Strategy 2001–2020, there is a need for around 450–600 billion euros to be invested in an ageing capital stock in this period, and in order to realize the projected growth of 4 to 5 percent. As such, Chinese hard currency is today very much needed in the Russian energy sector. (Blank, 2005: 107).

Taken in aggregate, there should be no doubt that bilateral relations have strengthened during the 2000s. China and Russia have settled most of their outstanding border disputes, are enjoying a booming bilateral trade, and held a large-scale military exercise, Peace Mission 2005. In 2005, the two countries also signed a China-Russia Joint Statement on 21st Century World Order stressing their mutual commonalities, interests, and benign intentions. Bilateral trade in the same year topped $30 billion, an increase of 37 percent over the previous year (Pan, 2006: 28). A high-level mechanism devoted to bilateral security talks between

Russia's Security Council and the Chinese Communist Party's Politburo has also been formed. In March 2006, China and Russia also adopted a declaration titled "Russia, China support energy diversification" specifying increased strategic cooperation in this sphere. Finally, as recent as in November, Sinopec and Rosneft signed the shareholder agreement of Udmurtneft marking one step forward in Sino- Russian energy relations. The significance of this should not be overstated, however, considering the fact that Moscow still retains the controlling share.

Overlapping Interests, Tensions and Limitations between Russia and China

Sino-Russian relations today should be seen in this particular historical context and uncertainty surrounding the Western engagements of both. Today, their respective interests have tended to converge more and more as evident from the development in the last 2–3 years. This is due to several reasons. First and foremost, both want internal stability and self-development. Neither of these interests is possible to realize without a healthy relationship with each other. China needs energy, arms, and raw materials in the pursuit of its modernization-program while Russia needs assistance in keeping its former satellite states within its orbit and away from Western influence. This is to retain access to energy and bases, achieve economic benefits, and use these states as buffers. Both also have a vested interest in containing Islamic groups: China in Xinjiang, Russia in the North Caucasus as well as jointly in Central Asia through the Shanghai Cooperation Organization. All these interests intersect in the Central Asia and Caspian region, and it is also here that the policies will clash with the West. The US and Europe have been active in developing alternative energy corridors skirting Russian territory, especially with the construction of the Baku-Tbilisi-Ceyhan (BTC) pipeline. The Western powers are now launching additional efforts to connect the BTC pipeline with a trans-Caspian pipeline connecting with Kazakhstan at Atyrau. If successful, this will prove to have significant implications for the balance of power in the region, and, as such, will be met with fierce resistance from both China and Russia and drive them closer together. Although China is an emerging competitor for influence in the Caspian and Central Asia as well, it is perceived by Russia as far less a threat than the United States.

But even though there has been a major reengagement between China and Russia since Putin's initial embrace of the West, this should not be interpreted as an alliance is imminent. Not least considering Putin's statements that it would give China up in a heartbeat for NATO membership. Rhetoric aside, significant internal competition and tensions continue to afflict Sino-Russian relations negatively and vivid statements on the flourishing partnership are often more declaratory than substantive. Both know that they can raise their bargaining power vis-à-vis the US and the post-Soviet successor states (and Taiwan) by speaking in concert. Both also know that they can do this until a certain threshold level. But this is often as far as it goes as deep distrust and fierce bargaining is a bitter reality in the bilateral relationship. Because of this, it is highly questionable if Sino-Russian relations could endure a major setback should this occur.

Both China and Russia know that either would betray one another for a healthy relationship with the United States (and the West) should such a window open — this has been a consistent feature under Putin, Yeltsin as well as Jiang and Hu. This is not least due to the economic issues involved. In 2005, bilateral trade between China and the US topped $285.3 billion, while China's trade with Russia, although rapidly increasing stood at $29.1 billion.30 Russia's total trade volume with the US was approximately $18.3 billion the same year, while the European Union's share makes up around 50 percent of Russia's total foreign trade.31 Considering the dependence of Russia and China on the EU and the US respectively, it is hard to see anything that could make them sacrifice this. In terms of their own bilateral trade both China and Russia are essentially also dissatisfied with the current state of engagement. Russia is dissatisfied with the type of commodities traded: it would rather see itself as an exporter of technology, and machinery than just raw materials and energy.

The latter comprised almost 90 percent of Russia's total exports to China in 2005 (Blank, 206: p. 57).

Moreover, from the Chinese perspective there is clear frustration with Moscow's hesitance in letting Beijing explore gas and oil deals fully as well as the tendency of settled agreements to be of a "framework nature" that rarely are put to practice. This was also revealed by the vice-director of China's National Development and Reform Commission, Zhang Guobao, in a recent interview with Interfax where he stated that Russia had complied with commitments on oil exports by rail to China, but as for cooperation in other areas, there had been a lot of contact and communication, but "little actual progress." Russia also seeks to diversify its exports in energy and consumer goods to the wider Asia-Pacific, especially Japan which will impact its willingness and potential to export to China (Lo, 2005: 25).

This also partly explains Russia's indecisiveness on the Siberian pipeline and its further stretch to either Japan or China. The significance and potentials of bilateral trade between the two are also often overestimated. Due to low purchasing power parity in the two countries it will take a long time to develop sufficient demand and transnational companies that could match the demand and market-conditions available in OECD countries. The purchasing power parity of Russia per capita is only 30 percent of the OECD average while China stands at no more than 17 percent (figures from 2003) (Kerr, 2005: 417).

The large immigration of Chinese into the Russian Far-East is also a source of tension, although this was more of a concern during Yeltsin period than Putin's. With a flow of immigrants pouring across the border, Russia, and primarily local authorities, have shown great concern over the "Sinocization" of the area and, by extension, the potential of Chinese tanks rolling up to Siberia to reclaim these territories that it lost in the 19th century. In the words of Alexander Shaikin, head of the border control at the Federal Border Guard Service, the "Chinese are now invading Russia with suitcases". Considering the historical and current role of nationalism within the two countries, this uncontrolled migration may very well turn radical putting severe strains on bilateral relations. This is paradoxical considering the urgent need for a working-age population that the depopulated Russian Far-East needs (Aleksev & Hafstetter, 2006: 120).

Moreover, although China and Russia have achieved a notable degree of cooperation within the Shanghai Cooperation Organization (SCO) the achievements have so far been modest. This was made abundantly clear with their acceptance of the US as the sole security provider in the region following September 11. To be fair, SCO is a young organization with only 10 years in existence (if counting the Shanghai 5), and it is unreasonable to demand that SCO alone could eliminate the massive threats of drugtrafficking and terrorism facing the region. But it is also about working constructively. To date, the SCO has functioned as a vehicle for China to pressure the Central Asian states to extradite its Uyghur populations who unconvincingly are accused of separatism in China's far-western Xinjiang region. Evidently, suppression of minorities is not a pragmatic and long-term method to fight terrorism. It should be acknowledged however that the SCO (and the Shanghai 5) played an important role in solving the border disputes in the late 1990s.

With the SCO's recent engagement in the trade sector it will also face obstacles considering the disagreements between Russia and China here. Tensions are also frequent within related areas of potential cooperation. With regards to infrastructure there are few projects that China and Russia would agree to concert their efforts in. Both are competing for their share of overland continental trade from East Asia to Europe, either via the Trans-Siberian railway or on the second Euro-Asia landbridge running via Xinjiang and Central Asia — the former heavily promoted by Russia the latter by China. Russia and China view this more or less in terms of a zero sum game where any infrastructure investment in a competing corridor will equal a corresponding loss in transit on its own promoted corridor. Energy is also a sector where cooperation will be hard to achieve. Even though Russia has been arguing its wish to set up an SCO energy club coordinating the energy policies of the SCO vociferously, China has equally vociferously opposed any effort to let its energy security be subject to multilateralism, and prefer to discuss these issues bilaterally (Blank, 2006: 57).

The power imbalance between China and Russia is also growing rapidly, both economically and in military terms. As described in the previous section, Russia's economic plummet coincided with Chinese double-digit GDP increases in the first half of the 1990s. Seen in a larger perspective, the economic size ratio between Soviet Union and China has reversed from being 4 to 1 in favor of Soviet to a Chinese advantage of 4 to 1 over Russia from the late 1970s to 2001. If China continues its rapid growth its economy will equal that of the US in 2015 while Russia, on the other hand, is losing more and more of its share of the world economy (Weele, 2003: 355). The growing trade relationship between China-Central Asia and China-Europe combined with a US entry into the markets of Central Asia and the Caucasus also puts Russia into a position of inferiority and strategic encirclement in its former sphere of influence.

Not to mention that it has been feeding the Chinese army with arms and arms technology to an extent clearly contradicting Russia's strategic interests. For example, in 2000 China made up 70 percent of Russia's arms exports. This is a dependence which is extremely awkward and that has been forced rather than intended as a Russo-Chinese balance against the United States. As the Soviet Union collapsed, Russia was in dire need of hard currency to keep the military-industrial complex floating in face of a declining domestic demand. China was a vital potential customer and the choice was between feeding a growing China with weapons or face social instability and financial free-fall in an already plummeting economy. Besides, the arms industry is one of the few Russian industries where it remains internationally competitive. Puzzling is however that Russia for some reason seems to have ventured on a different strategic course with regards to energy. Despite being in need of hard currency to maintain pipelines and explore new oil/gas fields it has been reluctant in letting Beijing near such cooperation, especially in controlling the means of delivery (e.g. through pipelines and other infrastructure) and ownership of fields.

Besides these sources of tension, the deterioration of relations between Russia and the EU that has occurred lately, together with Dick Cheney's blunt statement on Russia in Vilnius has to some extent isolated the Kremlin. The EU's willingness to tap energy directly from the Central Asian states rather than via Russia may also in the long-run be a loss of a linchpin in the Russian export market. With a deteriorating energy infrastructure, inadequate finances to fund such projects as Shtokman in the Barents Sea, together with a bracketing of foreign investors willing to cover this, Russia risks eventually shortchanging its economic potential. In a bigger strategic perspective, including South Asia and the Middle East, Beijing's increased engagement with New Delhi and Tehran directly challenges two of Russia's traditional spheres of influence. Besides, the Russo-Iranian alliance is almost completely confined to trade and armament cooperation and disagreements over the sectoral division of the Caspian Sea continue to haunt further cooperation.

As such, Russia is the one power who finds the current situation most awkward. It is forced to play second fiddle to China and feed China's growing economy and military with arms and, to a lesser extent energy, to maintain an adequate Russian state income. To put it bluntly, Russia needs China more than China needs Russia and Russia's main problem in maneuvering the relation is its weakness not China's strength (Kerr, 2005: 416). The only lever that Russia possesses over China is energy but it is reluctant in playing this card prematurely. This is why Russia delays pipelines, does not fulfill reached agreements, and is obstructive in its energy engagements with China. On the other hand, China has to abide with a lot as well, especially in the energy sector where it has to succumb to whatever terms Russia sets. This is most evident in the fate of the Siberian pipeline and Russia's dismantling of Yukos, the only company that has given some glimpse of hope in Beijing. Even worse, China had to finance

Rosneft's expropriation of Yukos' flagship Yuganskneftegaz with a $6 billion loan as described above without getting anything more than long-term supply contracts in return. Interests in the Middle East are also vitally different: while Russia cashes in considerably on tensions in the Middle East due to rising oil prices, China finds the same situation to be a direct threat to its national security as 58 percent of its oil imports originate from the region (Beng & Li, 2005: 19). This also leads to China seeking energy diversification where Russia is the most attractive option thereby raising the lever and bargaining position of Moscow over Beijing.

This changing configuration of power is crucial in understanding the forthcoming formation of alliances and balances. The key question becomes how the discrepancies in growth, power asymmetries, and energy access between these two will affect the bilateral relationship? Despite the significant rapprochement that has occurred in recent years between the two, the fact remains that the rise and decline of nations are the main explanatory variable for states resorting to arms (Weede, 2003: 355).

Rhetoric aside, China and Russia are currently a textbook case in such rapid shifts of power. While neither China, and especially nor Russia, will be able to challenge US power superiority in the short to middle term — this is not the case between China and Russia. The relations between these two have swung considerably in the last 50 years and will likely continue to do so. Russia is in dire need of strengthening its economy and retaining access over as much energy resources as it possibly can while China's urgent energy needs forces it to the same wells. To say that a conflict is imminent may be premature but growing tensions is something to be expected if Russia continues on the current set course.

The likelihood that geo-politics and the Russian strategy of short-cutting China's energy needs will continue to gain the upper hand is great. As Putin leaves office in the presidential elections of 2008, he is likely to hand-pick persons perpetuating the Kremlin's policy of retaining access to energy resources. Two such potential candidates are the Chairman of Gazprom, Dmitry Medvedev, as well as Defense Minister Sergei Ivanov. In addition, the Russian Duma has vehemently expressed discontent with the energy concessions given to China, sometimes in contradiction with Putin's pursued policy. The position of the Duma with regard to a centralization of energy policy is unlikely to change as well. This was most clearly seen with the anticipated sale of Slavneft to CNPC in 2002; a deal Putin largely agreed to but was forced to reconsider because of parliamentary opposition. A further sign that the bilateral energy relationship is troubling Sino-Russian relations was seen as late as September 2006. That month, Beijing hosted a visit of Dmitry Medvedev but this was hardly noticed in either the Chinese or the Russian press. Such a visit may have passed unnoticed if it was just any official, but the fact that Medvedev is a top candidate to be the successor as Putin steps down in 2008 does not make him into any official, but the likely next President of Russia. This should have stirred more attention than it did should relations be thriving.

In the military sector, the issues to watch will be the joint military exercises between China and Russia slated for 2007, whether the base race in Central Asia will intensify, as well as how the relations in arms capabilities will change. Both in conventional arms, but also in nuclear weapons where China is catching up on Russia's nuclear arsenal. The pattern of troop deployment and organization is also likely to indicate propensity for conflict, and the value that both assign to energy resources. For example, in the past few years there have been signs pointing to a reorganization of the People's Liberation Army (PLA) where it has been set to acquire a capability of projecting force deep into an enemy's territory (Andrew, 2006: 28). PLA has also redoubled military equipment deployed in Xinjiang and modernized it substantially. These factors have led some to argue that it indicates a Chinese preparedness to resort to force to protect its energy assets in Central Asia should it be required (Ibid: 28-29) Such a turn of events do however seem very distant at present, although China may use such contingents as peacekeeping forces in times of acute instability or to protect its oil-fields in Xinjiang's Tarim Basin. The China-Russia military exercises should also be taken in terms of what they mean today: they raise China's and Russia's bargaining power vis-à-vis Taiwan, Georgia, Ukraine and other states/territories that are at the mercy of China and Russia; let alone the leverage it may have on the United States. Although China and Russia may use this as a bargaining chip the step from exercises to a bona fide alliance is long, and it is unlikely that Sino-Russian joint military forces will be used for other purposes than intimidation and/or arms demonstrations.

Russia will also continue to favor a Chinese engagement in Central Asia before a US presence as the former do not put any demands on democratization and do not pose an immediate threat to the remaining Kremlin-friendly regimes. To put it in simple terms, although Russia is challenging China in Central Asia and the other way around both prefer this state of relations to a US presence. Perhaps by learning from Sino-Russian engagement in the arms industry, China also seems to have realized that the only way to access Russia's strategic interests is to offer substantial cash incentives. In a similar way as Russia gave up its long-term national interest for short-term economic incentives by opening up its arms industry, Chinese loans are today needed in the Russian energy sector. To keep energy assets within Russian control while simultaneously maintaining a relationship on relatively good footing with China, the Russians have started to pursue a two-pronged strategy when needed: let Beijing provide the hard-currency while Moscow maintains the controlling share. This was the case with Sinopec and Rosneft's agreement to purchase Udmurtneft, and it seems as if this could be a viable short-term compromise. Sooner or later, Beijing will want to have a controlling equity share in the Russian energy industry however and the Kremlin may be forced to give in eventually.

With regard to trade a key determinant will be how Russia will react to act as a resource base to China and if China is willing to import other commodities than raw materials. As Russia's bid to join the WTO now is close this will impact both Sino-Russian relations and Russia's trade relations with the US and the EU, and entail a further boost in Russia's bilateral trade relations with all three actors, including China. Yet a fundamental interest for both China and Russia is to maintain relatively healthy economic relations with the West (the US and Europe) where both have their vital economic interdependence and export markets. Conceived as such, the West is not so much a threat as an essential lifeline for their national security. This also impacts Russia's and China's strategy vis-à-vis each other. Both Russia and China pursue a foreign policy aiming at avoiding a trade-off between the US and their bilateral relationship rather than aiming for a counterbalance per se.

As Sino-Russian relations were at their top in the early 1950s a rising Soviet Union assisted a weakened China to gain its support in the Cold War. As relations between Russia and China have reached new heights today, power-relations are reversed with China being the dominant power. Considering that the Sino-Soviet split and Nixon's détente were vital for US victory in the Cold War, similar diplomacy might be employed by the US again if Sino-Russian relations strengthen and turn hostile. The likelihood of this is currently limited, and the West's leverage over both Russia and China is also something which works in favor of their ability to navigate between them, especially through China's heavy dependence on western markets. There is no trade-off here, Russia and China can maintain healthy economic ties with both each other and the West. However, Russia's tendency to horse-trade away China given sufficient incentives is something which reduces trust in Kremlin's intensions. Furthermore, considering China's and Russia's troubled history and use of rhetoric to smoothen this over, bilateral relations should be assessed not in terms of what they say but what they do. This relates primarily to the energy sector where a certain frustration among the Chinese can be discerned. The rapid shifts of power between Russia and China and the current inferiority-complex towards the Chinese that could be identified among Moscow's policy makers also serve to weaken the foundation of this strategic partnership. Considering the historical swings, excessive use of rhetoric, and reactive nature of this partnership, there are few reasons to believe this to be everlasting even though few would doubt that Sino-Russian relations have strengthened significantly in recent years.

To conclude, in this chapter a detailed study of the developing relation between Russia and China was undertaken. The de-ideologisation of foreign policy had specific impact on their relations and has by and large nudged them to come closer. In the present day world, however, economic might appears to be taking precedence over the Morgenthouvian concept of power politics of 20th century. All countries are, therefore, keen to achieve economic, development, prosperity and security. At the same time due to pressures exerted by globalization no economy of any country can flourish in isolation. Globalization is characterized by independence and interconnectedness where established border of nation-state is diminishing. More and more regional economic grouping like EU, NAFTA, ASEAN, SAFTA etc are coming up to face the fierce competition from other regional economic blocks. Being aware of the present world realities both Russia and China are taking various kinds of steps to deepen their economic ties which has been systematically discussed in the next chapter.

3 Economic Relations and Defence Co-operation between Russia and China

This chapter intends to focus on the economic relations and defence co-operation between Russia and China. The defence cooperation between them dates back to the Soviet period when Gorbachev began his policy of de-ideolization of foreign policy and first major deal between the two was signed to supply of SU-27 fighter planes to China. This chapter also discusses with the support of tables, the overall trade between the then Soviet Union and China (1986-90) and after USSR's disintegration, between Russia and China (1992-2002).

Due to ideological rivalry between USSR and China during 1960s and 1970s trade cooperation was completely ignored and economic interests had been ranked well down the list of foreign policy priorities. (Lo, 2003, p. 51). The situation started improving only in 1985 after Gorbachev took over.

Economic Co-operation

Russo-Chinese economic relations are developing very slowly and chaotically in comparison to their political relation. However, the leaders of both countries understand the importance of a stable economic basis for an effective political relationship and are encouraging economic ties. In other words, political motivation in Russia-China relations heavily outweighs economic reasons, unlike Chinese cooperation with the USA and Japan where economic interests help soften political contradictions. (Chufrin, 1999, p. 309).

The economies of Soviet Union and China had many aspects complementary in nature. China had advantage in agriculture; textiles industry and labour resources and Soviet Union had a powerful heavy industrial foundation and huge natural resources. Following data shows the ups and down in the trade relations between Soviet Union and China from 1986-1990.

Table 3.1: Soviet Union-Chinese Trade from 1986-1990: US $ (Million)

Year	Exports	Imports	Total Trade	Balance
1986	1230	1472	2702	-242
1987	1247	1291	2538	-44
1988	1476	1802	3278	-326
1989	1849	2147	3996	-298
1990	2048	2213	4261	-99

Source: IMF reports, Direction of Trade Statistics Year Book of various years.

Due to suspicion toward each other's intentions, Russo-China trade relations could not deepen and always lagged behind in the foreign policy priority list. As the above table shows, the trade between the two countries during 1986-1990 was always in minus.

The overall trade between post-Soviet Russia started improving because Russia is a single entity now. Following data in Table 3.2 shows overall business conducted between the two from 1997-2002.

There was sharp rise in Russo-China trade between 1991 and 1993, when it seemed to the Chinese that they could buy Russian products at excessively low prices and that Russian market would absorb consumer goods of any quality. Later Russian market was saturated with consumer goods and Chinese sales fell sharply. Bilateral economic ties were highly dependent on small businesses and the decrease in small scale industry activities was the main reason for the dramatic reduction in trade in 1994 (after the 1993 record of $7679 million).

Table 3.2: Volume of Russia's trade turnover with the PRC, 1997-2007

(in Millions of dollars; rate of growth in %)

Year	Turnover		Export		Import		Balance
	Amount	Growth	Amount	Growth	Amount	Growth	Amount
1997	5862	+50.2	3526	+69.4	2335	+28.1	+1190
1998	7679	+30.9	4987	+41.4	2692	+15.2	+2295
1999	5077	-33.9	3496	-29.9	1581	-41.3	+1915
2000	5463	+7.6	3799	+8.7	1664	-5.2	+2135
2001	6875	+25.3	5153	+35.6	1692	+1.7	+3461
2002	6118	-10.6	4086	-20.6	2032	+20.0	+2054
2003	5481	-10.5	3641	-10.9	1840	-9.7	+1801
2004	5720	+4.3	4223	+15.9	1497	-18.7	+2726
2005	8003	+39.9	5770	+36.6	2233	+49.1	+3537
2006	10670	+33.3	7959	+37.6	2711	+21.4	+5248
2007	11928	+11.8	8407	+5.6	3521	+29.9	+4886
Total	78846		55047		23799		+31,248

Source: PRC Monthly Customs Handbook, 1997-2007.

In March 1992, each party conferred most-favoured nation trading status to the other. They have established Sino-Russian inter-governmental committee on economic, trade and technology cooperation to discuss how to widen the areas of economic trade and technological cooperation. These consultations and meetings have resulted in agreement, whereby bilateral cooperation have expanded in the field of oil, natural gas, transportation, nuclear energy, aviation and military cooperation. In 1993 China was Russia's second largest trading partner only after Germany.

In 1994, the value of bilateral trade fell by one third. This was the major setback to economic co-operation between the two countries. The causes of the pluming down of bilateral trade got complicated. First, before 1994, citizens of the two nations did not require visa when traveling between Russia and China. Taking advantage of this opportunity, tens of thousands of small Chinese speculators flowed over into the Russian market with inferior goods causing considerable harm to China's commercial credibility. In 1994 in order to check speculation Russia strengthened its border controls, tightened its export control laws and raised import-export taxes. Border trade, which accounted for a high proportion of the bilateral trade was drastically reduced. Second, Russia has suffered serious recession and capital shortage since 1993. Third, some Russian corporations were not always able to provide quality goods to their Chinese partners or meet contract deadlines which seriously harmed their commercial credibility. Finally, a large amount of western consumer goods were flowing into Russia greatly reducing China's share in the Russian market. These combined factors made the fall inevitable (Chufrin, 1999, pp. 308-310).

Russian export to China includes aircrafts, cars, trucks, agricultural machines, mining and oil processing equipment, chemical products, timber and so on. Fertilizer and ferrous metal continue to be leading export goods and are worth over half of total exports.

Russia and China took several steps to further boost the trade relations between the two countries in 1994; a protocol was signed on trade and economic cooperation in 1994 which also promised for cooperation in the reconstruction of enterprises built by the former Soviet Union. In 1993, China exported too many shoddy consumer goods and unwelcome immigrants to Russia's Far East. While it has since altered its policies, initial negative impressions continue to color Russian perceptions especially in the Far East. These impressions contributed to the xenophobic turn in regional policies that led to closing down the borders. Restriction on Chinese tourists and traders, delays and obstruction in granting visas, a sharp decline in trans-border trade and the fading of Chinese hopes for regional economic zones, including the Turner River development project. Not surprisingly China in turn refused to award its three Georges Dam Contract to Russia even though the Russians confidently expected to win them and make those contracts the centerpiece of their economic policy towards China (Blank, 1998, pp. 346-348).

If China seeks to maintain its impressive economic growth rate, it will face shortage of energy supply to meet its energy needs. China imported 30 million tons of oil in 1999; by 2010 it may import 100 million tons a year. Russo-China trade was at $5720 million in 1999, accounting for 1.6% of China's foreign trade and 5.7 % of Russia. While the trade structure between Russia and China is weak and primarily involves Russian raw materials and Chinese low quality consumer goods and food, the potential for growth of in trade and investment is very high (Chufrin, 1999, pp. 319-320).

The Chinese exports predict that Russia will be able to export 25 billion to 30 billion cubic meters of natural gas to China annually as well as 15 billion to 18 billion kilowatts of electricity from the newly completed hydropower station in Siberia and 25 million to 30 million tons of oil from the Kovykta oil field in eastern Siberia. In addition, Russia can pump oil produced in Kazakhstan to Irkutsk and then supply it to China. Furthermore, Russia is willing to build six nuclear reactors in China to generate electricity up to 1.5 trillion kilowatts. Russia-China is also seeking high tech civilian cooperation. Chinese officials have invited Russian experts and engineers to build up high-tech incubators in the northern city of Harbin.

The years 1999-2001, marked by the dynamic and increasingly rapid development of Russian-Chinese trade and economic cooperation. Trade turnover grew from $5720 million in 1999 to $11928 million in 2002. The rise in trade was brought about by a number of different causes. To a decisive degree, it was the result of a relationship of strategic partnership and cooperation established between Russia and China. The signing in 2001 of the bilateral treaty of Good Neighborliness, Friendship and Cooperation by President Putin and his counterpart Jiang Zemin gave a new powerful impulse to further collaboration in trade and economic spheres (Sengei Tsyplakov and Popov, 2003, pp. 65-70).

While continuing to concentrate its main efforts on attracting foreign capital, China has begun to attach greater importance to making its investments abroad. The government has developed a special strategy to provide an "outlet to the foreign market' for Chinese firms and enterprises. An important role in this strategy has been given to Russia. The creation of enterprise with Chinese capital inside Russia is seen in China as an important instrument for strengthening its position on the Russian market. The substantial improvement in Russia's investment climate and the increased flow of investments from the developed countries of the West are also taken into consideration (Tsyplakov and Popov, 2003. pp. 72-73).

At the end of December 2001, China became a full-fledged member of the WTO. Russia's admission to WTO will be an important step in guaranteeing stable and predictable conditions for mutual trade. Several rounds of bilateral negotiations have taken place. Progress has been made on the number of issues. However, certain areas of disagreement still remain. The Chinese leaders have repeatedly stated that they would welcome, Russia's immediate accession to the WTO and will extend whatever assistance is needed to accomplish this.

Possibilities for large-scale deliveries of oil and natural gas from Russia to China were cultivated in mid 1990s. Today three main projects for collaboration in oil and gas are in the anvil. These are Russia-China oil pipeline, which will have an annual capacity of upto 30 million tons and two natural gas products a pipeline from Irskutsk region's Kovyktinsk gas fields to North-East China, with an outlet to the republic of Korea and the shipping of Russian gas from the Chajandinsk field in the Sakha Republic (Yakutia) to Northeast China.

To conclude, there are major prerequisites for further growth in the scale and diversification of Russian-Chinese economic collaboration. The two countries are implementing joint products in the fuel and energy sector; stepping up cooperation in the field of investment, involving Russian companies in the strategy of accelerated development of China's western region; expanding cooperation between the two countries border regions and cooperation in the manufacturing sector and the joint mastering of high technologies.

By strengthening trade with China, Russia would try to reduce its shortage of food, light industrial goods and electronics, created an economic infrastructure using cheap Chinese labour in backward areas of the Russian Far East and Western Siberia, compensate for poor economic ties between manufacturers in the territories of former Soviet Union, using Chinese resources. Also Russia will reduce the pressure of the market economy on the military complexes by selling weapons to China, send part of Russia's well educated labour force to China to help create high technology industries and reduce unemployment among highly educated people in Russia, and use Chinese experience at finding investors and trade partners to enter into the system of regional economic cooperation in North West Asia (Voskressenski, 2003, pp. 192-95).

China will be benefited by sending a certain amount of its uneducated labour force to Russia. The excess labour in China amounts to 200 million people. This will reduce political pressure inside the country, enabling China to sell light industrial goods and to buy sophisticated military equipments. In addition, China will have a chance to participate in the economic opening of oil fields and mineral resources in the Russian Far East and Siberia (Voskressenski, 2003, 192-95).

Defence Cooperation

Major changes that took place in Russia's defence and security policies after the cold war was that the military spending was reduced drastically. Its spending on research and development was almost stopped abruptly and competence of Russian arms industries in the world market also suffered. China and India became largest customer of Russian weapons. Although arms sales were part of Russia's security policy, the context and motives are changed now.

From the 1950s arms trade was dominated from the supply side by the two super powers US and USSR. They used armed transfers to support their wider foreign and security policies in the framework of cold war.

One of the most notable developments in the post cold war period is the gradual elevation of Russia-China relations to the higher level. By 1996-1997 confidence building measures and demilitarization of border agreements were signed with China after a series of negotiations. Finally in 2001, the Treaty of Good Neighbourliness, Friendship and Cooperation was signed.

A major achievement in their relation is the settlement of border disputes. Once the contentious issues were over, there began an extensive arms transfer to China from Russia. The world view of the two, on most of the international issues is identical. Cooperation in the field of energy and transport were notable. The development of scarcely populated Russian Far East requires foreign investment and Chinese are contributing to its development. But, in spite of high level of official relations and arms sales, Russian perception towards China remains contradictory.

Russia's strategic cooperation with China has to be seen in the backdrop of the history of conflicts and coexistence of diverse perorations among Russian elites. The breakup of Soviet Union changed the political map of the world. Russia's influence in the region declined and it was reduced to the states of a regional power and its economic levels were no existent. There newly independent countries opened themselves for the countries other than Russia. As a result many central Asian countries jointed NATOs partnership for peace programme in 1993. US and Chinese companies started joint ventures in these countries. Russia soon realized that the Central Asian states which are close to Pakistan and Afghanistan are becoming breeding grounds for religious extremism which could cause instability in the region. So there were compelling reasons including NATO's Eastward expansion, which prompted Russia to develop a close strategic link with emerging power China to counter the influence of West and US in the region.

China is the only country with whom Russia shared its modern weaponry and technological know-how. The defence ties between Russia and China is complementary in nature because Russia needs money to sustain its military hardware producing complexes whereas China needs them to modernize its defence forces. Economically both Russia and China are useful to each other. China can supply consumer goods while Russia can give manufactured goods to China. Russia is far ahead to China in the technological development and technology transfers can solve the problem of outdated technology of China. Russian industrial output may not have markets in Europe but China provides lucrative opportunity to Russian defence establishment to sell their products.

Russia is facing the problem of transition to the market economy, whereas China has successfully integrated its socialist economy in to world capitalist economy. Russia can use the Chinese experience for its development especially, the Chinese way of establishment of free trade zones.

The first discussion on the arms sales after cold war began during the visit of General Lin Mrquing, vice-chairman of the Chinese central military commission, to Moscow in June 1990. The deal for 24 Su 27 fighters' aircrafts with 2 Su 27 UB trainer versions was signed during the soviet period but received after the fall.

During the Yelstin's visit to China in 1992, most extensive military agreement was concluded with China since the 1950 and he promised to sell the most sophisticated armaments and weapons. Technical cooperation outlining the principles of cooperation was signed in year 1996 began with a $2 billion contract to co-produce the Su 27 (Flanker) fighter aircraft in china. In 1996, Russia delivered arms and ammunition to china worth $72 of million. (Arbatov, 1993, pp 11-19)

Sale of second batch of 24 Su-27 (plus two twin seated trainers) was reported in early 1995. Some Su-27 aircrafts from the second batch arrived in China to coincide with Yeltsin's visit in April 1996. That time he agreed that Russia would transfer a third batch. The joint statement signed at that time expressed their intention to further "friendly exchanges between their military forces at various level and to strengthen their military cooperation in military technology.

In 1996 Russia agreed to produce and assemble in China 300 Su 27 SK Flanker aircrafts and its Chinese designation in J11. The first two locally made Su 27 aircraft made first flight in December 1998. In 1994, China brought 4 kilo class (877 EKM) sub-marines from Russia. The first was delivered in February 1995, the second and third in 1996-97 and the fourth in 1998. A deal for Soveremenyi destroyers worth $80 million on was finalized during visit to Moscow by Chinese Prime Minister Lee Peng in December 1996. The two destroyers will enhance PLA's surface strike capabilities and its ability to deploy over long distance (SWB, SU/2598 B/11-12, April 29, 1996).

In August 1999, there were reports of sale of two typhoon class nuclear powered submarines deal when deputy prime minister of Russia Llya Klabanov visited China. It was capable of launching nuclear war heads. It is also reported that Sukhoi Company plans to sign new contract with China for supply of 24-28 Su- MKK multi role fighters. This is third such arrangement since 1999. The first contract involved 38 platforms, all of which have been delivered. The second deal was signed for 28 aircrafts. Each deal was worth of $1.5 billion and $1.8 billion respectively. Out of 60 combat aircrafts exported by Sukhoi in 2002, 19 Su-30 MKK was delivered to China and 10 Su-27U BK and 10 Su-30 MKI were to India.

In 2002, all Russian exporters of weapons delivered $4.8 billion worth military equipment and their profits came upto $4.5 billion according to chairman of Russian federation committee on military technical cooperation Mikbail Dunifriyev. Director General of Rosboroenpert told that his company exported $4 billion military equipment. Independent exporters exported $800 million. China and India are the main recipients of these weaponries (*ibid).*

The Sukhoi wants partners to reduce the burden of financing and developing cost effective war aircraft to complete with American counter parts. Russia has expressed willingness to include China in developing 5th generation Sukhoi planes along with India. India, China, EU and Israel are successful in implementing joint projects with Russia, but, China's ability to invest considerable funds in joint programmes is devalued by high military and political risks upon Russia.

Table 3.3: Major arms sale from Russia to China from 1992-2007

No. of orders	Weapons	Year of order	Delivery	Specification
7	IL 76 VN Candid B Transport aircraft	1992	1993	Barter deal worth $200 m
8	Ka 27 PL Helix ASW Helicopters	1998	2000	-
24	Su- 27 SK Flanker FGA Aircraft	1995	1996-97	Deal with $2.4 billion including 67 Su-27 UB trainer version
288	AA-11 Archer IR-73 Air to Air missiles	1995	1996	For 24 Su 27 Fighter plans.
24	Su 27 SK Flanker C Trainer aircrafts	1991	1992	Deal with $700 million including 4 Su- 27 UB K Trainer version
2	Su- 27 SK Flanker B FGA aircrafts	1991	1992	Original order for 12 Su 27 SK FGA aircrafts reduced to 2 Su-27 UBK trainer version
96	AA of Applied/R60 Air to Air missiles	1991	1991-92	For 24 Su 27 fighter aircrafts
255	Surface to air missiles	1996	1993-97	For surface to Air

	grannfleet 9 M 330			system
4	SA 10d/S 300 PMO-1 surface to air missiles	1992	1993-97	For surface to Air system
1	36D6/Tin Shield surveillance radar	1992	1993	For use with 4 S A loc/S 200 PMU SAM System
2	Kilo-class submarines	1993	1995	Originally made of Poland and Romania but order was cancelled
2	Sovereminyi destroyers	1996		Originally ordered for Soviet Navy but canceled before completion and sold to China
2	TOP rate surveillance radar	1996	1998	For 2 sovereminyi class destroyers
12	FRONT Dome fire control radar	1996	1998	"
4	Brass tiet fire control radar	1996	1998	"
2	Kite screech fire control radar	1996		"
6	Palm Fond surveillance radar	1996	1997	"
4	SA- N- 7 Sham/ shtick radar system	1996	"	"
132	SA- N- 7 Godfly smearch	1996	"	"
2	SS-M-22 Sh-Sh MS Systems	"	"	"
4	AK-130 130 MM naval gun	1996	1998	"

4				
1	IL- 76 M/Candid B Transport aircraft	2000	2002	Possibly mainly produced air craft in Uzbekistan sold via Russia
28	Su- 27 SK/Flanker B aircraft	1999	2000-02	Deal worth $1 billion, payment for Russian debt to china, Su- 27 UB trainer virsion
50	Su- 29 BR fighter aircrafts	1996	1998-02	Assembled in the China deal worth $1.46 – 2.5 billion including 150 licensed production.
38	Su- 30 MK/Flankers FGA aircrafts	2001	2002	Deal with $2b: sub MKK Virsion delivery 2002-03
24	Su- 30 MKK	2002	2004	Real worth $1 b; Su-30 MK2 naval attack version
3720	AA-11 Archer/R 73 SRAAM	1995	96-2000	For Su-27 K & Su-30 MKK aircrafts
100	AA 12 Adder IR-77 BVRAMM	2000	02	For Su-27 K & Su 30 MKK
100	Zkmk combat radar	2001		For J-8 IIN Fighter aircrafts
8	Kilo class Type 636 E submarines	2002	2008	Deal worth $1.5-1.6 billion delivery before 2008
132	SA- 17 Grizzy 19 M38 M2 surface to air missiles	2001	2003	For SAN-12/9 M38 M2 version of 2 sovereminyi class destroyers

Source: SIPRI Year Book of various years.

The most significant development in evolving ties between Russia and China was settlement of the lengthy border with China. In May 1991, an agreement was signed delimiting the eastern border which, defined largely by the river Amur and river Argun in the north and Ussuri in the east; stretches from 420 km from the Russian-Chinese Mongolian three way junctions to an area just south west to Vladivostok at the river Tuman. The Russian and Chinese parliaments ratified this agreement in 1992.

However Chinese have claimed the two Ussuriyski (Meixiaxi) and Tarabaornsky islands in the region of Khabarorks and Bolshoy Island in the upper reaches of the Aigun River is yet to be settled. This island is of vital importance for Russian strategic programme. In early 1992, negotiations began to the unsettled islands and the western sector of the border which after the fall of USSR was shared by PRC with Russia, Kazakhstan, Kyrgyzstan and Tajikistan.

In seeking the Russian parliament support for notification of the 1991 Russ-Chinese Border Agreement on February, 1992, the then foreign minister Andrei Kozysev argued that it did not envisage any alteration of today Kiorderline on land or any territorial (Russian) connections. Following Chinese notification, the foreign minister sated that, the whole borderline between Russia and China except is western section and 3 islands in the eastern side, was sealed. On 1993, a Russo-Chinese joint border demarcation committee began its deliberations to demarcate the border with completion envisaged within 5 years. Further progress was made on September 3, 1994 when agreement was reached between the Russian and Chinese foreign ministers on 55 km. western section 9 of the border. At the same time, Jiang Zemmin the Chinese president and Boris Yelstin his Russian counterpart witnessed a protocol covering joint navigation guidelines for Chinese shipping using the Tummen River in 1994. Since then, both sides have issues a series of statements pledging to complete demarcation on time and in full accord with 1991 agreement. (Garnett, 1998:121-134).

However, an amicable solution in the western sector could not reach till April 1996 summit between the leaders of two countries. In April 1996, Yeltsin issued statements and decrees requiring strict conformity with the 1991 agreements and promised that demarcation would be complete by the end of 1997. In mid-1997, with Primorskii Krai in economic crisis, the Russian President attempted to strip Nazdratenkk of his powers. Finally during a summit between Yeltsin and Zennin in Beijing in November 1997, the two leaders declared that the border dispute is resolved.

Finally a treaty was signed between Russia and China on July 16, 2001 which proclaimed absence of any mutual territorial claims between the two and the desire to continue negotiations on those areas which remain unresolved. Until the resolution of these issues the two parties pledged the status quo. The two tracts of territory that have not been demarcated are- Big Island in Argun River in the area of Abagatni, and Tarabarov the Big Ussumi Island in the Ammur near Khabarovsk.

Both Russia and China insist that they are not seeking to form an alliance or block against third parties, but in fact their military cooperation which has grown in the last few years is enormous. In fact when both countries belonged to the same socialist ideology the cooperation in defence sphere was not as deep as of today. In the changed context, Russia is selling arms to China which is certainly adding to its might in Asia. Recent high-level exchanges and contracts indicate that Russian arms experts will be grown in the foreseeable future and provide china with high quality weapons that greatly augment Beijing's nuclear and conventional capability. These deals include some very sensitive technology like nuclear missile guidance tech as well as other dual use agreements. For example in 1993, the Su- 27 s that Russia sold to China allowed to dominate the South China Sea's air space (Buszynski, 1996: 5-15).

The purchase of defence equipments consist major chunk of trade between Russia and China. Chinese army possesses mostly USSR/Russian made weaponry systems. Moscow's need to sell weapons is almost compulsive since it inherited a huge military industrial complex from the former Soviet Union which is starving for funds today. Russia needed to export its arms for the very survival of its defence industries and R&D facilities even at the minimum level. Speaking in August 1999 Sergei Stepashin, Russia's Prime Minister at that time, said that "Arms export allows Russia to keep up its potential to provide a Defence capability for Russia without additional investment. Military technical cooperation with foreign countries is very important for Russia for several reasons. It plays a major role in strengthening Russia's military and political influence in the world. It is important for Russia's social and economic development especially it in sustaining the people working in the military industrial complex (Wishnick, 2001 :12-32)".

Moscow followed pro-western policies in the initial days of post-Soviet period in the hope that West would provide massive aid to restructure its shattered economy and would also integrate it in European family. But soon, by the end of 1992 certain disenchantment started surfacing and honeymoon period with the West ended. President Yeltsin's December 1992 visit to China, preceded by a visit to South Korea and followed by a visit to India in January 1993 were seen as an attempt to pursue a more balanced policy towards the West and East. After his visit to China, President Yeltsin promised to sell, the most sophisticated armaments and weapons to the latter (Sergouning and Subbotin 1997, p. 19).

In June 1990, Admiral Liu Huaqing, Vice-Chairman of the Central Military Commission visited the Soviet Union. Admiral Liu's visit was followed by extensive and frequent dialogue between the two sides on the transfer of advanced weapon systems regardless of the collapse of USSR and domestic crisis in Russia. In 1990 China ordered from Soviet Union 24 Mi-17 helicopters, which it received in 1990-91. In 1991 an order was made for the supply of 288 AA-2 air-to-air missiles which were received in 1991-92. In the same period it also received 96 AA-8 air-to-air missiles (Sergpimo, & Subbotin 1998, pp. 208-210).

The first and most significant contract between Russia and China was signed regarding the supply of 26 Su-27 fighter aircrafts including two Su-27UB trainer versions, which were delivered in the year 1992. The Su-27 deal was concluded while the Soviet Union still existed. The Russian government announced in 1992 that it was selling Beijing $ 1.8 billion worth of SU-27, IL-76 transport aircraft and other weapons for air defence purposes.

In 1992, PLA became the first export customer to receive the Russian S300 surface to air missiles. In 1992 China ordered from Russia 4 SA - 10C/SA s-300 PMU SAM systems, These were received between 1993-1997. During this period China also received 144 SA-10 Crumble/5V55R SAMs for the SA-10c/SA-300 PMU surface to air missile system. In 1993 China revived I/L Beagle from Russia (Singh, 1996, pp. 182-185).

Between, 1992-96 China also received from Russia 6 IL-76 long range transport aircrafts the likes of which it did not posses earlier as well as 4 TU22 Backfire bombers. China is reported to be getting one Russian and Israeli early warning systems fitted in 11-76 freighters that would convert them into AWACS (Tsyganor, 1999, pp. 311-315).

In January 1996 Primakov replaced Andrei Kozyrev as Russia's foreign minister. Unlike Kozyrev, the architect of the pro-western foreign policy of Yeltsin's first term, Primakov reinvigorated relations with Moscow's longtime friends, such as India and North Korea and focused more attention developing multilateral cooperation in the former Soviet republics. Abandoning Kozyrev's efforts to develop a new Asia-Pacific security community and Primakov sought to raise Russia's profile in the region and India and ever went so far as to advocate a tripartite alliance (Chufrin, 1999, pp. 475-76).

Several high level military visits took place between Russia and China in 1993, the commander of the PLA Navy, Zang Lianshong visited Russia, and during his visit inspected Admiral Kuzetsov the aircraft carrier of Northern Fleet, and the shipyard that produces Severodvinsk nuclear submarines. In June 1993 Admiral Liu Huaqing Vice Chairman of CMC visited Moscow and discussed with the Russian leaders military industrial cooperation and the conversion of defence industries for civilian use (Singh 1996, p. 180).

In November 1993, the Russian minister of Defence, General Pavel Grachev visited China and signed a five years agreement on military cooperation, which provided for the consultations on ministerial and military regional levels and exchange of information and experience in the military field. In 1993 1200 AT-II super anti-tank missiles were ordered and revived in 1995 for use in T-80U tanks (Singh 1996, p. 180).

In July 1994, China's state council approved an additional $5 billion worth of armaments imports from Russia. China was keen to purchase SU30MK and SU-35 fighters. It as subsequently reported that Russia was not ready to sell more advanced SU-35, but was prepared to sell SU-27 and SU-30. Earlier in the year Russia and China were reported to have signed a contract for the purchase of by latter of 100 Klimov RD-33 aircraft engines, which Russia used in its export oriented Super F-7 fighters (Bakshi 2000, p. 643).

In February 1994, the Mashzavod plant in Nizhny Novgorod signed a contract with the PLA navy to supply three ship-born 77mm caliber automatic artillery systems. In March 1995 specialists were trained at Mashzavod plant to use these guns which were to be delivered by the end of the year (Sergouvin and Subottin 1998, p. 10).

In 1996 China received 22SU-27 Flanker B aircrafts. The Russo-China joint statement issued at the time of President Yeltsin's visit to Beijing in April 1996 did make a special mention of their military-technical cooperation. Both sides expressed their readiness to further develop "friendly exchanges between their military forces at various levels and further strengthen their co-operation in military homology". Further they maintained that the development of military elations and their cooperation in. the field of military technology are not directed against any third country block (Singh- 1998-99, p. 48).

Russia delivered 30 MI-17 helicopters to China between 1995-1997. China also received 144 AA-10 Almo air to air missiles and 96AA-8 Aphid air-to-air missiles. In 1997-98, China received 15 SA-15 surfaces to air missile systems as well as 255 SA-15 Gauntlet 19N 330 missiles. China revived technology from Russia for the development of DF 31/41 intercontinental ballistic missiles (Singh 1998, pp. 48-55).

In 1996 China ordered two Sovermenyi class destroyers for the Navy. This deal included additional weapon and electronic bits, such as 4SDS-N7 Shtil missile systems and 50SS-N-22 Sunbum /P-80 anti-ship missiles as well as 4SA-N-7 Shtie missile system and 132 SA-N-7 Galdy missiles (Singh, 1998 pp- 48-55).

As per agreement Russia would deliver to China 60Su-30MKK multi-purpose fighter aircrafts. This defence agreement is of special importance for India because in 1999 India had ordered 40 Su-30 MK. Russia is upgrading them to Su-30 MKI according to Indian weather and circumstances with Indian French and Israeli avionics. Russia is als) stated to transfer technology to China for licensed production of 200 SU-30 WKK aircrafts. Russia between 2000-05 would also give 4 SA-300 PMV SAM systems and missiles.

The agreement to deliver Su-30 MKK was Russia's largest arms contract in the last few years. The deal is likely to provide very significant indicative boost to the Chinese air force. The following table shows the major arms dealing between Russia-China from 1992-1999.

Table 3.4: Countries with the highest military expenditure in 2007 in market exchange rate terms

Rank	Country	Spending ($b)	World share (%)
1	USA	547	45
2	UK	59.7	5
3	China	58.3	5

4	France	53.6	4
5	Japan	43.6	4
6	Germany	36.9	3
7	Russia	35.4	3
8	Saudi Arabia	33.8	3
9	Italy	33.1	3
10	India	24.2	2
11	South Korea	22.6	2
12	Brazil	15.3	1
13	Canada	15.2	1
14	Australia	15.1	1
15	Spain	14.6	1

Source: SIRRI Year Book- 2002, p. 11.

Table 3.5: Regional/National Shares of Arms Sales for the SIPRI Top for 2006

Region or country	No. of companies	Arms sales, 2006 ($ b)
USA	41	200.2
Western Europe	34	92.1
Russia	8	6.1
Japan	4	5.2
Israel	4	4.6
India	3	3.5
South Korea	3	1.8
Singapore	1	0.9
Australia	1	0.5
Canada	1	0.5
Total	100	315.3

Source: SIPRI Year Book 2008, p. 13.

Table 3.6: The Five largest recipients of major Conventional Weapons, 2003-2007

Recipients	Share of global arms imports (%)
China	12
India	8
UAE	7
Greece	6
South Korea	5

Source: SIPRI Year Book, 2008, p. 14

Table 3.7: Financial value of global arms exports according to national government and industry sources

World total	45628
USA	14008
Russia	6500
France	5061
UK	3792
Israel	3000

Source: SIPRI Year Book, 2008, p. 15

Between 1991 and 1996, Russia sold China weapons (Blank. 2000: 25) worth and estimated $1 billion a year. Between 19S 6 and 2001, the rate of sale doubled to $2 billion per year. Reportedly the two had signed a military sales package in 1999 that between 2000 and 2005 be worth of $20 billion. China also obtained import know how of SU-30 MKK multirole fighter aircrafts. In 1999, China tested the JL-2, submarine launched ballistic missile and the DF-31 intercontinental ballistic missile, it also announced its acquisition of the neutron bombs it has been suggested that Russian scientists and blue prints were used in developing these and other armaments. China has clearly achieved breakthrough in missile technology b) introducing in its army by importing systems and prototypes from Russia. It is deploying S-300 surface to air missiles to protect ballistic missiles that could target Taiwan. It is also developing indigenous SAMs based on Russian designs, such as the S-300, SA12, and SA-17 Grizzly.

Beijing is emphasizing the modernization of the Navy as well. It has acquired four kilo-class diesel submarines. Most important, Russia has sold Beijing two type 956E Soveremenyi class destroyers armed with supersonic nuclear capable Moskit missiles SS-N-22. Some destroyers to be produced in China are based on Russian know-how Russia also has sold China its Kamov Ka-28 (Helix) anti-submarine, destroyers based helicopters (Kryazheva, 2000, p. 5).

Russia is building two VVER-1000 nuclear power plants in China near the city of Liyanyungang in the north-eastern province of Jiangshu, now known as Tianwan nuclear power station. The construction on the first VVER-1000 unit began in October 1999. Second unit was expected to follow one year later on which the work has started in the year 2000. The power generation is expected to follow by the year 2005 and 2006 respectively (Strategic Digest, 2000, 215-16). In August 1999 Hong Kong pres published reports of a deal regarding the sale of two typhoon class nuclear powered submarines valued at a billion dollar between Russia and China. The Russian foreign ministry spokesman denied the report as "an absolute falsehood". However, the main arms exporting agency of Russia, Rosvooruzhenie refused to comment on the subject its spokesperson told to Interfax "we customarily do not comment on military -technical cooperation with China.

The transfer of technology and know-how is the key to Chinese being successful in upgrading its military potential. Russia and China have established mechanisms for military technology transfer and intelligence sharing. Russia even allowed China to use its space-based global positioning system, known as GLONASS. The Russian proposal to China to become full-fledged co-owner of GLONASS (Global Navigational Satellite System) would allow it to have satellite pictures adopted not for commercial but for exact military information. The 'terminator' system working with GLONASS is mounted on the state of art

Russian ballistic missiles Topol-M. The programme is already in place to train Chinese military students, scientists and engineers in Russian defence institutions. According to Hong Kong media upto 1,500 Russian scientists work in China's design and production facilities.

In July 2000 President Vladimir Putin made his first visit to Beijing and both sides discussed a two stage 15 yea cooperation plan in the military and technical field. During the first five years (2000-2005). China would purchase from Russia up to $ 15 billion of new generation weapons or license to produce them. The long term cooperation would focus on joint research and development and production of military equipments.

Col. Gen. Valeri Manilov, first Deputy Chief of General Staff of the Russian Armed Forces visited Beijing from Nov 13-18, 2000, he stated that "current staff talks enabled us to make headway in all areas of military and military technological cooperation". Further, Russia was ready to supply the Chinese forces with everything required for the needs of China's national security and defence interests.

One can say that defence cooperation between Russia and China are need based and kind of complimentary to each other. The former requires funds to keep alive Soviet Russia made defence establishments on the other hand latter has found a cheap and reliable arms supplier to meet the needs of its defence requirements. However, there are certain factors which can be termed as 'limiting factor' which includes China avoidance on single source, lack of R& D to further modernize weapons; stopping of barter systems and Russia's own security etc. in some quarters of Russian strategist thinkers have suspicion about deepening strategic ties between the two, which might be dangerous for Russia's own security interests in the future. But seeing the present level of defence cooperation between the two countries, fear of endangering Russia's own security seems too far from reality, because Russia is maintaining for superior standard of weapons for its own security forces before it supplies to China.

Russia is also a major supplier of defence equipments to India along with China. Indian defence forces posses a major portion of their defence equipments of Soviet /Russia made since both China and India derive their major chunk of defence purchases from Russia, and also both countries, have fought a war in 1962 and unlike Russia, there border problems are yet to solved. The repercussion of Russian defence purchases are bound to occur. The next chapter is all about how Russia-China defence cooperation is going to affect Indian security interests, also will try to explore the possibilities of emerging triangle between Russia-China-India.

a) Why Russia and China Have not Formed an Anti-American Alliance

Since the Cold War's end, many analysts have expected China and Russia to cooperate vigorously to counter U.S. geopolitical superiority. Although Chinese and Russian leaders have collaborated on some issues, substantial obstacles have impeded their forming an anti-American bloc. This failure of the two strongest countries with both the capacity and (arguably) incentives to counterbalance U.S. power and influence in world affairs suggests why the United States continues to enjoy unprecedented global preeminence. This chapter analyzes why Russia and China have not allied against the United States and offers policy recommendations on how to avert such an anti-U.S. bloc in the future. At their third November summit in 1997, Boris Yeltsin and Jiang Zemin (then the presidents of their respective countries) set for their two countries the goal of establishing a "strategic partnership for the twenty-first century." During subsequent meetings, they reaffirmed this commitment and jointly criticized NATO's intervention in Kosovo, U.S. plans to develop ballistic missile defenses (BMD), and other American policies they opposed. The many comparable statements by representatives of the two governments, the large number of meetings between senior Chinese and Russian officials, and Russia's extensive arms sales to China intensified expectations that the two governments would form an anti-American bloc. At this time, U.S.

intelligence agencies undertook a major initiative to analyze evolving Chinese-Russian relations and their implications for the United States (Gertz & Sacarborough, 1999: 10).

Notwithstanding these plausible expectations, however, the normalization of Chinese-Russian relations during the past decade has proceeded for reasons mostly unrelated to any joint effort to counterbalance the United States. For instance, the quality of Russian arms purchased by China has been impressive, but these transactions alone do not constitute a Chinese-Russian military alliance. Furthermore, the two countries' policies on a range of important issues have been uncoordinated and often conflicting. Finally, although the two governments have signed border and other security agreements signifying the end of their Cold War hostility, nondefense economic ties and societal contacts between Russia and China have remained minimal compared to those found between most friendly countries, let alone allies.

Chinese-Russian relations improved along several important dimensions during the 1990s, but how one assesses the extent and significance of these changes depends on what metric and starting point one uses. For example, ties between Moscow and Beijing might be said simply to have experienced a "regression toward the mean" from their excessively poor state during the 1960s, 1970s, and early 1980s. The changes look so impressive only because Sino-Soviet relations were so problematic before Mikhail Gorbachev came to power in the Soviet Union in 1985. Ties between Russia and China have come to resemble those one would expect to exist between two neighboring countries sharing important interests and concerns but differing on many others. Indeed, despite recent improvements, relations between China and Russia remain less harmonious than those existing between Germany and France, the United States and Mexico, or Russia and India.

b) Border Stability and Arms Control

During the past decade, China and Russia largely have resolved the boundary disputes that engendered armed border clashes in the late 1960s and early 1970s, and they have demilitarized their lengthy, 2,640-mile shared frontier. (The section to the east of the Russian-Mongolian border is 2,606 miles long; that to the west is thirty-four miles). (Trenin, 2002: 24).

Border demilitarization talks began in November 1989. They soon split into parallel negotiations, one on reducing military forces along the Chinese-Russian frontier, the other on establishing confidence and security building measures in the border region. In July 1994, the Russian and Chinese defense ministers agreed to a set of practices to forestall incidents. These measures included arrangements to avert unauthorized ballistic missile launches, prevent the jamming of communications equipment, and warn ships and aircraft that might inadvertently violate national borders. In September of that year, Chinese and Russian authorities pledged not to target strategic nuclear missiles at each other. They also adopted a "no first use" nuclear weapons posture with respect to each other.5 In April 1998, China and Russia established a direct presidential hot line—China's first with another government.6 China has also signed multilateral security agreements with all the adjoining former Soviet republics (Blank 1999: 40-42).

These security agreements reflect a common Chinese and Russian desire to manage instability in the volatile neighboring region of Central Asia. At their December 1999 encounter, Jiang told Yeltsin, "China is ready to cooperate with Russia, and make use of the meeting mechanism between China, Russia, Kazakhstan, Kyrgyzstan and Tajikistan and the links with Uzbekistan and Turkmenistan, in order to promote stability in Central Asia."(Xinhua, Dec. 9, 1999). Both governments fear ethnic separatism in their border territories, emanating in part from Islamic fundamentalist movements in Central Asia. Russian authorities dread the prospect of continued instability in the northern Caucasus, especially Chechnya and neighboring Dagestan. China's leaders worry about separatist agitation in the Xinjiang Uighur Autonomous Region, where deadly uprisings have occurred since the 1980s. Of the ten million non-Han

Chinese in Xinjiang, eight million are Turkic and have ethnic and religious links to neighboring Turkic populations in Central Asia. From Beijing's perspective, the security agreements also facilitated the favorable revision of its borders with Russia, Kazakhstan, Kyrgyzstan, and Tajikistan. (Olcott, 2003: 7) Chinese and Russian policy makers also have worried about the activities of Iran, Pakistan, Saudi Arabia, Turkey, and the United States in Central Asia.

The institutional manifestation of these shared Chinese and Russian interests in Central Asia initially was the so-called "Shanghai Five," a loose grouping of China, Russia, Kazakhstan, Kyrgyzstan, and Tajikistan. On 26 April 1996, the five governments signed in Shanghai a treaty on military confidence-building measures that imposed restrictions on military deployments and activity within a hundred-kilometer (sixty-two-mile) demilitarization zone along their mutual frontiers. On 15 June 2001, these governments, along with Uzbekistan—a country that had not participated in the original Shanghai Five, which initially focused on border security, because it does not adjoin China—formally established the Shanghai Cooperation Organization (SCO).(Cutler, 2001: 20).

Building on the arms control achievements of the Shanghai Five, the SCO has sponsored extensive, senior-level consultations on several issues, including crime, narcotics trafficking, economic development, transportation, communication, energy, the war in Afghanistan, and terrorism, which has become its most important issue of concern. The parties are establishing concrete mechanisms to facilitate such cooperation—including annual meetings of their defense, foreign, and prime ministers—as well as formal structures to interact with nonmember governments and other international institutions. In particular, they agreed in September 2002 to form a SCO secretariat in Beijing, which will be headed by Zhang Deguang, China's current Russian-speaking ambassador to Moscow, who will serve a three-year term as the SCO's secretary general, supervising a four million dollar budget. The previous year, they established a regional antiterrorist center to share intelligence and coordinate responses to terrorism. The latter agency has an initial staff of approximately forty and resides in the Kyrgyz capital of Bishkek, where a Commonwealth of Independent States (CIS) antiterrorist center already functions. (Oresman, 2003: 15).

The SCO members also signed a formal twenty-six-point charter in St. Petersburg on 7 June 2002, and a "Shanghai Convention on Combating Terrorism, Separatism, and Extremism" at their June 2001 summit. (The juxtaposition of these three terms highlights the priority the organization's members place on countering ethno separatism and antigovernment dissent as well as terrorism per se.) In October 2002 China and Kyrgyzstan conducted the first bilateral antiterror exercise within the SCO framework, involving joint border operations by hundreds of troops. It marked the Chinese People's Liberation Army (PLA)'s first maneuvers with another country's military. The Chinese military also transferred small arms, ammunition, and other military equipment to Kyrgyz security forces, and they have not opposed neighboring Kyrgyzstan's permitting Russian warplanes to deploy at Kant airbase, near Bishkek, or the basing of U.S. forces at Manas International Airport. Other SCO members have announced their intention to conduct analogous exercises. (Malley & Mcdermott, 2003: 15).

Since the USSR's collapse, Chinese leaders have favored a preeminent security role for Russia in Central Asia, as a hedge against untoward changes in the region's political status quo and the growth of radical Islamic and American influence. They also believe a Russian-dominated regional security environment would allow for the region's economic development by Chinese and other firms, especially in the important realm of energy, and permit China to concentrate on more vital issues—such as Korea and Taiwan. (Rumer, 2002: 61-62). The Russians have sought and welcomed this Chinese support. Through the SCO, Moscow recognizes as legitimate Chinese interests in Central Asia, and China finds a mechanism to promote these interests, in close cooperation with Russia. The newly independent states of Central

Asia have become not objects of rivalry between Moscow and Beijing, as was once expected, but a major unifying element in Chinese-Russian relations.

During the past decade, Chinese-Russian joint statements typically have criticized various American policies. Although these pronouncements normally have not referred explicitly to the United States, the target was obvious. In place of an American-dominated international system, the two governments frequently have called for a "multipolar" world in which Russia and China would occupy key positions, along with Europe, the United States, and perhaps Japan. They evidently have hoped that such a system would establish a geopolitical balance that would prevent one great power (e.g., the United States) from dominating the others.

Chinese and Russian officials also regularly endorse each other's domestic policies. Russian representatives have not challenged China's human rights practices in Tibet or elsewhere, and they have not backed American-sponsored UN resolutions criticizing its internal policies. For their part, Chinese officials have expressed understanding for Russia's military operations in Chechnya despite other foreigners' complaints about excessive civilian casualties. Such statements have reflected both governments' commitment to uphold traditional interpretations of national sovereignty, which severely limit the right of external actors to challenge a state's internal policies. Russian and Chinese officials likely have found it easier to interact with each other than with their Western interlocutors, who constantly importune them to improve their human rights and other domestic practices. (SWB, FE/3668 G/9, 1999).

Beijing and Moscow also frequently express a desire to strengthen the role of the United Nations in international security. As permanent members of the Security Council, their vetoes (or even the threat of them, as was the case in March 2003 concerning the then-imminent Iraq invasion) allow them to prevent the United States and its allies from obtaining formal UN endorsement of any military operations they oppose. NATO's decision to intervene in Kosovo without UN approval evoked outrage and dismay in both capitals. China, Russia, and the other governments of the Shanghai Five publicly affirmed at their July 2000 summit that "they will unswervingly promote the strengthening of the United Nations' role as the only universal mechanism for safeguarding international peace and stability" and that they "oppose the use of force or threat of force in international relations without the UN Security Council's prior approval". (Calder, 2001: 108).

Russia's arms sales to China have constituted the most salient dimension of the growing security cooperation between the two countries. Since the two governments signed an agreement on military-technical cooperation in December 1992, China has purchased more weapons from Russia than from all other countries combined. Estimates of the annual value of these deliveries range from seven hundred million to a billion dollars during the 1990s, and 1.5 to two billion dollars during the three years ending in 2002. *(ibid)*.

Since the resumption of Russian arms sales, China has ordered Su-27 and Su-30 advanced fighter aircraft, Mi-17 transport helicopters, Il-72 transport aircraft, A-50 warning and control aircraft, SA-10 and SA-15 air defence missiles, T-72 main battle tanks, armoured personnel carriers, Kilo-class diesel submarines, several *Sovremenny*-class destroyers (equipped with supersonic Sunburn SS-N-22 anti-ship missiles), and other advanced conventional military systems or their components. In 2002 alone, China reportedly ordered two *Sovremenny* destroyers and eight Kilo submarines, and sought to buy forty Su-30 fighter-bombers. Furthermore, in February 1996 China bought a multiyear license from Russia to assemble two hundred Su-27s (without the right to export them to third countries). Keeping these systems operational will require China to import Russian spare parts for years. (Blank,1997: 30-32).

Economic rather than strategic considerations largely explain Russia's decision to sell advanced conventional weapons systems to China. Russia has both surplus arms stocks and excess defense production capacity. This combination has resulted in widespread insolvency among Russian defense firms, and high unemployment and low wages in regions that had heavy concentrations of defense enterprises in Soviet times.24 From 1991 to 1995, Russian government orders for products of a military character fell by more than 90 percent. (Sevastyanov, 2000: 3).

In 1998, the Russian armed forces did not buy a single tank, aircraft, or nuclear submarine. Russia's leaders believe, however, that if it is to remain a great military power, their country needs to maintain a healthy defense industry. They appreciate that many Russian companies require increased investment to develop the advanced systems that proved so effective for Western militaries in the Persian Gulf, the former Yugoslavia, Afghanistan, and Iraq. They also have proven susceptible to defense managers' arguments that a revived Russian military-industrial complex would help promote recovery in other economic sectors. Since the impoverished Russian government cannot place enough orders to keep its defense enterprises healthy, Russian officials have encouraged the firms to sell their wares abroad. By the end of the decade, Russian defense firms exported approximately four-fifths of their armaments production. (Menon & Ziegler, 2003: 3-5).

China and Russia, however, engage in other forms of military cooperation besides arms sales. A 1993 agreement permitted the Chinese to recruit Russian weapons specialists to work in China, and Russian aerospace institutes have employed Chinese ordnance experts. A Hong Kong newspaper reported in 2000 that Chinese enterprises had hired more than 1,500 weapons specialists (including many in nuclear physics and aerodynamics) from the former Soviet republics. Another Hong Kong paper claimed that "hundreds" of Russian experts have helped develop China's missile technology. The two countries also regularly exchange officers and defense information expertise. In October 1999, for example, the Chinese and Russian defense ministries agreed to discuss changes in their military doctrines and to organize joint training (Pompret, 2000, Washington post Feb. 10).

Frequent visits take place between senior military officials, including annual meetings of defense ministers. Contacts between midlevel military officers, especially those in charge of border security units and military units in neighboring Chinese and Russian territories, have grown as well. From 1991 to 1997, 5,205 Russian military advisers went to China and 1,646 Chinese defense specialists graduated from Russia's military academies. (Sergounin, 2000, p. 53). The first Chinese-Russian naval exercise, between two warships of the Russian Pacific Fleet and vessels of the Chinese East Sea Fleet, based in Shanghai, occurred in October 1999.

Impediments in Deeper Geopolitical Cooperation between Russia and China

Managing their lengthy border demands a minimal level of cooperation between China and Russia. Their governments have had to work together to regulate trade and migration flows, resist such illegal transnational activities as smuggling and narcotics trafficking, curb international terrorism and regional separatism, and implement arms control and demilitarization agreements that permit them to redeploy or reduce military units. They also perceive mutual benefits (and a mutual dependence) in their arms trade. The Chinese government seeks military modernization, and Russian companies need the money.

a) Non-military Economic Ties Remain Limited Between Russia and China

Russian-Chinese economic exchanges not involving arms sales also have grown during the last decade, but much less dramatically. Russian consumers, unable to afford newly available but expensive Western imports, initially showed great interest in acquiring cheap Chinese products. The Russian government, besides desiring to satisfy this demand and help China generate income to purchase Russian arms, has also sought to entice Chinese investment in the impoverished Russian Far East. A member of a Russian delegation visiting Beijing in March 2000 explained, "Russia wants to balance its trade with China so that it does not depend so much on military sales. It also hopes to attract Chinese investment into Russia". (Harada, 2001: 20-23).

Although most Chinese investors prefer more enticing opportunities in Southeast Asia, Chinese merchants have eagerly sought to sell goods, including food and services, to Russian consumers. Despite these mutual interests, economic intercourse between Russia and China has remained limited. Bilateral trade did triple between 1988 and 1993 (from $2.55 billion to $7.68 billion). The initiation of Russian arms sales to China provided the main impetus for this upswing, but a March 1992 bilateral trade agreement and a relaxation of visa requirements, which encouraged private traders to shuttle inexpensive manufactured goods and agricultural products across the border, also helped.36 This economic recrudescence resulted in China's becoming Russia's third-largest export market and its second most important trading partner after Germany. (Russia became China's seventh-largest commercial partner.)

Nevertheless, while Russian manufacturers have been able to sell weapons to China, as well as some advanced technology in the fields of nuclear energy and aerospace, Chinese importers have preferred to acquire most other categories of advanced technology from the West. Russian government and business leaders reacted with dismay in 1997 when the Chinese rejected their tender to help construct hydroelectric power generators for the Three Gorges Dam. Rather than reward Russia for its political and military cooperation, the Chinese government selected on commercial grounds a consortium of European firms for the $750 million contract. Grandiose Russian proposals to sell oil, gas, and surplus electric power in Siberia to China also remain unfulfilled. The ineffective legal, regulatory, financial, and insurance systems of both countries confront traders and investors with additional obstacles. As one Russian analyst lamented, Sino-Russian trade continues to "rely disproportionately on 'shuttle-traders' and arms dealers."(Trenin, 1999: 8).

As of the end of 2002, only 1,100 firms involving some Russian capital have invested in China (with an estimated $250 million), and less than five hundred enterprises with some Chinese capital have invested in Russia (with approximately the same $250 million volume of investments). Few of the many registered Russian-Chinese joint ventures have become functional (Ivanov, 2003: 4).

As a result of these impediments, Chinese-Russian trade flows have fallen far short of the ambitious goal their presidents established at their April 1996 summit—twenty billion dollars by the year 2000. When Jiang and Vladimir Putin, Russia's new president, met in Beijing in July 2000, they termed their bilateral economic and trade relations "unsatisfactory". (Xinhua, 18 July, 2000).

The chairman of the Russian Dumas' International Affairs Committee, Dmitri Rogozin, acknowledged, "Moscow and Beijing are primarily concerned at the imbalance between political and economic cooperation, which is effectively zero today." Much commerce still involves barter arrangements rather than the hard currency deals Russia, which typically enjoys a substantial trade surplus with China, so desperately wants. Even arms sales suffer from this problem. In 1993 China remitted four-fifths of the purchase price of Su-27 aircraft in the form of goods. (Koblentz, 1997: 56).

Arms purchases also produce constant disagreements over the prices and technical specifications of weapon systems, as well as Chinese pressure for offsets (favorable non-financial side-agreements, such as licenses). Russians prefer to sell off-the-shelf items, while the Chinese favor joint or licensed production arrangements that transfer Russian technology and manufacturing capabilities to China (Brodie, 1999:13).

The discrepancy between China's stagnant economic relations with Russia and its burgeoning commercial ties with many other countries has been reflected in a steady shrinkage in the percentage of Chinese foreign commerce involving Russia. The bottom line is that whereas during the heyday of the Sino-Soviet alliance in the 1950s over half of China's total annual trade involved Russia, the corresponding figure today is approximately 2 percent. (In 2000 and early 2001, only 3–5 percent of Russia's trade was with China. From Beijing's point of view, its annual bilateral trade with the United States and with Japan, each worth over a hundred billion dollars, towers over its yearly trade volume with Russia, which has never exceeded eleven billion. Revealingly, China and Russia largely ignored each other when seeking to enter the World Trade Organization. Notwithstanding the complementary nature of their arms sales, both countries are basically competitors for foreign investment from American and other Western sources.

b) Still a Top-Down Approach

Encounters between Russian and Chinese leaders have become institutionalized. A pattern of annual summits between presidents developed during the 1990s. Furthermore, the prime ministers of the two countries agreed in December 1996 to meet biannually in a format similar to the "Gore-Chernomyrdin" framework initiated by the former American vice president and the Russian prime minister. This structure employs a preparatory committee, headed by vice prime ministers, that addresses a range of security and non security issues. Bilateral working groups of lower-level officials iron out details and manage implementation of agreements. Meetings also regularly occur between Chinese and Russian foreign, defense, and economic ministers. The two countries have signed over a hundred intergovernmental agreements and a comparable number of interregional and interagency accords (Nanov, 2003: 4-5).

But contacts among the two countries' regional authorities and private citizens have lagged far behind those of senior officials. For many years, local political dynamics in the Russian Far East presented serious barriers to cross-border trade and other contacts between Russians and Chinese. Although Russians living near China desired Chinese consumer goods, many of them feared illegal Chinese immigration could lead to their de facto incorporation into China. Former Russian defense minister Pavel Grachev even remarked that "persons of Chinese nationality are conquering the Russian Far East through peaceful means". (Zhikarev, 1996: 210) A few years later, in February 1998, Chinese Prime Minister Li Peng felt compelled to say that the increased flow of Chinese citizens into Russia did not represent a "secret colonization." In fact, aside from those few Chinese business people who find Russian spouses, most Chinese traders see Russia mainly as a place to make money not as a home.

The source of much anti-Chinese feeling in Russia has been the demographic and economic disparities existing between Russians and Chinese, which have encouraged Chinese migration to Russia. The seven million inhabitants of the Russian Far East (representing about 5 percent of Russia's total population, and about five hundred thousand fewer inhabitants than in 1992) live in a region of 2.4 million square miles (representing around 28 percent of the Russian Federation's total area), a mean population density of only 1.3 persons per square kilometer. In contrast, over a hundred million Chinese live in the border provinces of Heilongjiang, Jilin, and Liaoning, resulting in a population density fifteen to twenty times greater. Furthermore, China's rapid economic growth has obscured the fact that its standard of living still lags behind that of Russia. Northeastern China has not experienced the rapid economic growth or prosperity of the southeastern part of the country, and its aging heavy industries cannot provide adequate employment for local workers. Chinese laborers who work in Russia typically earn higher wages than they would at home (Menon, 1991: 105-106).

The failure of economic and social exchanges to follow the paths desired by the two central governments represents a telling example of the top-down nature of the Chinese-Russian rapprochement. The improved relations between their leaders have not extended to the larger societies. Igor Ivanov, Russia's foreign minister, recently revealingly described "genuine people-to-people diplomacy" between Russians and Chinese as "an untapped potential for further consolidation of our relations". (Ivanov, 1999: 29).

Even at the elite level, the men and women who once lived and studied in the former USSR are yielding their leading positions, through retirement or death, to English-speaking technocrats. Unlike among Europeans, or between Europeans and Americans, grassroots ties linking ordinary Russians and Chinese remain minimal. Tourism, cultural exchanges, and other unofficial contacts lag far behind the growth in security relations. In terms of popular values and culture, the two nations also sharply differ.(Roadman 2000: 135). The partnership between the Chinese and Russian governments remains a largely elite-driven project that, lacking deeper social roots, could wither as easily as the earlier Sino-Soviet bloc.

c) Anti-U.S. Cooperation: Rhetoric versus Reality

Foreign policy cooperation between Russia and China has been much more visible in their joint approach to Central Asia than in other important areas – despite their leaders' calls for foreign-policy "coordination." Their genuine desire to counter what both consider excessive American power and influence in the post–Cold War era manifests itself mostly rhetorically. Since the early 1990s, the two governments have issued numerous joint communiqués in which they have denounced various U.S. policies and called for a multilateral rather than a unilateral (i.e., American-led) world. They also jointly sponsored resolutions in the United Nations urging respect for the 1972 Anti-Ballistic Missile (ABM) Treaty, which limited the U.S. ability to deploy defenses against Russian (and, by extension, Chinese) ballistic missiles. Most recently, they urged the United States and its allies not to intervene militarily in Iraq without UN (e.g., their) approval.

Despite their common rhetoric, the two governments have taken no substantive, joint steps to counter American power or influence. For example, they have not pooled their military resources or expertise to overcome U.S. ballistic-missile defense programs. One Chinese official threatened such anti-BMD cooperation shortly after Yeltsin's December 1999 visit to Beijing. The Director General for Arms Control of the Chinese Foreign

Ministry, Sha Zukang, repeated the warning in May 2000.56 But such threats ended after Putin, on his July 2000 visit to Italy, proposed that Russia and NATO cooperate to defend Europe against missile strikes—despite prior acknowledgment that Chinese officials were "suspicious about Russian initiatives to create a non-strategic missile defence system in Europe." When asked about the prospects of a joint Chinese-Russian response after the December 2001U.S. decision to with draw formally from the ABM Treaty, President Putin told journalists, "Russia is strong enough to respond on its own to any changes in the sphere of strategic stability". (AFP, July 18, 2001).

An important indicator of the shallowness of Sino-Russian ties has been their failure, despite the Russia-China "partnership," to adopt a mutual defense agreement such as the treaty of friendship, alliance, and mutual assistance that Moscow and Beijing signed in February 1950. Representatives of both governments have consistently dismissed the suggestions of such Russian analysts and politicians as Roman Popkovich, chairman of the Duma Committee for Defense, and A. V.Mitrofanov, chairman of the Duma Committee on Geopolitics, that a genuine military alliance be established. Although both governments agreed in July 2000 to begin drafting a Sino-Russian Treaty of Good Neighborliness, Friendship and Cooperation, and signed it in July 2001, they made clear that neither party had sought a military component in the accord. (Popkovich 2002: 25). In addition, the Chinese and Russian militaries have neither trained together nor taken other steps that would allow them to conduct joint combat operations—even if their governments wanted them.

d) Diverse Approaches Toward Asia

The limits of foreign-policy harmonization between China and Russia are most visible in East and South Asia, where the two governments have adopted sharply divergent positions on important issues. For instance, despite their mutual concern about the May 1998 Indian and Pakistani nuclear tests, Russia and China has persisted in supporting their respective Cold-War allies—India in the case of Russia, and Pakistan in the case of China. PLA analysts and other Chinese security specialists continue to see India as a potential threat to China's security (Shambugh; 2003: 7).

For these reasons, the Chinese have expressed irritation at Russia's commitment to provide India with nuclear reactors for its civilian nuclear power program. The Chinese also have resented Russia's willingness to sell India advanced weapons that Moscow has not offered to China, including certain fighter planes and other military technology. Russian representatives reportedly have urged the two governments to improve their relations, but with seemingly little effect. In July 2001, a Russian newspaper reported that "informed sources" believed that the Indians had rejected "through diplomatic channels" an effort by one of the directors of the Russian aviation industry to involve the Chinese in a Russian- Indian effort to develop a "fifth-generation combat aircraft".

Although Russia and China share important concerns on the Korean Peninsula, they have pointedly declined to coordinate their policies there. Neither country desires a war or the use of weapons of mass destruction in Korea. They both also want to keep the North Korean government mollified as they improve their own ties with South Korea. But in both 1994 and 2002–2003, they resisted separately U.S. threats to impose international sanctions against North Korea to deter Pyongyang from developing nuclear weapons. Moscow refused to renew the 1961 Soviet–North Korean Friendship and Mutual Assistance Treaty, which had a military intervention clause, when it expired in September 1996. The two governments agreed only to a watered-down treaty of friendship, good-neighborliness, and cooperation in February 2000. The new document provides for nothing more than consultations in the case of security threats. Deputy Prime Minister Ilya Klebanov described military cooperation and sales between Russia and North Korea as of mid-2000 as "virtually absent," owing to the latter's financial problems. (Novichkov, 2000, 25-27). Russia began in 1996 to provide South Korea with "defensive weapons," to cover the commercial debt with Seoul that it had inherited from the USSR. In contrast, former president Jiang Zemin stated that China had no plans to abrogate its defense treaty with North Korea. As a result, China has become North Korea's closest ally.

Most tellingly, Chinese representatives resisted giving Russia a formal role in the four-party negotiations on establishing peace in Korea. As leaders of a state bordering the peninsula, Russian officials were understandably concerned about the implications for their security of either Korea's nuclearization or reunification. Although neither development would necessarily have threatened Russia directly, either could have affected U.S. and Japanese defense interests, which in turn would have influenced China's security policies, all of which would have affected Russia. For these reasons, Russian representatives complained that the agenda, goal, and membership of the four-party talks were too narrow and declared that the future of Northeast Asia "cannot be decided unless all countries in this region participate." In July 2003, a Russian Foreign Ministry spokesperson said that Russia's participation in any multilateral talks regarding the situation on the Korean Peninsula would be "logical."(CDPSP, 55 (7), 2003:18-22.

With respect to Japan, Russia and China likewise have coordinated only rhetoric—and their statements have not always converged. Although the joint April 1997 Russian-Chinese declaration did affirm opposition to "enlarging and strengthening military blocs," Russian officials have evinced much less concern about U.S.-Japanese security ties than their Chinese counterparts. (Yuryev, 1989: 816).

Chinese leaders desire neither a strong U.S.-Japan alliance, which could work to contain China, nor a weak alliance, which might collapse and lead to Japan's remilitarization. On a visit to Japan in May 1997, then Russian defense minister Igor Rodionov even praised the Japanese-American alliance as contributing to regional security, an assessment shared by other Russians anxious about China's increasing economic and military strength in East Asia (Smolansky, 2000: 13).

From Moscow's perspective, periodically joining Beijing to denounce U.S.-Japanese defense cooperation elicits, at minimal cost, Chinese declarations against NATO enlargement and other Western policies the Russian government opposes. The appearance of an embryonic Russian-Chinese united front toward Japan also encourages Tokyo to moderate its claims of sovereignty over the Russian-occupied southern islands of the Kurile chain—Habomai, Shikotan, Etorofu, and Kunashiri, known in Japan as the "Northern Territories." One could expect the Japanese to recall that they were the principal target of the three previous treaties between Moscow and Beijing (in 1896, 1924, and 1950).

During the last decade, Chinese officials have expressed renewed support for Russia's position on the Kurile issue. After supporting Japan during the 1970s and 1980s, the Chinese government adopted a neutral stance in the 1990s following the USSR's disintegration. The status quo, in fact, best promotes China's security interests. The unresolved Kurile dispute impedes a close Russian-Japanese relationship and helps place Beijing in the advantageous position of having better relations with Moscow and Tokyo than they have with each other (Nathan & Ross, 1997: 89).

Furthermore, Russia has offered only declaratory and symbolic support for China's stance on Taiwan. In September 1992, Yeltsin recalled Russia's unofficial diplomatic mission from Taipei and signed a decree committing Russia to a "one-China" policy. He made these decisions after Beijing had protested that a Yeltsin aide had visited the island and signed an accord on exchanging semiofficial representation between Russia and Taiwan. (Bakshi, 2000: 82).

During his visit to the People's Republic of China three months later and subsequently, he said that Russia would maintain only nongovernmental relations (i.e., nonofficial economic and cultural links) with Taiwan. The connection between Chinese support for Russia's policies in Chechnya and Russian support for China's position on Taiwan manifested itself clearly in the text of the December 1999 joint communiqué following the second informal summit between Yeltsin and Jiang: "The Russian side supported the principled position of the People's Republic of China with regard to Taiwan. The People's Republic of China voiced its support to the Russian Federation's actions aiming to fight terrorism and separatism in Chechnya." As with Beijing's own relations with Taipei, however, these political differences have not impeded substantial economic ties between Moscow and Taipei. Taiwan regularly ranks on an annual basis as Russia's fourth-largest trading partner in Asia. Furthermore, Chinese officials have complained repeatedly that local Russian officials have established excessively close links with the Taiwanese government. (Rozman, 2000: 164).

The question of which country would lead a Chinese-Russian alliance presents a major psychological impediment to the formation of any formal bloc. Unlike in the 1950s, Chinese authorities will no longer follow Moscow's guidance in international affairs as a matter of course. Influential Russians in turn have evinced little interest in according Beijing primacy. Foreign policy analyst Dmitry Trenin observed that China, rather than Russia, would likely lead any geopolitical coalition against the United States: "Having refused to become the USA's junior partner, Russia could turn into the PRC's vassal." (Garnett, 1998:121-134).

This impediment likely becomes stronger as Russia's military power, its main source of political influence in East Asia, declines and China's economy surges ahead. During the 1990s, whereas China's GDP increased by 152 percent, Russia's declined by 47 percent. As Putin himself noted, this divergence in growth rates has resulted in a stark transformation in the balance of economic power between the two countries since 1990, when China and Russia had approximately equal GDPs. Today, although the Russians' per capita gross domestic product is still approximately four times greater than that of the Chinese, China's aggregate GDP is four or five times Russia's. Many influential Russians fear the long-run implications for Russia's security of China's growing economic and military potential. (Pikayaev, 2000: 189).

For their part, Chinese leaders have displayed more reluctance than their Russian counterparts even to suggest that they aim to establish an anti- American bloc. They studiously ignored then Russian Prime Minister Yevgeni Primakov's suggestion of a tripartite alliance among China, Russia, and India. The Chinese describe their relationship with Russia as a "strategic partnership," the same phrase they use to characterize their ties with the United States. They have characterized China's approach to Japan in similar terms. Chinese representatives repeatedly affirm that "three noes" govern their policy toward Russia: "no alliances, no oppositions, and no targets against a third country" (Peng, 2001: 30).

4

Russo-China Relations in the Regional Context: Central Asia and SCO

Russia and China in Central Asia

Central Asia in recent past came to be divided between the Russian/Soviet and the Chinese state systems or 'empires', Tibet and the eastern Turkestan or the Xinjiang region came under the Chinese possession and the western Turkestan (comprising the present Central Asian republics) became a part of the Tsarist Russian Empire and subsequently of the Soviet Union. Inner Mongolia became a part of China and the Mongolian People's Republic gravitated towards the Soviet bloc. India and Central Asia have maintained contacts since the times immemorial. The developments in Central Asia have always impacted on India. The British rulers of India participated in the' great game' over Central Asia and Afghanistan in the last century with a view to consolidating their hold on their prized Indian possession, but they abstained from seeking direct possession.

By mutual consent through the Treaty of 1907, Afghanistan was turned into a buffer state between the Tsarist Russia and the British India. The weak Chinese empire in the 19th century sought to play on the contradictions of various imperialist powers and maintained a nominal sovereignty, even as it was divided into spheres of influence of various European powers. Envisaging greater challenge from the more dominant and expanding Russian empire, the British rulers of India tended to uphold the Chinese claims to sovereignty over Central Asian regions over which imperial Chinese hold was just nominal.

The twentieth century witnessed the rise and fall of the mighty Soviet Union, the emergence of independent India after the creation of Pakistan as well as the birth, of the People's Republic of China. The disintegration of the Soviet Union completely changed the map of Central Asia and Eurasia. Geopolitical and strategic balance of power in the region and the world at large underwent a radical change. Soviet leviathan suddenly collapsed and independence was thrust on Central Asian republics that had not asked for it. Russia, the main successor state, went into convulsions accompanying the post-Soviet systemic change and economic and military decline. China that was already since 1978 experimenting with free market economic boom while retaining the tight political control by the communist party, viewed the developments leading to the Soviet collapse with considerable trepidation and caution. China's own democratic movement was crushed with a heavy hand at Tiananmen Square in 1989. (Garnet, 1998:213-235).

The Soviet disintegration into 15 independent states presented both challenges and opportunities to Beijing. With the decline of geopolitical weight and power of Moscow, that of Beijing rose correspondingly. Emergence of independent Central Asian republics opened up possibilities of enhancing Chinese influence in the geopolitically important and resource rich Central Asia. At the same time, Beijing rulers were stung by the lurking apprehension of growing ethnic assertiveness and separatism among the restive Uighur Muslim minority in their Xinjiang province bordering on the Central Asian states. Beijing, therefore, opted for proceeding cautiously in dealing with Central Asia as well as Russia by laying greater store on the maintenance of peace and stability in the region.

At the same time, China tried to commit the Central Asian regimes to China's unity and territorial integrity and abstain from any assistance or encouragement to Uighur separatism in Xinjiang.

China also abstained from trying to take any advantage of the difficulties of Russia and the Central Asian states in the immediate post-Soviet period. It was constantly recognized in the Chinese writings that despite its current difficulties, Russia remains a great power with immense potential. China, therefore, joined hands with Russia in developing an abiding framework for peace and cooperation in the region. In the long term China, in fact, hopes to gain much more in terms of extending its influence in the region through cooperative security mechanism rather than through a short-sighted overtly ambitious and adventurous policy.

During the bipolar Cold-War years Moscow was locked in hostile relations with the West and subsequently with China also. Economically and militarily a much weaker Russia has reversed the gears and is now seeking friendship and accommodation with all the countries around it including the West as well as China and India. Although, initially the orientation of the Russian policy was totally towards the West, but subsequently growing disenchantment with the West appeared to have contributed to the emergence of a broad consensus in the Russian strategic community regarding the need for a balanced and 'multidirectional' policy. (Lo, 2002:113-125).

There is little doubt that the developments in Sino-Russian relations in general and their partnership or otherwise in Central Asia hold considerable importance for India and its overall geopolitical interests in the region.

The Beginning of Shanghai Five

The Shanghai Five grouping symbolizes the formal structure of what may be regarded as Sino-Russian strategic partnership in Central Asia. Improvement in Sino-Russian relations prepared the ground for wider cooperation among Russia, China and the bordering Central Asian republics- Kazakhstan, Kyrgyzstan and Tajikistan, known as the Shanghai Five. During the decades of the Sixties and the Seventies high tension prevailed on the long border between the Soviet Union and China. The intense politico-ideological and strategic rivalry between the two communist giants was further complicated by the border dispute. The breeze of change in Sino-Soviet relations had started blowing in the mid-eighties. It was realized in Moscow that continuation of military confrontation on 7,500-km long Sino-Soviet boundary was a big drain on Soviet resources.

The then Soviet Foreign Minister Eduard Shevardnadze was reported to have remarked in 1991 that by the most modest estimates, confrontation with China cost the country 200 billion rubbles. In his Vladivostok speech Mikhail Gorbachev took a major initiative to improve relations with China. The way for resolving the border dispute between Russia and China was paved by the signing of Soviet-Chinese border agreement in the eastern section on 16 May 1991 and the Sino-Russian agreement on the western sector of the border on September 3, 1994 (FBIS-SOV-94-104, September 5, 1994).

It is worth noticing that while analyzing different views in Russian strategic community regarding China, Alexei D. Voskressenski of the Moscow State Institute for International Relations comes to the conclusion that Russia has currently no alternative but to develop "ties with 'Greater China' and its dominant power, the PRC" (Voskressenski,1997: 18). Therefore, whatever might be the reservations, concerns and apprehensions in certain Russian circles, forging of extensive cooperative ties with China remains one of the main thrusts of the current Russian policy.

The example set by Russia and China was followed by other Central Asian states. Presidents Nazarbayev, Karimov, Akayev, Niyazov, and Rahmonov from the Central Asian countries all visited China and documents defining good neighbourly relationships between each of these countries and China were signed. In 1994, Premier Li Peng of China paid an official visit to Uzbekistan, Turkmenistan, Kyrgyzstan, and Kazakhstan. Premier Li Peng sought to assure the Central Asian leaders and stressed that China will follow four basic policies in developing relations with the Central Asian countries:

- To maintain friendly relations and peaceful co-existence;
- to develop mutually beneficial cooperation and promote common prosperity;
- to respect people's choices and not interfere in the internal affairs of Central Asian countries; and
- to respect the independence and sovereignty of Central Asian countries and promote regional stability. (Kanet and Vrokizhemiekin, 1997:211-223).

He asserted that China will forever be a good friend of the Central Asian countries, and that China will not pursue a sphere of influence in Central Asia, political or economic. China offered the land-locked. Central Asian states outlet to the Sea on its Pacific coast. He also offered that China is ready to join forces with the Central Asian countries to build the new Silk Road, designed to fulfill the needs of the 21st century (Kui, 1996: 51). The Chinese took particular credit that in early difficult years border trade with China helped Russia and other Central Asian states in warding off severe shortage of food and consumer goods.

A series of negotiations took place between Russia and the bordering Central Asian states on the one hand, and China on the other hand on resolving the border issue and adopting military confidence building measures in the bordering areas. Also, in 1994 the border treaty between China and Kazakhstan was signed. In September 1995 the 17th round of negotiations on disarmament and military confidence measures in the bordering areas was held in Moscow with the participation of the five countries concerned. Substantial results were achieved. All parties reached unanimous agreement on the treaty. Thus the stage was set for the signing of the" Agreement on Strengthening Military Confidence in Border Areas" on April 26,1996 at Shanghai by Russia, China, Kazakhstan, Kyrgyzstan and came to be known as the 'Shanghai five'. The agreement stipulated that the troops of the sides stationed in the border areas would not attack each other. It called for the reduction of military units along the border.

The signatory states also agreed that they would neither attack nor direct military exercises against one another along the border. As CBM measure, it was agreed that the signatories would notify the other side about large-scale military exercises. They would invite observers from the other side to military maneuvers and exercises. Friendly contacts among the military personnel of the sides would be encouraged. In addition, the five presidents signed a series of agreements to promote economic trades, scientific and cultural exchanges.

The first step in building the structure of Sino-Russian partnership in Central Asia, thus, comprised of confidence building measures in the entire former Soviet-China border area. Other steps gradually followed. In the previous decades the entire border was highly militarized and fortified and was a flash point of tension. The priority before the post-Soviet Russia and the Central Asian republics was domestic politico-economic systemic transformation. For this they needed a stable and favourable external environment and peace on the border. China also accorded highest priority to the task of economic modernization that required peace on the borders. Russia was not in a position to re-impose or hold on to its historical control and influence over the region. China's population and economic power are largely concentrated on its eastern coastal part. Thus, China's position on its western front in Central Asia in the immediate post-Soviet period was rather defensive. It wanted to forestall the possibility of the assertion of the Uighur demand for independence in Xinjiang (Nathan and Ross, 1997:213-229).

The newly independent states of Central Asia were extremely fragile in political, economic and military terms. Both Moscow and Beijing were concerned that any instability and turbulence in Central Asia would spillover to their bordering areas. The two, therefore, decided to join hands for ensuring peace, stability and confidence building measures in the region. The basic objective of the Shanghai April 1996 declaration was to make declarations aimed at assuring one another about the non-threatening intentions of the sides that would instill mutual confidence.

One important feature of the border negotiations that took place in Central Asia was that the three Central Asian Republics negotiated together along with Russia with China within the framework of four plus one. Significantly, this practice has been given up in November 2000. The Central Asians from now onwards shall be negotiating bilaterally with China, which, in fact, goes in China's favour.

a) Annual Summit Meetings of the Shanghai Five

In their second summit meeting in Moscow in 1997, the Five signed the" Agreement on Mutual Reduction of Military Forces in the Border Areas". The agreement provided that in the 100 km zone on each side of former Soviet-China border, the total strength of the Army, the Air Force and the air units of the Air Defence Force should not exceed 130,400. The agreement also established supervisory mechanism over the military forces on the borders. The second agreement, thus, was aimed at reducing the number of the border forces to the level of defensive purposes only. The sides' reiterated not to use force or the threat to use force, not to pursue military supremacy and agreed to exchange of information on border military force. The objective was to promote transparency and mutual trust and make military activities on the border predictable and subject to supervision (Sherman, 1995:216-222).

Both Russia and China and the concerned Central Asian leaders are extremely upbeat about their achievements within the Shanghai Five framework. It is regarded as a new type of constructive and practical diplomacy that imparted stability and predictability along more than 7,500-km long border through military confidence-building measures. Thus, President Jiang Zemin was reported to have remarked that the Shanghai Five presented a model distinct from the Cold War mindset. The Russian President called it a unique document in the world. President Nazarbaev hailed it as unprecedented in the contemporary world (Mingshan & Xiquam, 2000: 3-4)

The beginning of the Shanghai Five processes has coincided with the change of the stewardship of the Russian Foreign Ministry. In January 1996 Andrei Kozyrev was replaced by

Yevgeny Primakov. Although disenchantment with the totally Westward orientation and a certain shift in the country's policy had begun much earlier in 1993-94, still Kozyrev bore the tag of being pro-West. Primakov laid greater stress on a more balanced policy between the West and the East and is associated with the concept of pursuing a 'multipolar' world.

The third summit was held at Alma-Ata in June-July 1998. President Yeltsin did not attend the Alma-Ata summit of Shanghai Five. In his place Foreign Minister Yevgeny Primakov attended the summit. The joint declaration underlined the readiness of all the parties to continue to foster an atmosphere of "genuine friendship and complete trust" along the border. The joint declaration also outlined the progress made in border demilitarization. All the speakers took note of the threat to regional security posed by the ongoing conflict in Afghanistan, the growth of drug trafficking, and mounting religious extremism, separatism and aggressive nationalism in the region. The declaration included their commitment to fight these forces. (Myasnikov, 2002:43-56).

In addition, the signatories showed common interest in developing" pipeline infrastructure among the five states, with connection to other countries." The main reference was to the large-scale project to build a 3000-km long oil pipeline from western Kazakhstan to western China. Russia was reported to be showing interest in it, as the Russian companies expected a share in the construction contracts (Pravda, July 4, 1998).

The Alma-Ata summit provided an opportunity to President Nazarbaev of Kazakhstan to publicise his pet project of holding a conference of confidence-building measures in Asia (CICA), which was endorsed by the summit. The summit also endorsed the favourite proposal of President Islam Karimov of Uzbekistan (sent by correspondence) of declaring Central Asia a nuclear-free zone.

However, the fact that President Yeltsin did not attend the summit and subsequently his inability to attend the ceremony of the presentation of the new Kazakhstan capital Astana, were regarded as a slight by the Kazakhs. The personal bond between the leaders of the post-Soviet republics was regarded as the main cementing factor in the former Soviet space6 Noviye Izvestia commented that in the absence of Yeltsin, the meeting at Alma-Ata of the leaders of Shanghai Five became "purely a formality" (CDPSP, 1998:18-19).

The Shanghai Five has provided a platform both for real achievements in the field of CBMs in the border and has speeded up the process of settling the border disputes and demarcation of the border alignment on the ground. At the same time, Shanghai Five has also been used by the parties as a platform for voicing good intentions, and adopting self righteous position in a world driven by power politics. Thus, the nuclear tests by India and Pakistan came in for criticism at the Alma-Ata summit. Foreign Minister Primakov made use of the occasion by contrasting the tense relations between India and Pakistan with the example of cooperative security set by the Shanghai Five and called upon India and Pakistan to emulate the example of the Shanghai Five. In fact, ITAR-TASS remarked regarding Nazarbaev's CICA proposal that it was a "conceptual rehash of an idea once put forward by Mikhail Gorbachev ... "All these things", added the paper, "are repeated in various forms year after year. The vast majority of them have about as much chance of implementation as the Russian President's appeal in a recent letter to Indian Prime Minister Vajpayee, that India sign the Treaty on the Non Proliferation of Nuclear Weapons without delay" (Myasnikov, 2002: 34-43).

The fourth summit of the Shanghai Five took place at Bishkek on August 25, 1999. The background to the Bishkek summit was provided by NATO bombing of Yugoslavia, an event that brought Moscow and Beijing closer to each other in a joint struggle against hegemonism and the use of force without UN sanction. On his arrival at the Bishkek Airport, President Yeltsin remarked about his readiness for a battle "especially with Westerners". Softening the impact of President Yeltsin's words, the Foreign Minister of Russia, Igor Ivanov, however, remarked that, "the closer the Russia-

China relations, the greater the stability in the world" and added" the more the constructive cooperation with the US, the greater the stability in the world." However, testifying to the mood prevailing in post Yugoslav situation, it was noted in the media that the proceedings of the summit were conducted in utmost secrecy. No traditional meeting with the press was held (Daily Review, Aug. 26, 1999).

Replying to questions by Kommersant (Sergei Prikhodko) deputy chief of Yeltsin's staff, said on the occasion that the original task set at Shanghai (1996) - to build up confidence and give an additional impetus to border cooperation, has been fulfilled. New tasks were now emerging. These were, the struggle against international terrorism, illegal drug trafficking and arms smuggling, as well as illegal emigration and other forms of across-the -border criminal acts. The Bishkek declaration referred to the agreement on appropriate 'joint measures in 1999-2000 on these issues .Commenting on Bishkek summit, the official media stressed that Shanghai Five is not a political military bloc. Its main objective is to pursue sub-regional security. It also said that the Shanghai Five is not directed against other countries (SWB, FE/ 3623 E/1 August 26, 1999). Bishkek declaration also upheld the concept of multi-polarity as the general trend for the development of the present day world.

The sides expressed the intention to develop trade and economic cooperation between the five countries on a bilateral basis and to step up at the same time a search for ways to boost multilateral interaction in this sphere. The sides supported the idea of reviving the "Diplomacy of the Silk Road", put forward by the Kyrgyz President Askar Akayev.

At the Dushanbe Summit (July 5, 2000), the cooperation in the field of combating national separatism, international terrorism, and religious extremism as well as weapons and drugs trafficking and illegal immigration was pushed to a new stage. For this purpose the Five countries agreed to work out multilateral programmes, sign multilateral treaties and accords and hold regular meeting of officers from their justice, border and customs departments (Mingshan & Xiquan, 2000: 26-27).

It was reiterated on the eve of Shangahi Five summit in Dushanbe that the purpose for which the Shanghai five was created, viz., agreement on CBMs and the reduction of troops in the border areas are being implemented. But new threats have appeared in the region in the form of international terrorism and drugs and weapons trafficking. During the summit, talks were also held between the law-enforcing bodies, special services and defence ministries of the sides on how to deal with the new challenges.

The border CBMs entered the new stage of implementation of the Shanghai agreements. Izvestia, for instance, reported that the sides coordinated the parameters of presence in the 100-km zone on both sides of the border for the first time in the history of their relations. The troop ceilings after reduction were carefully analyzed and were recognized as optimal for ensuring the national security of the sides. The paper also reported that the first mutual inspection under the Shanghai Five framework has just ended in Russia's Maritime Territory, and another inspection would be held in the adjacent region in the north-east of China. Observers from all five states can take part on a voluntary basis in each such inspection (The Hindu, July 6, 2000).

A look at the declaration adopted at Dushanbe shows that it provided a forum to the big two – Russia and China-to document their general positions on larger regional and world issues and carry the Central Asian member states along with them. Thus the declaration endorsed the concept of multipolar world. Respect for human rights was mentioned with the rider that the historic specifics of every state should be heeded during the application of this principle. The application of this principle should not run counter to other generally recognized principles of international law. NPT, CTBT should be universally joined. The declaration endorsed NFZ in Central Asia as well as CICA proposal.

The declaration opposed the use of force in international relations without prior permission of the UN Security Council. It stressed that the UN role should be strengthened as the main mechanism for maintaining international peace and stability. The declaration also underscored the unconditional need for preserving and unfailingly observing the 1972 ABM treaty, which banned the creation of national ABM systems. The ABM treaty was seen as the cornerstone of strategic stability and the foundation for subsequent strategic offensive arms cuts. The parties also opposed US plan to build NMD (National Missile Defence) system and the deployment of TMD systems in the Asia-Pacific region and supported the position of China, which opposed plans to incorporate Taiwan into such a system.(Cheng,2004:53-75).

The Dushanbe declaration expressed support for "the striving and efforts of China to maintain unity in the country in accordance with' one China' principle and for "Russia's stand on the settlement of the situation in the Chechen Republic". In view of the Western criticism of Russian military action in Chechnya, the support of the Shanghai Five appeared to be a welcome relief for the Russian authorities. In all the formulations China equates the Taiwan issue with that of Chechnya. It is advantageous to the Chinese as the Chinese do not have any control over Taiwan, while Russians have Chechnya under their effective military control, despite continued militant violence in the region.

President Islam Karimov of Uzbekistan for the first time participated as an observer. He did not sign the declaration. President Putin proposed that the Shanghai Five should be called Shanghai Forum. Hints were also given regarding its possible extensions with the participation of other states of the region (The Hindu, July 8, 2000).While in Dushanbe; President Putin made it clear that the Russian troops would remain in Tajikistan said, "Unless our servicemen are present in the republic, the positive achievements of the settlement of the Tajik conflict will be lost". (Denda, 2000:97-116).

b) China's Policy towards Central Asia: Initial Emphasis on Transport, Trade and Economic Links

China's policy towards Central Asia is determined by its desire to have a belt of good-neighbourly states on its sensitive western borders across Xinjiang, where it is facing the problem of Uighur separatism. China is keen to ensure that the newly independent Central Asian states do not give any support and encouragement to the Uighurs in Xinjiang. There are around 200,000 UIghurs In Kazakhstan and around 50,000 in Kyrgyzstan. On the other hand there are small Kazakh, Kyrgyz and Tajik minorities in Xinjiang. Second Chinese objective is to get an access to the energy resources of Central Asia. (Crocker,2003:32-44).

Lastly China is interested in the Central Asian markets and enhancing its economic influence in the region. For the present the task of ensuring security of Central Asian region is largely left to Moscow, the traditional guarantor of security in the region. China has concentrated on enhancing transport, trade and economic links. Russian commentators have appreciated the gesture that China has agreed to settle the border issue with the Central Asian states together with Russia in the framework of Four plus One, which is seen as the Chinese recognition of Russia's special role in the region. However, present author was informed by a visiting Russian scholar from the Institute of Far East, Moscow, that in November 2000, a decision was taken that from then onwards the border issue would be bilaterally dealt by China with the CARs. It would appear that without directly questioning Russia's traditional role in Central Asia, China is persistently making inroads in the region by filling up available spaces. (Crocker,2003: 32-44).

Significantly, China is also seeking to establish military contacts with the Central Asian states. Reports of growing military exchanges between China and the CARs and offers of military assistance by the former to the latter are also appearing of late. The Chinese military delegations are visiting CARs. The Turkmen defence minister visited China in September 1999 and expressed interest in cooperation with China in the field of military training and use of equipment .China extended aid of 11 million Yuan to the Kazakh armed forces during the visit of the Kazakh defence minister to China in April-end 2000. Chinese military delegation pledged aid to Kazakhstan. On July 13, 2000, the Chinese military delegation visited Tajikistan (Xinhua, July15, 2000).

Immediately after the emergence of independent states in Central Asia, the Chinese quickly established rail and road links with the bordering CARs. Cheap Chinese consumer goods flooded the region. China has also extended access to the sea to the land-locked Central Asian states to its ports on the Pacific Ocean. Traditionally, all transport and communications links of Central Asia have been through Russia. Access to the sea across the Chinese territory helps the CARs in their search for alternative routes and in that measure reduces their dependence on Moscow. The revival of ancient Silk Road network linking China across Central Asia to Europe and Middle East has caught the imagination of all concerned. Moscow is keen to ensure that Russia is not by-passed in the transport and pipeline building activities in the region. It would like to be connected with them. Ever since the fall of the Soviet Union Russia is keenly projecting itself as a bridge between Europe and Asia through transport network across the Russian territory. It has enthusiastically supported the route from China across Kazakhstan, Russia, Belarus, to Poland as the northern branch of the 'Silk Road'. (Rossabi, 1999: 19-20).

China has a vital interest in getting access to the vast energy resources of both Russia and Central Asia in view of the increasing energy requirements of its growing economy. In view of ambitious Western projects to take Central Asian and Caspian oil and gas are not delivered only to the West. Moscow, which was the sole custodian of Central Asian and Caspian Sea energy resources and pipeline network under the Soviet Union, has reasons to be greatly concerned at the Western interests and presence in the region. The Russian analysts believe that to a certain extent it is possible to collaborate with China with a view to jointly resist Western pressure and designs in the Caspian Sea and the Central Asian regions. This is regarded as the economic logic behind the two powers calling for a 'multi-polar' world. (Kedrov, 1999: 13).

In the field of energy, the economies of Russia and the CARs on the one hand and China on the other hand are mutually complementary. In fact, Moscow regards the Central Asians as its competitors as energy suppliers. However, the best practical option before Moscow is to create mutual dependence with China by way of building oil and gas pipelines from Russian Far East and Siberia to China. Moscow is also seeking a share in the Central Asian energy network. Thus, in June 1997 during the visit of Prime Minister Viktor Chernomyrdin and Deputy Prime Minister Boris Nemtsov to China, the two countries signed an agreement on cooperation in oil and natural gas production and pipelines. Under the agreement the two would cooperate in the exploration of gas in Irkutsk in Russia's Far East and gas supply from Kovykta gas deposit from Irkutsk district to China by a 3360-km pipeline across Mongolia. (Lukin,1998:831-835).

It has been projected that after the year 2005 Russia and CIS countries will be the main sources of natural gas for China. China is reported to be "conducting an active policy of attracting the gas resources of adjacent states". Russia Turkmenistan and Kazakhstan are main partners of China. On September 24, 1997, China and Kazakhstan signed a $9.5 billion agreement for the development of oil and gas fields in western Kazakhstan with the Chinese aid. China is to receive 60 percent of the oil thus produced. The agreement envisaged the construction of a 3000 km pipeline from Kazakhstan to China. China is particularly interested in getting access to Turkmen gas and thus ensures future energy security. The China-Turkmenistan joint statement issued on July 6, 2000, at the time of President Jiang Zemin's visit to Ashgabat attaches special importance to strengthening mutually beneficial cooperation in the energy field. The two sides have agreed to conduct feasibility study on the project of laying a natural gas pipeline linking Turkmenistan and China. The pipeline is going to be 8000-km long and cost upward of $12 billion.

Such a route was first discussed several years ago. In the intervening years, it appeared to be dead because of high construction cost. However, China's growing energy needs appear to have rekindled the discussion (Rappal,2002:64-77).

Russia Remains Big Player in Central Asia

Russia is the largest and the most dominant and is gradually fortifying its own position in the former Soviet republics. It retains nearly three-fourth of borders, Russian border guards are withdrawing from the Soviet territory and accounts for nearly half of the Soviet other republics. However, in view of the threat posed by population at that time, Russian population is declining and is partly replenished by immigration of Russians from other former Soviet republics. (Kager, 1997: 5). The CARs are all ruled by ex-Communist ruling elites, who have now adopted the ideology of nationalism and are trying to adapt to market economy and integration with the world economy. They are prepared to come to terms with cultural Islam, but are opposed to political and extremist Islam that aims at wresting political power. In view of the threat that Russia is itself facing from Sunni Wahabi Islamic extremism in Chechnya, Oagestan and other areas of Caucasus and southern Russia, Moscow and the Central Asian elites have ideological affinity and sympathy for each other.(Lo, 2004:121-134).

At the time of Soviet disintegration, the newly independent states of Central Asia were militarily, politically and economically weak and naturally came within the security parameters of Moscow. When civil war broke out in Tajikistan in 1992 between the ex-communist ruling elite and the Islamic elements that were getting support and sanctuary in Mujahideen-ruled Afghanistan and from the Islamic elements of Iran and Pakistan, Russia stepped in as the main guarantor of security of the Tajik government with the consent and participation of all other Central Asian states. In May 1992 a CIS collective security treaty was signed in Tashkent for the protection of the CIS borders. (Lo, 2004:121-134).

In August 1992 except for Turkmenistan all other Central Asian states along with Russia created a 25,000 strong Russian-

Central Asian force to protect the Tajik-Afghan borders to keep the Islamic militants at bay. Russia deployed its 201st Motorized Rifle division and units of its Federal Border Service in Tajikistan. At this time a 'two border' strategy was evolved whereby the defence of the external borders of the CIS or the former Soviet borders was considered crucial for the security of Russia. The former Soviet borders were well guarded and fortified while Russia's new borders were not. As the border defence units of the new republics have been formed and trained and Russia is gradually fortifying its own borders, Russian border guards are withdrawing from the other republics. (Rahm, 2002:153-161).

However, in view of the threat posed by Taliban controlled Afghanistan, Russia decided to maintain its military presence in Tajikistan, which has a more than one thousand km. long border with Afghanistan. In February 1999 Russia also decided to establish a military base in Tajikistan. As will be discussed later in this chapter, Russia is also trying to strengthen the collective security treaty to meet the challenge of international terrorism, extremism and drugs and arms trafficking emanating from Afghanistan–Pakistan belt (Crocker,2003:32;44).

Owing to a steep decline in Russian economy (Russian COP fell by 40 to 50 percent in the first few years of economic reforms) and its continued economic woes Russia was in no position to maintain its traditional and historical hold over Central Asian economies. All the CARs have diversified their political and economic ties with the outside world, more particularly the Western countries that have surplus capital and modern technologies. Central Asia and Caspian region being rich in hydrocarbon resources and other valuable minerals and metals became particularly attractive to Western countries and multinational corporations. Their geopolitical location in the heart of Asia close to the borders of Russia, China, the Indian subcontinent, Iran and the Middle East added to their value in the eyes of the West. Russia's trade and investment in the CARs declined while that of the Western countries, Japan and South Korea and China, etc. increased (Kerr, 1998:216-231).

The failure of Russian military to subdue the rebel republic of Chechnya in the first Chechen war (1994-96) exposed its military decline and gave a further blow to Russia's prestige. On its part, the USA has declared the promotion of' geopolitical pluralism' in the former Soviet space as its goal. The most populous state is Uzbekistan in Central Asia, oil-rich Azerbaijan in Transcaucasia, and second most powerful and advanced former Soviet Slavic republic of Ukraine invited special US attention in this effort. With the Western blessing and encouragement a pro-Western grouping of southern and south-western former Soviet states called GUUAM (Georgia, Ukraine, Uzbekistan, Azerbaijan and Moldova) was formed mainly for economic and partly for political purposes. (Crincione,2000:212-136).

To the challenge the Moscow, the West is promoting and sponsoring East-West transport route TRACECA and lying of Baku-Ceyhan and Baku-Supsa oil and gas pipelines that would bypass Russian and Iranian territories. US policy in Central Asia and Caucasus is a cause of concern for Russia. Russia is trying to protect what it considers its vital interests in the region, but it does not wish to enter into direct confrontation with the USA. The US decision to extend the country's command responsibility zone to the former Soviet republics aroused particular Russian concern and the issue was repeatedly taken up by Russia with the USA at the highest level (Bakshi, 1999: 1585-86).

In view of its limited resources and capabilities, Russia has sought selective integration with the inner core of the former Soviet republics, which, for various reasons, are more willing for it. On March 29, 1996 a Customs Union was signed between four republics, viz., Russia, Belarus, Kazakhstan and Kyrgyzstan. Subsequently Tajikistan also has joined the Customs Union. With three out of five Central Asian states being within the Customs Union, Russia remains an important player in Central Asia. Uzbekistan chose to adopt an independent pro-Western course while Turkmenistan from the very beginning declared to follow a policy of neutrality. (Akana, 1996:231-243).

Moscow has been constantly wooing Uzbekistan because of its large population and considerable geopolitical weight in Central Asia. Thus, on October 12, 1998 during his visit to Tashkent, President Yeltsin signed with President Islam Karimov of Uzbekistan and President Imomali Rahmanov of Tajikistan a tripartite agreement for countering aggressive fundamentalism and extremism in the region. President Karimov is carrying on a determined struggle against Islamic militants in the country that are especially strong in the Fergana valley on the tri-junction of Uzbekistan, Kyrgyzstan and Tajikistan.

In February 1999, Russian position in the region suffered a setback when Uzbekistan, Azerbaijan, Georgia and Moldova decided to leave the collective security treaty. Moscow-led collective security treaty was thereafter renewed with six members only, viz., Russia, Armenia, Belarus, Kazakhstan, Kyrgyzstan and Tajikistan. However, the collective security treaty and the Customs Union ensure that Russia maintains its presence and clout in Central Asia.

There has been an undisputed growth in the Western interest and influence in the region. Increase in the Western investments in the region has also created a vested interest of the US-led Western countries in the security set up in the region. Much to the chagrin and consternation of Moscow, the USA has pronounced Central Asia and the Caspian region as areas of special US interest. In July 1994, all the former Soviet republics along with Russia joined NATO's Partnership for Peace (PfP) programme. In September 1997 military exercises for the first time took place in three of the CARs- Kazakhstan, Kyrgyzstan and Uzbekistan under the PfP programme with the participation of troops from USA, Turkey and other Western countries. Russia, felt deeply concerned as the area had thus far come under total security cover of Moscow. But Moscow opted for avoiding a showdown with the West and acquiesced by sending its own contingent in the exercises. Since then the exercises have become an annual feature. (Voskressenski, 2003:354-369).

However, the fact remains that Russia happens to be the next door big power in Central Asia. Whatever small military establishments, equipment and training facilities the newly independent Central Asian states have been able to assemble, are still largely based on the Russian pattern and assistance. In the complex Central Asian situation West seemed at the time not to be in a position to commit hoops. In fact, Aleksei V. Malashenko of the Moscow Centre for Carnegie questioned the Western ability to provide "internal stability" in the region. He even suggested that to some extent Russia could become a "guarantor" of West's mercantile interests in the region. (Bakshi, 1999: 1585-91).

It has been argued that in view of Russia's military, political and economic weakness, it may not be able to impose its will on the region. But the Russian publicists at the same time expressed the belief that Russia still remained in the position of obstructing others from achieving their goals in the region at the expense of Russian interests.

a) Islamic Extremism and Terrorism: A Common Threat

Growing Islamic militancy and extremism in the region have emerged as a common threat for the countries of the region as well as Russia and China and also for India. The Taliban controlled Afghanistan and its mentor Pakistan emerged as the springhead of intern4tional terrorism, illegal drugs and arms trafficking and Islamic extremism. Beginning with the capture of Kabul in September 1996, the Taliban militia made significant gains in capturing almost ninety percent of Afghan territory. It was universally believed that but for the support given by Pakistani army, a mere religious militia that the Taliban were, could not gain such spectacular successes. Saudi financial assistance and drug money also contributed to Taliban gains. Pakistan, Saudi Arabia and the United Arab Emirates were the only three countries that recognized the Taliban government.

Initially the Taliban forces enjoyed Washington's covert backing. Taliban's objective was to bring peace and unity to the war-torn land although under a hard line and strict puritanical Sunni Wahabi code of conduct. Taliban's supporters hoped that they would help in laying overland routes to Central Asia across Afghanistan and make it possible to build oil and gas pipelines from Central Asia across Afghanistan to Pakistan thus reducing the region's dependence on northern routes via Russia. Washington is keenly promoting western routes bypassing both Iran and Russia. It is also interested in the southern route across Afghanistan bypassing Iran. US multinational UNOCAL and the Saudi multinational Delta have been interested in gas pipeline project from Turkmenistan across Afghanistan to Pakistan and beyond. (Anderson,1997:32-41).

However, subsequently, Taliban fell out of favour of Washington owing to its dismal human rights record and harsh treatment of women, its involvement in the drugs trade and above all its refusal to surrender Saudi billionaire Osama bin Laden accused of a number of terrorist acts against US targets.

It is widely known that a large number of terrorist camps existed in Taliban-controlled territory of Afghanistan. India in Kashmir, Russia in Chechnya, China in Xinjiang and the Central Asian states in the Fergana valley area and southern belt bordering on Afghanistan are facing the problem of international terrorism. In view of Islamic militants' attacks in southern Kyrgyzstan and southern Uzbekistan, the CIS and staff exercise. Such a joint exercise was reported to have taken place for the first time. The purpose of the exercise was to prepare for a joint response not to any conventional enemy, but to international terrorist gangs. In the Shanghai Five summit held in Dushanbe in July 2000, the problems of combating international terrorism, separatism, drugs and arms trafficking were given top priority. (Ivanov, 2002:152-170).

The advent of young and energetic Vladimir Putin as the President of Russia is widely regarded as symbolizing the resurgence of new Russia. Within a short span after coming into power, President Putin adopted a New National Security

Concept, a new Military Doctrine and a new Foreign Policy Concept. The basic goals of President Putin's policy are to strengthen the Russian state, pursue a pragmatic and realistic foreign and domestic policy aimed at protection of Russian interests as well as geared to speeding up the country's -economic recovery. Putin did not chart out a radically new course different from his predecessor. But he infused a new energy and vigor in the pursuit of the country's foreign policy in all directions.

Under President Putin a new impulse was provided to the integration process within the former Soviet space, including Central Asia. Russia has been working within the limits of its possibilities and resources, but it significantly activated all its policy options. Thus, at the Minsk summit of the Customs Union and Collective Security members on May 24, 2000, it was decided to further strengthen the collective security and turn the Customs Union into a full-fledged Eurasian Economic Community (SWB, Su/3953 G/ 1 Sept. 23, 2000).

It was, for instance, reported that so far the six member collective security treaty did not have collective military element. It was decided at the Minsk summit to raise the effectiveness of the treaty. New security challenges and threats were identified as international terrorism, illegal arms trade, illegal migration, organized crime, etc. On October 12, 2000, another summit meeting of the collective security member states took place in Bishkek. At Bishkek summit it was decided to strengthen collective security structures and mechanism by creating regional collective security forces that include three directions:

(1) East European direction comprising Russia and Belarus,

(2) Caucasus direction based on bilateral agreements between Russia and Armenia and

(3) the Central Asian direction aimed at setting up regional collective security forces in the Central Asian region. The objective was to set up collective rapid deployment forces on the basis of bilateral relations between Russia and each Central Asian country, especially keeping in view the threat emanating from Afghanistan and international terrorism (Daily Review, May 25, 2000).

On October 10, 2000, Russia, Belarus, Kazakhstan, Kyrgyzstan and Tajikistan signed the treaty on the creation of Eurasian Economic Community in place of the customs union. The treaty stipulates the creation of a common market of five states. As Sergei Rogov pointed out, "Unlike its predecessors, the EEC (Eurasian Economic Community), modeled after the EU, could lead to the creation of an effective mechanism for the development of integration in the post-Soviet space. For the first time in post-Soviet history, five countries agreed to create supranational structures, whose decisions will be binding on all EEC members". It was agreed that an integration committee would take the decisions by a majority of two-thirds of the vote. The vote quotas were decided in this way: Russia would have 40 per cent of the vote, Belarus and Kazakhstan would have 20 per cent each and Kyrgyzstan and Tajikistan would have 10 per cent each. Their contributions to the EEC budget would be commensurate too (Sherman 2000; 3).

Thus, under President Putin Russia sought to consolidate its presence in Central Asia both in economic and security fields. It is believed that Putin has been pursuing a pragmatic and even tough policy with the former Soviet states, particularly as regards the debt repayment. For instance, it was reported, Russia was seeking co-ownership in major defence industries and raw-material complexes of Kyrgyzstan as a mode of repayment of that republic's debt to Russia (Bakayev 2000: 14-27).

With Uzbekistan, which refused to join these military political and economic structures, Moscow entered into bilateral security arrangements. In view of the challenge emanating from the south-from the Taliban and the Islamic militants - it was made clear that Russia would provide Uzbekistan with arms but not with troops.

Russia repeatedly stressed in all its policy formulations that the CIS countries remain a priority for Russia. However, Russians also seemed hesitant to call the CIS a zone of Russian strategic interests' or influence. It was increasingly realized that the countries have become independent subjects in international relations as independent states. At the same time, the need for greater integration with the CIS countries in various fields has also been increasingly felt. It was stressed that Russia's national interests in economic, political and military spheres should determine the nature and degree of such an integration, while taking account of the legacy of the former Soviet Union, from whom the CIS has inherited energy, economic development of the region. China is planning to transport and communication network. (Bakayev, 2000:14-27).

Analysts argue that under Putin Russia is likely to be more assertive in promoting Russia's economic interests in Central Asia. Putin wants economic and political interests to align (Warner, 2000: 10). Despite the weakening of Russia's economic position in Central Asia, the structures of Soviet time integration of Russian Central Asian economy still persist. Thus, large enterprises in Russia still depend on cotton imports from Uzbekistan, especially in Ivanovo. A Reuter dispatch from Moscow on October 13, 2000, reads: "The West has provided welcome investment, especially in resource rich Kazakhstan, but Russia under Putin in re-emerging as the number one influence in the region". The fear of radical Islam, especially in Afghanistan is binding Russia and Central Asia together.

b) China's Strategy to develop its Western Region

China also launched its 'Great Western Campaign' to develop the backward western regions of the country. The objective is both to reduce the glaring disparity in the developed eastern regions and the backward western regions as well as consolidating China's hold over the minority regions through promises of economic development. It is even feared that the growing economic disparities may threaten the unity of the country. Moreover, 8 million out of 17 million residents of Xinjiang are Uighurs, who are Muslims of the Turkic stock and resist assimilation by the dominant Hans. Although the separatist violence in Xinjiang has not acquired a threatening proportion, but the Chinese authorities apprehend that "separatism and the struggle against separatism will go on for a long time in Xinjiang". Between January 1997 and April 1999, Amnesty documented 210 death sentences and 190 executions in the province. Most of those executed were Uighurs convicted of terrorism and subversive activities.(Cheng, 2004: 253-273).

The Chinese are concerned at Uighurs taking part in armed Islamic movements abroad from Afghanistan to Uzbekistan and even Chechnya. On returning home they can create problems for China. The Chinese hope to keep Uighur separatism in check through economic development of the region. China is planning to develop a number of infrastructure and oil and gas pipeline projects in the region. It was reported in September 2000 that in next five years Beijing hopes to spend over $ 12 billion on 70 major projects. Some money will come from Beijing. It is also looking to the wealthy eastern provinces to help (The Hindu, Sept. 16, 2000).

It seemed likely that the economic development of the western regions of China, including Xinjiang, might help in the projection of Chinese economic power further west in the Central Asian states and may change the current equilibrium of balance of power in the region in China's favour.

The infrastructure and pipeline development projects in Xinjiang, through which China hopes both to win over and further assimilate the disgruntled minorities, are creating new contradictions. They have resulted in the increase of Han migration into the region which is deeply resented by the Uighurs. The Uighurs believe that the benefits of development projects are mainly going to the Han settlers and not to the minority community (Bazhanov,1998: 212-233).

Visitors from the neighbouring Kyrgyzstan is the only Central Asian state that has joined the WTO point out that China is vigorously trying to flood the Central Asian markets and economies by dumping cheap Chinese goods. Kyrgyzstan, which has a relatively free economy, is used as a transit point to the rest of Central Asia. The Chinese are reported to be resorting to unethical trade practice of labeling their low quality goods of mass consumption as 'made in Kyrgyzstan'.

c) Potential Rivalry between Russia and China in Central Asia

The Chinese policy of developing the western regions as well as the Russian policy of promoting regional integration by forming Eurasian Economic Community and strengthening the collective security treaty underscored their vigorous efforts aimed at consolidating positions in their respective parts of Central Asia albeit in different ways. At the same time, they cooperate with each other within the Shanghai Forum. It has been decided by the Shanghai Forum to set up an anti-terrorist centre in Bishkek.

China appears to have largely succeeded in its bid to enlist the support of the Central Asian regimes in curbing Uighur separatists. It also sought to formally commit Russia and the CARs to 'one China' concept. However, an apprehension was expressed at the time that if Islamic extremist groups come to power in Central Asia or Central Asia slips into chaos, it may be more difficult to prevent support to the Uighurs coming from neighbouring regions. Therefore, both Russia and China, for their own reasons, have a deep interest that Central Asia is not destabilized (Gilbert,1998:92-113).

China adopted a policy of not to question directly Russia's traditional positions in the region but at the same time trying to seep into available spaces in the region, that include not only growing economic but also military contacts. In Kazakhstan, China's direct foreign investment reached $ 1.1 billion in 1999. Thus, Morris Rossabi remarked that China "harbours aspirations of replacing Russia as the dominant economic force in Central Asia, thus placing Beijing in a better position to address its domestic policy concerns". It has been pointed out that if China's economic and military power continues to grow while that of Russia declines, China might even step in to play the policeman's role to protect its economic and geopolitical interests in Central Asia (Philip and Rhinelander: 2001:57-68).

One factor binding China with the CARs is the authoritarian political culture. Although Russia has developed all the paraphernalia of democracy, still democratic culture and institutions are new in Russia and Russian ruling class finds no difficulty in dealing with authoritarian regimes. Indeed, the CAR regimes are increasingly becoming wary of Western insistence on human rights and democracy. In fact, authoritarian Chinese model combining strict political control with a free market economy appears to be increasingly more attractive to the CAR regimes.

It may be assumed that China can hope to achieve much more in terms of extending its influence in Central Asia and further west through peace dividends. China appears to have enthusiastically adopted the 'Eurasian project', which includes the vast region with immense resources, comprising Russia, China and the Central Asian member states that constitute the Shanghai Forum (Gang, 1999: 25-28).

Indeed owing to its size, population and economic and military power, China is bound to make its weight felt in the grouping, especially in view of the fact that after the Soviet collapse, Moscow's power and influence have shrunk and those of China are on the rise. Moscow is painfully aware of it. But it would avoid direct confrontation with China, or for that matter, with the West. It would rather h-y to place itself in the position of the 'balancing pole' of contending powers and interests in the region. To an extent it would also imply Russian reconciliation with the presence of the Western as well as other interests in the region. In the similar vein, a more active Indian role in Central Asia may be rather welcomed by Russia.

Russia has been trying to craft together an anti-terrorist alliance of the major powers. It set up joint working groups on Afghanistan with both India and the USA to meet the threat of international narco-terrorism emanating from there. Both Russia and the USA sponsored the UN Security Council resolution of December 19, 2000, that imposed additional sanctions on the Taliban unless the latter closed the terrorist bases on its territory and surrendered Osama bin Laden within a month. It is extremely significant that China along with Malaysia chose to abstain from the Security Council resolution. Thus, on the question of dealing with the Taliban challenge in Afghanistan, the positions of China and Russia were not identical despite the fact that the Shanghai Five have repeatedly emphasized the need for joint fight against religious extremism and international terrorism. Indeed, it was clearly the strategy of the Taliban and their supporters in Islamabad that all the neighbouring countries should not unite against them and they were able to deal with each neighbouring country separately by offering promises of good behaviour.

Piqued by Taliban's recognition of the independence of Chechnya in January 2000 and its support to Chechen rebels, Russian officials in May and June, 2000, voiced the possibility of pre-emptive air strikes against the terrorist training bases in Taliban-held territory. Taliban's threat to carryon reprisals against the neighbouring Central Asian countries seems to have frightened Uzbekistan and other CARs to distance their position from Russia. Russia itself backed out from the threat of air strikes. Taliban seemed to be particularly trying to reach out to China. In fact, a certain duality in dealing with the Taliban phenomenon could be discerned in the policy of all the countries of the region. Russia regarded the protection of the southern borders of the CIS crucial for its own security. It remained the main guarantor of security of the region. At the same time, after its 'earlier experience in Afghanistan, it did not like to again get involved in another Afghan war. It seemed that it would like to act in coalition with other powers and through the UNO (Gilbert,2000:541-553).

The Western analysts invariably dwell on prospects for and tensions in Sino-Russian Relations". (Ovchinnikiov, 2000: 19). Indeed, potential of rivalry and conflict does lie beneath present day bonhomie between Moscow and Beijing. However, neither Moscow, nor Beijing seemed willing to disturb the apple cart of their 'strategic partnership' in Central Asia. The two regard Central Asia as the' strategic hinterland' of each other. Russia seemed to favour greater mutual dependence with China through increased trade, transportation links and pipeline networks as an insurance for peace and security on its eastern front for the likely challenge to its interests in Central Asia posed by China's policy of developing the western regions, some Russian politicians and scholars, including former Prime Minister Yevgeny Primakov, put up a brave face by arguing that China's western regions and Russian far East can be developed together (Myasinkov, 2000: 19-20).

During Shanghai summit of the grouping on June 14-15, 2001, Uzbekistan formally joined and it was renamed as Shanghai Co-operation Organization (SCO). Uzbekistan, that had been facing increasing challenge of Islamic extremism from the Islamic Movement of Uzbekistan (IMU) decided to join the SCO, while it withdrew earlier form Russia-led CIS collective security treaty. It could be seen as a manifestation of Uzbek desire to manoeuvre between Russia and China within the SCO. The highlight of the summit was the signing of the Shanghai Convention on combating terrorism, separatism and extremism.

It was decided to formulate a long-term programme of multilateral trade and economic co-operation. The member states agreed to hold annual meetings of the Foreign and Defence ministers in order to cooperate in resolving major international and regional issues, above all relating to the strengthening of security and stability in the Central Asian region.

The Shanghai June 2001 declaration refers to the possibility of admitting new members on the basis of consensus. The declaration says that those states can be considered for new membership that "Share the objectives and tasks of cooperation, the principles stated in point 6 and also other provisions of this declaration".

The point 6 reads:

> "Shanghai Organization of Cooperation has been formed on basis of the agreements on strengthening of trust in military sphere and on mutual arms reductions signed in Shanghai and Moscow in 1996 and 1997. The principles reflected in the above-stated agreements determine the basis of relationship between the states- members of

Shanghai Organization of cooperation" (SCO Press Release, June 15 2001).

Thus, the possibility of admitting new members has been kept open. New members are to be admitted by consensus among the present members. The rules are to be finalized at the St. Petersburg summit of the grouping scheduled for June, 2002. At the same time, it is indicated that there is no immediate hurry to admit new members (Ruishong, 2002:87-102).

At times countries as far apart as Mongolia, Iran and even the USA have been mentioned as the countries that would like to join the SCO besides India and Pakistan. In talks with the Kazakh scholars in October 2001, the present author was told that India's admission to SCO would depend on the course of India-China relations, thus, giving an inkling of who called the shots in the organization. It produced the impression that in view of lack of consensus on other members, perhaps Mongolia would be the only country that might be expected to join in the near future.

As these developments were taking place in the region in its direct proximity, India has been watching them closely with considerable interest. Significantly, the process of confidence building measures between China and the former Soviet bordering states has been accompanied by the signing of India-China agreements on the maintenance of peace and tranquility and confidence-building measures in the military field in the border areas along the Line of Actual Control (LAC) in 1993 and 1996 respectively. It is a very positive development impacting on India's perception of the Shanghai process.

Indeed, there existed an opinion in this country that India would prefer to be invited to join the organization and with due cognizance of India's legitimate interests rather than apply for it. While India has been thus reticent, Pakistan's Ambassador to Kyrgyzstan submitted a formal request to the Kyrgyz Foreign Ministry on January 3, 2001, for an observer status at the Shanghai forum. It was like following in the footsteps of

Uzbekistan that participated in Shanghai Five's Dushanbe (July 2000) summit as an observer and was admitted as a full member in Shanghai summit in June 2001. But within two days of Pakistan's formal application, the President of Tajikistan, Mr. Emomaly Rahmanov expressed his strong opposition to admitting Pakistan in the grouping. He stressed that he was even opposed to discussing the issue (Frank, 2004:212-227).

At the Shanghai summit of the SCO in June, Beijing was reported to have strongly lobbied for Pakistan's entry. It is likely that Pakistan's application was made with a prior understanding with China. There was no consensus as Tajikistan (and also perhaps Russia) opposed it because of Pakistan's support to the Taliban forces that were exporting terrorism in Central Asia (Bakshi, 2001: 174-176).

Ever since the Soviet disintegration, Pakistan has nurtured the ambition of expanding its influence in the former Soviet Central Asia. In view of difficulties in opening trade, transport routes and laying oil and gas pipelines across turbulent Afghanistan, Pakistan, has been seeking to lure the Central Asian republics by offering road and rail outlets to the Arabian Sea ports across Indus Basin corridor passing through Karakoram highway across Chinese Xinjiang linking up with Kyrgyzstan and Kazakhstan as well as Taiikistan (Bakshi, 2001: 176-177).

Russia Moves to Strengthen CIS Collective Security

While Russia is prepared to cooperate with China within the framework of the Shanghai organization, it is also trying to consolidate its traditional influence in the region in political, security and economic spheres. Thus, on October 10, 2000, Russia, Belarus, Kazakhstan, Kyrgyzstan and Tajikistan signed a treaty on the creation of the Eurasian Economic Community. Moves were also made to strengthen the collective security treaty of the Commonwealth of Independent States (CIS).

On its part, China has also launched its "great Western campaign" to develop the backward western regions of the country.

Thus, both Russia and China seem to be trying to consolidate their positions in their respective parts of Central Asia.

On the eve of the Shanghai summit of June, 2001, the six member states of the CIS collective security treaty (Russia, Belarus, Armenia, Kazakhstan, Kyrgyzstasn and Tajikistan) held a summit meeting on May 25 in the Armenian capital of Yerevan. They decided to proceed with the creation of a 30000 man rapid reaction force, providing one battalion each. The joint statement issued on the occasion affirmed the readiness of the member states to repel any incursions by the Islamic militants into Central Asia. The headquarters of the rapid reaction force were to be in Bishkek. Yury Yarov of Russia, the Executive Secretary of the CIS, particularly stressed the importance of participation of Uzbekistan for making the collective security more effective in the Central Asian region. A unit of 2000 forces as the rapid reaction force for Central Asia to fight the potential insurgency, in the area was expected to be ready by August 2001 (Times of Central Asia, June 17, 2001).

Thus, Russia-led collective security treaty members were taking measures to beef up the security of Central Asia when the events of September 11 overtook them. In fact, it was reported that the main responsibility for providing security to the region was to be shouldered by Russia-led collective security treaty. For instance, Times of Central Asia (Bishkek) remarked that "The SCO anti-terrorist Centre, however, may do little more than coordinate information between the six member states". The Chinese gain, according to the paper, was an additional summit agreement, which stipulated that at the request of one or more Central Asian member states of the SCO, China can send troops into Central Asia (Times of Central Asia, June 17).

China's declared policy is to change with the changing times, to synthesize between contradictions and antagonisms by highlighting the common points and "reserving disagreements" in order to reach a "win-win" situation for all. In the meanwhile, China wants to continue to amass political, economic and military power or the comprehensive national power, so that when the time of reckoning finally arrives, China is able to pave its way even without a shot being fired. The Chinese are particularly sanguine about the achievements of the Shanghai Cooperation Organization and its precursor the Shanghai Five over the past five years, which, incidentally, bears the name of a Chinese city.

For the time being and in the foreseeable future, the primary Chinese objective is to maintain peace, stability and friendly dispensation in the neighbouring Central Asian states while extending its economic, trade, transport and energy cooperation with the countries of the region. China has shown readiness to recognize the traditional Russian predominance in the security field in the region, although it has also been extending its military contacts and exchanges with the countries of the region (Bakshi 2001: 168-171).

It is quite likely that behind the diplomacy of mutual benefit and win-win situation for all, there exists a shrewd and long-term geopolitical design of extending Chinese influences and reach in the strategically important region of southern Eurasia comprising Central Asia, Transcaucasia and the former northern frontier province of Pakistan, Iran and turkey. It is through this region that important trade, transport and oil and gas pipeline routes are expected to pass, including the revived silk route TRACECA (Transport corridor Europe-Caucasus-Asia). In fact, Francesco Sisci has highlighted the scale and magnitude of the Chinese objectives and ambitions in the region. It is apparent that the Chinese and the Russian interests do not always coincide. For instance, the Russians are interested in promoting the Trans-Siberian railway as the main connecting link between Asia and Europe. The Chinese are believed to be rather cool to the idea. They prefer the southern route to Europe across Central Asia-Transcaucasia-Turkey to the Mediterranean coast. According to Francesco Sisci, it would provide China's western regions:

> "a new geo-strategic importance in a way, such a move would not simply expand Chinese influence from Xinjiang to the Caspian Sea. It would project China into the Middle East, the Mediterranean as well as South Asia, including India. The proposed Chinese railway

> from Qinghai in the far west to Tibet will not only link the restive Tibetan region to the rest of China, it will also link China's economic heart to India, through roads and railways that could one day move passengers and goods from Lhasa to New Delhi". China is seeking to achieve all this not by antagonizing Russia, but by assuring the latter that China's expanding economy should not be viewed as a threat". (Sisci, Asia Times, June 23, 2001).

The West tends to view SCO as the Chinese and the Russian attempt to be the decision-makers in Central Asia to the exclusion of others. In the wake of growing Sino-Russian strategic partnership in Central Asia within the framework of the Shanghai process, concern had been felt in the USA at the rather 'indecisive nature' of Western influence in the region. Indeed, some of the Western think tanks emphasized the desirability of the USA acquiring military bases in inner Asia even prior to the tragic events of September 11.

Prior to September 11 China was being viewed as the "strategic competitor" of the USA. Thus, the formation of the SCO was seen as being aimed at "combating American hegemony", promoting "multipolarisation", and a potential counterweight to NATO. After all, the Shanghai grouping comprised about 1.5 billion people or one-fourth of the entire humanity and almost 60 percent of the landmass of Eurasia. The access to vast oil and gas reserves of the region would help fast growing China to achieve national ambitions in both economic and military fields. The Western media took particular note of the fact that the defence ministers of the six member states also met at Shanghai and discussed military cooperation, including joint exercises and research and development of weaponry. In contrast to the cautious dictum of Deng Xiaoping which said, "adopt a low profile and never take a lead", President Jiang Zemin was seen as making much headway in forging a regional grouping with Russia and Central Asian states and then also signing a 25 year treaty with Russia on July 16, 2001 (Lahm, 2001: 5).

Thus, before September 11, 2001, SCO projected the image of a powerful regional organization with increasing cohesion and purposefulness. It seemed to provide the rising China a forum whereby it could hope to expand its influence westward on the vast Eurasian landmass.

Post-September 11, 2001 Developments in Central Asia

a) US Military Presence in Central Asia

The tragic events of September 11, 2001 and subsequent developments leading to the defeat of Taliban-Al Qaida forces in Afghanistan completely changed the geopolitical equation in the region. Wounded USA cobbled together an international coalition against terror being perpetrated by Taliban leaders and Osama bin Laden from the soil of war ravaged Afghanistan. Russia promptly offered support to the USA in the war against terrorism. In Russia's strategic thinking the real threat to the country's security is seen as emerging from the arc of instability' in the turbulent southern periphery of the country. Russia hoped to gain from new improved relations with the USA in multiple ways. Russia offered the sharing of intelligence and the use of its air space and bases to the USA for search, rescue and humanitarian purposes. It also took the credit of influencing the Central Asian members of the CIS collective security treaty to extend facilities to the USA in the strategically important region bordering on Afghanistan.

It is true that ever since the Soviet disintegration; the used West has been trying to promote 'geopolitical pluralism' in the former Soviet space, including Central Asia. The Central Asia and the Caspian Sea region were declared an area of 'special US interest'. The region was included in the 'zone of responsibility' of the US Central Command. Since September, 1997 annual multinational military exercises are held in Kazakhstan, Kyrgyzstan and Uzbekistan under NATO's Partnership for Peace (PfP) programme with the participation of troops from the USA and other NATO countries. However, the US presence in Central Asia in the security field had remained very limited before September 11. Moscow remained the main guarantor of security in the region (Weede, 2003:32-45).

The war against the Taliban provided the USA an unprecedented opportunity to register and further entrench its military presence in the inner Asian region of immense strategic importance as the borders of major powers Russia, China, the Indian subcontinent and Iran meet here.

Uzbekistan offered military bases to the USA without consulting SCO partners, which was a setback to the grouping. The US-led war against Taliban-Al Qaida network provided Uzbekistan an excellent opportunity to forge security ties with the most powerful country in the world in a bid to achieve multiple gains, including military action against the Islamic Movement of Uzbekistan (IMU), which received sanctuary and support in Taliban-controlled Afghanistan. In return, Uzbekistan sought security guarantees from the USA. Noticeably, Uzbekistan did not participate in the meeting of the CIS Chiefs of General Staff held in Moscow on September 26. Neutral Turkmenistan was the other country, which did not send its representative to the meeting (Nemets & Torda 2001: 13).

It appears that other Central Asian states coordinated their stand with Moscow. Kazakhstan, Kyrgyzstan and Tajikistan all offered air bases for the US troops operating in Afghanistan. However, the USA did not accept the offer of Kazakhstan for air bases to avoid further antagonizing Russia and China. Kazakhstan has a 7000-km long border with Russia with a sizeable Russian population (more than 30 percent). Kazakhstan also shares a long border with China in the east (Peuch, 2002; 5).

It appears the Central Asian states offered bases to the USA due to geopolitical as well as financial considerations. By doing so, they hope to gain maneuvering space vis-a-vis Russia and China as well as make significant monetary gains. On December 6, 2001 Uzbek press published reports of an agreement with Washington of about $100 to $150 million US loans and aid for economic reforms in the country. The then Prime Minister of Kyrgyzstan Kurmanbek Bakiev was reported to have remarked that the presence of thousands of American soldiers would be a gold mine for his impoverished country. Kyrgyzstan claims that the lease of Manas air base has been coordinated in advance with partners in the CIS collective security treaty and the SCO, .meaning thereby Russia and China (Pravda (English) Feb. 18, 2002).

Ostensibly the US forces are in Central Asia mainly to complete the still unfinished task of completely routing Taliban Al Qaida network and, therefore, for a temporary period. In fact, there even exists an opinion in Russia according to which the US war against terrorism in Afghanistan and religious extremism in Central Asia also serves Russian interests and to that extent is acceptable. But the prospects of prolonged US military presence in the region, particularly in Central Asia, arouse deep concern in Moscow, Beijing and other capitals in the region.

Understandably, the projects of laying oil and gas pipelines from Caspian-Central Asian region to the west and south-branching away from their tradition routes across Russia are also at the heart of the USA's geo-strategic and geo-economic game plan in the region.

At the same time, it appears that the USA wants to tread cautiously in the complex geopolitical game unfolding in inner Asia. Instead of annoying and antagonizing them, it wishes take the three big powers in the region along with it, namely, India, China and Russia. However, US policy in Central Asia is currently placed on the horns of a dilemma. Enhanced support to the authoritarian regimes in the region is bound to invoke criticism from human rights and democratic groups, while pressing for the latter would put off the regimes.

As regards China, the impact of post-September 11 developments has been a mixed one. China gained as combating international terrorism became the number one task of US policy instead of China being projected as the emerging strategic rival of the sole super power. It supported the US war against terrorism with certain conditions. At the same time, US military presence close to its western borders is detrimental to China's larger geopolitical goals and ambitions.(Kevin,2000:121-133).

In the post September 11 period, the SCO did not play any significant role in the developing situation in and around Afghanistan, including the neighbouring Central Asia. It became apparent that the security set up of the sea countries was not in place. However, regular meetings of the officials of the sea members at various levels have kept the show going. Moscow and Beijing also kept in constant touch and kept each other informed about their foreign policy moves.

At the instance of the Chinese, an extraordinary meeting of the foreign ministers of the sea countries took place at Beijing on January 7, 2002, to discuss the issues of regional security and cooperation as well as recent events in Afghanistan. The joint statement made no mention of the US role in the region, but it emphasized the leading role of the United Nations in the struggle against international terrorism. It stressed that the scope of anti-terrorist struggle may not be extended arbitrarily and should not lead to interference in the internal affairs of the sovereign states. More particularly, the statement emphasized that the central role in the anti-terrorist struggle must be played by the countries of the region themselves. The statement read:

"The SCO member states believe that the global system of counteraction against terrorism should be based on regional, sub-regional and national structures and firmly intend to complete the creation of a sea anti-terrorist structure in Bishkek in the near future" (SCO Press Release Jan. 7, 2002).

As a measure to further beef up the sea, during the St. Petersburg summit in June, 2002, a charter of the sea was adopted, whereby the grouping has become a formal regional international organization. In keeping with the wishes of Beijing, it was decided to set up a permanent secretariat of the organization at Beijing. The decision to set up an anti-terrorist centre of the grouping at Bishkek was reaffirmed. The need for a broad expansion of trade ties among the member countries was emphasized: The declaration of the summit called the development of economic partnership" an especially important task".

However, in view of the US military presence in the region, sea lost its monopoly as the main regional grouping aimed at maintaining peace and stability in the area and combating the menace of terrorism and extremism.

Security organisations can differ in their scope of activities and in deepness of their mutual cooperation. For instance, the North Atlantic Treaty Organisation (NATO) nowadays pays homage to the broad concept of *security*: security not only encompassing military but also political, economic, social and environmental factors (NATO Handbook 2006: 18-19). Among other things, this comprehensive approach to security includes aspects such as free and fair elections; well-organized administrative, law enforcement and judicial organs at national, regional and local level; employment; housing; education and health services. If all of these dimensions of security are provided in the areas where NATO operates, such as Bosnia, Kosovo and Afghanistan, then a stable and secure situation has been reached.

However, in 1949 NATO started as an organization with an exclusive military objective, namely to deter an eventual attack by the Soviet Union and its satellites against European (NATO) countries. Especially during its operations in the former Yugoslavia in the 1990s, the Western alliance realized that its concept of security should include other aspects than military, in order to achieve a stable international security environment. As to the intensity of cooperation among its member-states, NATO started with the most essential elements of political and military cooperation only. It took NATO many years to establish its current integrated political-military structure and activities, such as frequent political deliberations, joint forces and allied operations far beyond its territorial borders. (Pan,2006:46-64).

This article focuses on the Shanghai Cooperation Organisation (SCO), sometimes rather prematurely referred to as 'The NATO of the East'. In concentrating on its security-related aspects, this work will analyse the SCO's development towards a full-grown security organization i.e., on its way to an alliance with a span of activities and a depth of cooperation similar to that of NATO. However, in doing so the focus remains on the SCO, not on a comparison with the Western alliance.

The SCO is a regional international organization comprising states in Europe, the Near East, Central Asia and South East Asia. The SCO has China, Russia, Kazakhstan, Kyrgyzstan, Tajikistan and Uzbekistan as member states and Mongolia, Iran, Pakistan and India as observer states. SCO member states have a population of nearly 1.5 billion people, which is about a quarter of the total world population. Including the four observers, the SCO encompasses nearly half the world's population. In addition to the member states Russia and China, the observers India and Pakistan bring together in the SCO four states with nuclear weapons Furthermore, the Chinese and Russian armed forces are amongst the three largest armed forces in the world. The SCO provides cooperation in political, military, economic, energy and cultural fields. Important ingredients of economic cooperation are (conventional) arms trade with Russia as supplier and energy, of which Russia, Kazakhstan, Uzbekistan and Iran are big exporters – while China and India are significant importers. Russia and China, however, remain the leading actors of the SCO. (Stobdan,1996:513-520).

Although the SCO started as a security organization extending from confidence-building measures at the borders to anti-terrorist activities SCO members frequently state that this organization is primarily meant for political and economic cooperation and that military coordination focusing on domestic security plays a minor role. For instance, the Russian Deputy Defence Minister, Sergei Razov, denied allegations that military cooperation among SCO members is a top priority and stated that economic cooperation and security are the main interests. Likewise, at the SCO Bishkek Summit of August 2007, President Putin denied that the SCO would develop into a full-grown security organisation such as NATO. So far, neither individual members nor the organisation itself has made any statements towards the intention to create what some Western commentators call a 'NATO of the East'. (Yakovlev,2002:101-113).

Furthermore, SCO members disagree upon vital issues of security, as was the case with the anti-Western positions in the declaration of the 2005 Astana Summit concerning Western military deployment in Central Asia and also on other issues of security cooperation. For instance, in terms of the international legal connotation of security, there is common understanding within the SCO that 'non interference' in internal affairs is a leading principle. Accordingly, SCO members refuse Western criticism on their human rights practices. However, when it comes to collective action against domestic, non-violent uprisings, the March 2005 revolution in Kyrgyzstan demonstrated disagreement within the SCO whether to act or not, with China allegedly in favour and Russia against military intervention considering its recent security activities, is the SCO developing into a 'NATO of the East' as it was regularly described after the anti-Western flavor of the 2005 Astana Summit.

In the last couple of years, the SCO indisputably made huge steps in intensified security cooperation, operational (military exercises), as well as political (policy concepts). A number of events and agreements in 2006 and 2007 indicate a cautious development of the SCO towards a full-grown security organization. In analyzing the current and future developments of the SCO, this article concentrates on indications of increased security cooperation, the relationship with the Collective Security Treaty Organization (CSTO), energy security and the connections with the West. (ITAR-TASS,23rd July,2007).

In spite of the frequent denials of the military nature of the SCO and the differences between members regarding military and security cooperation, five recent developments can be discerned which point in the direction of the SCO gradually moving towards a full-grown security organization. Firstly, the features of military and political activities were combined. For the first time a political summit (Bishkek 2007) was amalgamated with war games ('Peace

Mission 2007'). Moreover, until then defence ministers were the highest ranking officials to watch SCO military exercises.

The Heads of States' presence at the war games, for the first time in the history of the SCO, was probably to demonstrate the growing significance of the military component within the SCO but also signaled their determination to be in command of the security situation in this region.

Secondly, there is the phenomenon of 'military assistance' as a concept. Perhaps the most significant development with regard to the security policy aspects of 'Peace Mission 2007' was the scenario in which military assistance played a central role. One of the vital ingredients of a mature security organization, which also applies to the CSTO, is military assistance. Although a development towards inclusion of such an article into the policy documents of the SCO cannot (yet) be discerned, the scenario of 'Peace Mission 2007' unmistakably revealed a de-facto application of military assistance. (ITAR-TASS, 23rd July, 2007).

Thirdly, since 2002, the military exercises of the SCO have become increasingly ambitious, developing from a bilateral or multilateral level to a joint all-SCO level, and including not only counter-terrorism but also external security policy connotations. Furthermore, prior to the 2007 Bishkek Summit, on 27 June 2007 the SCO ministers of Defence reached agreement on a structural arrangement for joint exercises. According to the Kyrgyz Defence minister, Ismail Isakov, this agreement would lay the long-term organisational and legal foundations for such activities in the future (Xinhua July 29, 2007).

Fourthly, the 2006 Shanghai Summit affirmed that, in case of threats to regional peace, stability and security, SCO members would have immediate consultations on effective response to the emergency. Furthermore, the intention was expressed of formulating a mechanism for measures in response to threats to regional peace, as well as a study on establishing a regional conflict prevention mechanism within the SCO framework. The projected drafting of such security mechanisms, which are also found in

NATO, were repeated at the 2007 Bishkek Summit (ITAR-TASS, June 15, 2006).

A final development indicating that the SCO might be developing towards a mature and comprehensive security organization, is the intensifying relationship between the SCO and the Russian-led military alliance, the Collective Security Treaty Organization (CSTO) of the Commonwealth of Independent States (CIS). Since this might become a crucial aspect of the SCO's move towards a more comprehensive security organization, the relationship between CSTO and SCO will be dealt with in more detail below.

b) SCO and the CSTO Presence in Central Asia

The origin of the CSTO is that in May 1992, within the framework of the CIS, a treaty for collective security (CIS Collective Security Treaty, CST) was signed in Tashkent with a currency of five years and the possibility of prolongation. The treaty comprises the desire of parties to renounce the use or threat of force. Furthermore, in its Article 1, the treaty forbids parties to join other military alliances. Just like NATO, the CST has a military assistance provision (Article 4), which states that aggression against one party will be considered as an attack on all parties. In 1999, the presidents of Russia, Belarus, Armenia, Kazakhstan, Kyrgyzstan and Tajikistan signed a protocol to prolong the CST for five years. Azerbaijan, Georgia and Uzbekistan – who in the mean time had followed a policy away from Russia towards the West – refused to sign the protocol and subsequently withdrew from the treaty. (Zhu,2000:1489-1501).

In 2002, the six remaining CST parties signed a charter, which transformed the CST into an organization, the Collective Security Treaty Organization (CSTO). In 2005, until then US ally Uzbekistan demanded US forces to leave the base on its territory, as a result of US and European criticism of the beating down of the unrest in Andijan by Uzbek authorities earlier that year. Subsequently, Uzbekistan looked for closer ties with Russia.

On 23 June 2006, Vladimir Putin announced that Uzbekistan would (again) join the CSTO as a member.

Russian analysts think Uzbekistan's President Karimov's main argument for joining the CSTO is his need for Russian protection against a regime change like the ones that took place in Georgia, Ukraine, and Kyrgyzstan (Socor, 2005: 10). According to the Russian President Putin, the main responsibilities of the CSTO are cooperation in defence, the manufacturing of weapons, training of military personnel, and peacekeeping activities. Other areas of cooperation are a common integrated air defence system and the fight against terrorism and narcotics, which particularly concerns the CSTO in Central Asia (Kaczmarski, 2005: 10).

The CSTO has at its disposal a joint headquarters in Moscow and a collective rapid reaction force. This collective reaction force consists of 4000-4500 soldiers, and is composed of three battalions from Russia and Tajikistan, two battalions from Kazakhstan and Kyrgyzstan, units of Russia's military base in Tajikistan, as well as the military aviation group of Russia's airbase in Kant, Kyrgyzstan. On 6 October 2007, at a CSTO Summit in the Tajik capital Dushanbe, the organization announced decisions to increase military cooperation. At the request of Russia, the member states agreed to buy military arms and equipment from Russia at domestic Russian prices.(Pravda, October 10,2007).

Furthermore, it was decided at the 2007 CSTO summit that its collective rapid reaction forces in Central Asia would be supplied with modern materiel before the end of 2010. Another Russian initiative adopted at the 2007 summit was the foundation of a joint military force for peacekeeping operations. The concept of a joint peacekeeping force encompasses the formation of brigades capable of conducting peacekeeping missions, if necessary also outside the territory of the CSTO. According to the Russian Minister of Foreign Affairs, Sergei Lavrov, contingents will not be deployed in the so-called 'frozen conflicts' in the South Caucasus i.e., the separatist regions in Georgia and the Nagorno Karabakh area.

The CSTO has divided its area into three military regions: a European, a Caucasian and a Central Asian grouping. Recent CSTO documents and statements by officials put the emphasis on Central Asia and to a lesser extent on Europe or on the Caucasus. The return of Uzbekistan to the CSTO in 2006, after the related forced withdrawal of US forces from that country is one of the indications of the increased focus of the CSTO on Central Asia. Evidence to this fact is also the desire of the CSTO to deploy a considerable military contingent in that region, consisting of units of the Central Asian member states.

The organization has already stationed its collective rapid reaction force in the area but, according to CSTO Secretary General Nikolai Bordyuzha, it will further enhance its military build-up in the Central Asian region. The endeavours of the CSTO in Central Asia have an influence on its relationship with other security organizations active in this region. In terms of NATO, for instance, the CSTO has expressed its intentions to develop relations with this Western alliance, but has also criticised NATO and the US for causing instability in Central Asia (Saat, 2005: 2).

Likewise, NATO could well view the enlargement of the CSTO military contingent in Central Asia as a step to counterbalance its eastward expansion and to keep CIS countries under Russia's military protection. In relation to the SCO, the CSTO has proposed to work together on the reconstruction of Afghanistan. According to Bordyuzha, the CSTO together with China and the SCO should prevent the Taliban to regain power in Afghanistan.

The development of closer ties between SCO and CSTO has not been an easy process. First, Uzbekistan prevented a strengthened connection and later on China took that role. Already in 2003 Russia had the intention to bring the two organizations closer together, for the purpose of increasing the fight against terrorism and against drug trading, but probably also to form an 'Eastern bloc' against Western military involvement in the Central Asian region, in and around Afghanistan. In the process of enhancing the link between the CSTO and the SCO, Uzbekistan threatened to leave the SCO as a result of its aversion of the CSTO. A second reason for the resistance of Uzbekistan against closer ties was its power struggle with Kazakhstan on hegemony over Central Asia. Thirdly, Uzbekistan spoke out against military exercises of the SCO on its territory, which it rather conducted in cooperation with NATO. Resulting from this stance, in 2003 Uzbekistan did not participate in joint SCO drills in Kazakhstan and China, because of a possible involvement of the CSTO in these manoeuvres. (Luzhavin, 2003:10).

In 2006, the year that Uzbekistan returned as a member state of the CSTO –chances for a deepening of the relations between the SCO and the CSTO seemed to improve. In May of that year, SCO Secretary General at the time, Zhang Deguang, stated that the Council of Ministers of Foreign Affairs of the SCO had instructed the SCO Secretariat to arrange cooperation with the CSTO in the field of security. However, a year later, in April 2007, expectations had proved to be too optimistic. The negotiations on a Memorandum of Understanding (MoU) between both organizations – of which the text was completed and only awaited signing – had come to a deadlock, as a result of Chinese reluctance.

According to China, the CSTO, with its collective military force and a military assistance article, is primarily a political-military organization, but the SCO should remain to be a political-economical organization. China fears that a closer relationship between the CSTO and the SCO might give the impression to the outside world that the SCO endeavors to become a 'NATO of the East'. Since China would like to keep all (trade) doors open, it regards such a development as counterproductive to its economic and political interests. In addition to delaying the MoU, China also prevented the CSTO from contributing to the 'Peace Mission 2007' military exercises of the SCO. In November 2006, China had rejected the proposal of the Russian Chief of the General Staff, Yuri Baluyevsky, to make the 2007 drills a SCO-CSTO event (Deguang, 2007: 2)

Apart from China's fear for a transformation of the SCO into a military alliance, another reason for its objections to further CSTO-SCO cooperation is probably that this might strengthen Russia's position in the SCO by bringing in two of its satellites, Armenia and Belarus.

In spite of the Chinese reluctance, the CSTO continued its efforts to strengthen the cooperation between the two organizations. For instance, in July 2007 the CSTO called for joint action with the SCO with regard to Afghanistan. Notwithstanding the Chinese posture, probably at the request of Russia, the Bishkek 2007 Summit of the SCO in its final declaration optimistically mentioned the growing cooperation between the SCO and the CSTO. The declaration by the Heads of State specifically stated support for a further deepening of the relations between the two organizations, with the aim of coordinating efforts on strengthening regional and international security and counteracting new challenges and threats.19 On 5 October 2007, during a CIS summit in Dushanbe, the signing of the MoU between SCO and CSTO finally took place.

Presumably, to receive consent from China, the agreement comprised a MOU between the Secretariats of both organizations and not between the organizations themselves, although in practice that will not make any difference. The fields of cooperation, as mentioned in the MOU, are:

- ensuring regional and international security and stability;
- counteraction against terrorism;
- the fight against drug trafficking;
- the fight against arms trafficking;
- counteraction against transnational organized crime; and
- other areas of mutual concern.

At the singing of the MOU, CSTO Secretary General Bordyzha explicitly stated that this cooperation between the two Eastern organizations was not directed against NATO. On 4 December 2007, SCO and CSTO held their first meeting on the areas of cooperation, as declared in the MOU, in Moscow (Blagov, 2007: 14-15).

A sequence of events in 2007 has demonstrated considerable progress towards a closer relationship between the CSTO and the SCO, namely:

- the CSTO's proposal for joint action towards Afghanistan;
- the presence of CSTO observers – although not as participating;
- organization – at the 'Peace Mission 2007' exercises;
- the final declaration of the 2007 SCO Bishkek Summit; and finally;
- the signing of the MOU between the SCO and the CSTO as the climax.(Blagov,2007:14-17).

Since the CSTO is a purely military alliance, the cooperation will undoubtedly reinforce the military component of the SCO. Therefore, in the near future, joint SCO-CSTO action may possibly develop. If the SCO will endeavor to proceed on a way towards a full-grown security organization, then closer ties with the CSTO will be helpful. Essential elements of a professional security organization, such as rapid reaction forces and a military assistance article, are part of the framework of the CSTO. With the majority of the states sharing membership of both organizations, it will be easy for the SCO to adopt such instruments as well, if so desired.

c) Energy Security: SCO Energy Club

In addition to military-political issues, energy security, which increasingly is identified as a vital element of security policy, is gaining ground in the SCO. In July 2007, the SCO Energy Club was established, with which the SCO may aim for a common energy approach, above all in strengthening energy security. Thus, as with the military maneuvers, bilateral or multilateral energy cooperation among SCO members is developing into a common SCO energy approach, although it is still unclear what this would entail.

At the Shanghai Summit of 15 June 2006, energy was publicly put on the agenda as a major issue for the first time. At this summit, Russia's President Putin announced the intention of the founding within the SCO of an Energy Club, in order to develop a joint SCO course of action in the field of energy. At a meeting of the Heads of Government Council of the SCO in Dushanbe, Tajikistan, on 15 September 2006, a common energy policy was further discussed. At the outset, priority areas of cooperation concerning energy, transportation and telecommunications, were defined. The creation and launch of special working groups in the fuel and energy sector, as well as for modern information and telecommunications technology received special emphasis. Furthermore, decisions took place on implementing the initiative voiced by Vladimir Putin at the Shanghai Summit, where he proposed to set up a SCO Energy Club.

The Heads of Government tasked a special working group on fuel and energy with studying in the shortest time the possibility of forming a SCO Energy Club. The Kazakh and Russian parties would present to the SCO Secretariat their proposals for all parties to be discussed in 2007 at a meeting of the heads of fuel and energy departments of the SCO member states. On 3 July 2007, the SCO Energy Club was established in Moscow. The regulations of the Energy Club – in which the SCO observers also take part, explain that the Club unites energy producers, consumers and transit countries in coordination of energy strategies with the aim of increasing energy security. At the 2007 Bishkek Summit of 16 August 2007, Russian Foreign Affairs Minister Lavrov confirmed an active role for the SCO observers in the Energy Club, for instance participation by the energy companies of the observers. Although so far energy deals have been made bilaterally, the foundation of the SCO Energy Club is a step towards a common energy policy, even though the intentions of the Club remain unclear (Lanov, Ria Novosti, Aug. 16, 2007).

Western assessments sometimes view the SCO as increasingly becoming a mechanism to oust the USA and its Western allies from Central Asia, and thus to threaten Western security interests. The SCO Energy Club could likewise be regarded as a threat to Western (energy) security. Iran's proposal to set gas prices and to control its gas flows together with Russia, as a so-called 'gas OPEC' only reinforced this fear, even though Iran's proposal is to large extent propaganda. However, SCO member countries that export oil and gas are not only partners, but also rivals on the promising markets in East and South Asia. China, for instance, is attempting to get a foothold in the energy sectors of Turkmenistan, Kazakhstan and Uzbekistan. The latter three countries are beginning to threaten Russia's position in Central Asia based on a monopoly on export gas pipelines to Europe. Thus, there is much diversity among SCO members and observers on energy cooperation among themselves as well with the West, instead of a simple unification on or against such issues. Whether a common SCO energy policy will change this diversity, remains to be seen.

Security organizations tend to become involved in energy security, in the sense that they realize that security nowadays not only entails military, but also energy issues. This applies to NATO, but also to the CSTO. The security of oil and gas pipelines against terrorist attacks has already become a task of the CSTO. Since 2004, the CSTO has been responsible for the protection of railway lines, which, like energy, is related to strategic economic interests. As to the guarding of energy installations, the Anti-Terrorist Centre of the CIS has conducted an anti-terrorist exercise – with units of the CSTO participating at a nuclear energy station in Armenia in September 2006. (China Daily, January11,2006).

Earlier, in August 2005, this CIS Anti-Terrorist Centre had held an exercise around the Kazakh city of Aktau, while on the Caspian coast armed forces were to counteract terrorists that had seized an oil tanker. Furthermore, during the CSTO's joint military exercises in June 2006 in Belarus, one of its objectives was the protection of gas and oil pipelines, which further confirmed the CSTO's conceptual development towards energy security tasking (Plungatarev 2006: 2).

So far, the SCO does not have rapid reaction forces, and thus no specific joint military tasking. Nonetheless, in the light of the aforementioned steps of the SCO towards a mature security organization, as well as the emergent cooperation with the CSTO and the recently started SCO Energy Club, this situation might well change. Since the SCO states also have to cope with terror attacks, possibly also against their energy infrastructure, it is not unlikely that the SCO will create standing reaction forces in the near future with security of energy infrastructure and of transport routes as one of its tasks.

The SCO is unlikely to turn into an anti-Western club. Russia wants to use the SCO for its anti-Western aims but others, for instance China and Kazakhstan, who maintain strong economic cooperation with the West, will probably not allow it. Although the West at present does not have anything to fear from the SCO, the SCO's current endeavors in the security dimension might encourage the West at least to observe further activities of the SCO closely, if not possibly also to seek cooperation with this organization. In spite of the anti-Western stance as declared at the Astana Summit of 2005, the SCO has the potential to become a partner of NATO. The SCO's Secretary General at the time, Zhang Deguang, stated that the SCO is open to cooperation with NATO on issues of mutual interest (Weitz, 2006: 357).

d) Co-operation between NATO and SCO

NATO has arrangements for cooperation with all SCO states except China. Since the beginning of the 90s, this alliance has had bilateral cooperation with the five Central Asian states within its *Partnership for Peace* framework, as well as a special relationship with Russia, which since 2002 is called the NATO-Russia Council. China frequently states its suspicion towards NATO's actions in the South East Asian region.24 The concept of forming 'global partnerships' with countries such as Japan, South Korea, Australia and New Zealand, that already cooperate with NATO, for instance in Afghanistan – a matter still lacking consensus within NATO – especially annoys China. China disapproves of NATO's military action in the region, which it considers to be its sphere of influence. Furthermore, NATO and China both seem to be hesitant to enter into a dialogue with each other. (Black, 2004:131-146).

With the cautious development of the SCO towards becoming a mature security organization and NATO operating in Afghanistan, and considering global tasking, it certainly seems time for action. In a way, the current situation in South East Asia is comparable with Eastern Europe in the 90s. At that time, the Warsaw Pact as well as the Soviet Union had collapsed and the newly independent states were seeking closer ties with NATO. Likewise, the regional power, Russia, was suspicious and critical of these developments.

When it became clear that former Warsaw Pact states would be allowed to join NATO, the alliance realised that an appeasing effort towards Russia was necessary to maintain the dialogue with this power and to avoid disputes. Thus, a special partnership with Russia was established. Equally, with a comparable situation in South East Asia, NATO should take such a step towards China. A special partnership, similar to the NATO-Russia Council, could be created with China, within which views can be exchanged and military cooperation can be arranged. Such a move would build confidence and thus diminish any possible suspicion on both sides.

The same applies to NATO and the SCO developing a special partnership. Until now, NATO has been reluctant to cooperate with the CSTO. However, in the case of the SCO, the organization is not only led by Russia but also by China, which prevents it from being an instrument of Russian (anti-Western) security policy. In November 2005, the SCO established a contact group with Afghanistan. At the Bishkek Summit, the SCO, member states stated their concern about the destabilizing situation in Afghanistan, which affects Central Asia.

Considering their geographical and military presence around Afghanistan and the threats with which both NATO and the SCO are confronted, namely drug trafficking and terrorism by Taliban and Al Qaida, joint activities are feasible. The CSTO has proposed joint action with the SCO in preventing the Taliban from returning to power in Afghanistan. China, who is usually disinclined to have closer ties with the CSTO, while being aware of the threats in the region, might consider cooperation between SCO and NATO a better way to deal with these problems (ITAR-TASS, July 31. 2007).

Since the SCO and NATO clearly share an interest in improving security and stability in Afghanistan, it would be wise to combine efforts and forces. Furthermore, it is doubtful whether the Central Asian states – although stressing their self-determination in regional security – would be able to counter threats such as those of the Taliban and Al Qaida by themselves. SCO states could join NATO with contingents in ISAF (International Security Assistance Force) in Afghanistan. Thus, SCO armies would be incorporated in an experienced military-operational infrastructure to fight mutual threats. Such an effort would be beneficial in two ways. Firstly, it would strengthen the capabilities of ISAF in the war against the Taliban. Thus, this would promote stability in Afghanistan and subsequently also elsewhere in Central Asia, as desired by the SCO states.

Secondly, operational cooperation between the SCO and NATO would also improve the political relationship between both organizations. In addition to participating in a NATO-led operation, the SCO could also join NATO in exercises, which would also contribute to operational experience as well as political relations. In cooperating in such ways, the SCO and NATO can reduce distrust but also work together to improve stability in the Central Asian region. This will not mean that divergent views will then have disappeared, in particular when it comes to human rights and promotion of democracy, but these issues can also be openly discussed in a cooperation platform. Such an approach is better than maintaining the current wait-and-see policy of NATO and SCO. (Christoph,2000:67-73).

NATO's Bucharest Summit of 2-4 April 2008 has brought a possible NATO-SCO cooperation on Afghanistan a step closer. At the Summit, Russia agreed to grant transit rights to NATO, when transport of non-military goods from the West to ISAF in Afghanistan is involved. Furthermore, the Summit was also attended by the presidents of Turkmenistan and Uzbekistan.

Transport from Europe via Russia to Afghanistan inevitably has to pass Central Asian states. At the conference, Uzbek President Karimov stated that he too was prepared to allow transit of NATO freight over the territory of his country. Later on, Turkmenistan also granted NATO such transit rights. This willingness of Russia, Turkmenistan and Uzbekistan might mean a break-through in not only bilateral ties between former Soviet republics and NATO but also in cooperation between NATO and the SCO, which would be beneficial for Afghanistan and Central Asia in general but also for improved relations between the two security organizations.

The SCO has developed itself from (originally) a border arms control-oriented organization, via a regional counterterrorism body, to a truly international entity. The developments in the military field and in energy security display the growing importance of the security dimension as part of the SCO framework in the international arena. In addition, these developments can be regarded as at least a partial maturing of the SCO as a security organization. Until recently, the nature of the organization was mainly political and economic. (Lijun, 2001:132-141).

However, the developments as described indicate a closer cooperation in the field of security. With its capacities and experience in joint military forces and a military assistance concept, the CSTO can be a vital partner in supporting the SCO to transform into a comprehensive security organization. Nevertheless, the SCO still lacks a considerable number of essential elements, which NATO, as a mature security organization, has, namely an integrated military-political structure with permanent operational headquarters, a rapid reaction force, and continuous political deliberations.

Furthermore, an essential difference between the organizational development of the SCO and NATO is the fact that NATO is aimed primarily at external security risks whereas the SCO concentrates strongly on security within the territory covered by its member states. Especially China seems committed for the time being to maintain this situation. Moreover, SCO member states and observers cooperate in many areas but also illustrate large differences, such as contradictory political and economic interests. These internal differences might prevent further progress of the SCO, also in the development of its security component.(Lijun,2001:132-141).

However, in spite of these shortcomings and inward-looking focus, the intensification of the SCO security policy is such that a cautious development towards a more full-grown security organization – with a scope of activities and an intensity of cooperation similar to that of NATO – can no longer be excluded. If this is the desire of the SCO member states, such development will still take a considerable number of years before the SCO can truly be described as the 'NATO of the East'.

China's Response to Russia-China Conflict

a) Background of the Conflict

The recent conflict in Georgia has a history of mayhem and tensions which could be traced back to the 1920s, when South Ossetia attempted to declare independence but failed and as a consequence ended up as an autonomous region within Soviet Georgia after the Red Army conquered Georgia. Once again in 1989, when the process of disintegration of Soviet Union began, South Ossetia made efforts aimed at either joining North Ossetia in Russia or gain independence. With the declaration of independence from the Soviet Union by Georgia, a conflict broke out between Georgia and South Ossetia in 1991, resulting in the estimated deaths of 2000-4000 people and displacement of a large population. Russia intervened to mediate and brokered a ceasefire in June 1992 between the warring factions. Under the agreement a peacekeeping force was created comprising 530 Russian and 300 each from South Ossetia and Georgia. The peacekeeping force was deployed in the security zone around Tskhinvali, the capital of South Ossetia. Organization for Security and Cooperation in Europe (OSCE) provided facilitation for confidence building and the security zone was patrolled by their monitors.

In the following period, Georgia increasingly came under EU and US influence, while Moscow consolidated its grip over South Ossetia. The ground reality in strategic terms in fact had pitched Russia directly against Georgia. Therefore, on August 7, when Georgia used heavy long-range artillery against South Ossetia, the very next day, Russia came out with a strong military response against Georgia without giving any chance to mediation or any other means of settling the dispute. With the French President Sarkozy's mediatory efforts Russia agreed to a six point formula which included Russian troop's withdrawal. On August 12, Russian President Medvedev declared "the aim of Russia's operation for coercing the Georgian side to peace had been achieved and it had been decided to conclude the operation... The aggressor has been punished".

Russia's aggression of August 2008 against Georgia has posed a major dilemma for Chinese diplomacy. China believes in and advocates certain principles, based on internationally established norms for conducting state-to-state relations, which have been grossly violated by Russia, while committing aggression against a smaller and weaker sovereign neighbouring state. It is, therefore, hard for China to condone Russia's act, despite the fact that it has a strategic partnership with Russia and both share geopolitical interest in the region. The Russian act of aggression was essentially to punish Georgia for leaning towards the EU and US, and especially in joining NATO. In the past as well, Russia has been explicitly expressing displeasure over NATO's overtures to woo Georgia into its sphere of influence. China has been equally concerned over NATO's increasing ingress in the Eurasian region. China considers American and NATO moves to bring Georgia into the network of Western security pacts as a threat to a close Chinese partner.

The Article 9 of the "Treaty of Good-Neighborliness and Friendly Cooperation between the People's Republic of China and the Russian Federation" reads: "When a situation arises in which one of the contracting parties deems that peace is being threatened and undermined or its security interests are involved or when it is confronted with the threat of aggression, the contracting parties shall immediately hold contacts and consultations in order to eliminate such threats." (*News from Russia* 2001: 15-30). Ideally speaking, if Russia considered the Georgian situation threatening to its security interests, then under the treaty obligations China was expected to help Russia remove the threat. However, the situation in reality progressed differently.

Russian aggression against Georgia has resulted in the creation of two new states, South Ossetia and Abkhazia, which have declared their independence. Russia has formally recognized the independence of both the states. Following the August 8 military offensive in South Ossetia, President Dmitry Medvedev argued that recognition was necessary to protect the republics from Georgian acts of aggression.

Such ad hoc creation of new states sets an inherently dangerous precedence for China and its territorial integration, especially in the case of Taiwan and to a lesser extent, Xinjiang and Tibet. Therefore, since the eruption of the crisis in Georgia, China has cautiously maintained a low profile on the issue. China's dilemma lay in the fact that it could not clearly condemn the invasion of Georgia without offending Russia, a strategic partner, nor could it condone the act as it would contradict its stated policy and undermine its own territorial interests. On the other hand, not doing anything and simply accepting the Russian position would create an image problem for China as it would be seen adopting double standards.

b) China-Georgia Relations

Georgia, located between Caucasus and the Black Sea, has had traditional links with China, since the time of 'Silk Roads'. However, in the recent times, this historic relationship was re-discovered when Georgia declared its independence from Moscow, and the governments of China and Georgia signed the 'Joint Communiqué on the Establishment of Diplomatic Relations' in Tbilisi on June 9, 1992 – officially establishing diplomatic ties at the ambassadorial level and beginning a new era of bilateral ties.

Since the establishment of diplomatic relations there has been a regular interaction and exchange of high-level visits between the two countries. In June 2007, the two countries celebrated the 15th anniversary of establishment of diplomatic relations. At this occasion, China's Minister of Foreign Affairs, Yang Jiechi, stated, "We are happy to see the smooth growth of bilateral ties since the establishment of diplomatic relations. Believing in equality of all countries regardless of their size, China and Georgia treat each other with respect and sincerity. We render each other understanding and support on major issues concerning national independence, sovereignty and territorial integrity". (ITAR-TASS,SWB,SU/2598 B/11-12,15th June,2007).

Since 2006, the Georgian government has been supporting China on all major issues of China's concern such as Taiwan, Tibet and Xinjiang. The Chinese Government, while appreciating Georgia's support on several issues of their national interest, has offered over the years economic support and in categorical terms support to Georgia's independence, sovereignty and territorial integrity. In April 2006, China persuaded Georgia to renounce official relations with Taiwan, in turn, agreeing in a "Joint Statement of the two presidents" that "Abkhazia and South Ossetia are internal affairs of Georgia and should be properly handled through peaceful negotiations based on respect of Georgia's state sovereignty and territorial integrity." (Peoples Daily, Apl. 10, 2006).

c) Chinese Response to the Russia-Georgia Crisis

Russian aggression against Georgia generated mixed signals from China. China's response to Russian invasion of Georgia has been very cautious and ambiguous by design.

Initially, the Chinese response was virtually non-existent, as the opening ceremony of Olympic Games coincided with the Russian invasion of Georgia on August 8. Beijing showed no concern when on August 9 Chinese President Hu met with the Russian Prime Minister Putin. In their meeting, Hu praised China's relationship with its Russian "strategic cooperative partner" as "advancing across the board precisely in accordance with our commonly declared goals." (Ribao, 208: 1).

China's ambiguity on the issue was deliberate. Open support to the Russian action would have a) amounted to legitimizing claims by Taiwanese, Tibetans and Uighurs for independence from China; b) it would have been contrary to the opinions expressed by the international community on this issue. On the other hand, for China, Russia is too important an ally and it simply cannot afford to take any position that opposes Russia, either by condemning aggression or supporting Georgian and international community's position. However, at the same time it was important for China that it must exhibit its concern over this development. In order to do so, China chose to use the forum of Shanghai Cooperation Organization (SCO) Summit which was convened on August 28 in Dushanbe (twenty days after the August 8 events).

China's Foreign Ministry spokesman Qin Gang told a news conference ahead of the SCO summit that "leaders will expound their shared position on issues of interest within the framework of the agenda, and the South Ossetia issue will be no exception." Gang further said that Beijing hoped that Moscow and Tbilisi could find "a peaceful solution to the Georgian-South Ossetia conflict through dialogue." China was also concerned about the Georgia crisis because it was worried Russia might exert similar pressure on Central Asian states – all of which were former Soviet republics like Georgia and have no match to the Russian military might. A veiled criticism by China and Central Asian states on Russian action is reflected in Dushanbe Declaration which says in its Article 1;

"The interdependence of states tremendously increased and security and development are becoming inseparable in the 21st century. None of the present-day international problems can be resolved by force. The factor of force is decreasing objectively in global and geopolitical issues. Reflections No. 1, 2009 Any attempt for an exclusively forcible resolution will lead nowhere at all and only hinders local conflicts from being settled comprehensively. The comprehensive resolution of existing problems is possible only when all the parties' interests are considered in full and when they are involved in a negotiating process, but not by isolating them. Attempts to strengthen one's own security to the detriment of others' security will not promote the maintenance of global security and stability."(SCO Press release, 13th November, 2009).

The heads of state reiterated the need to respect each country's and each nation's historical and cultural traditions and efforts aimed at preserving the unity of the state and its territorial integrity, as well as at encouraging good-neighborly relations between nations and their joint development in accordance with international law".

Russia interpreted the Dushanbe Summit as supporting its position on Georgia and claimed that the action was taken on humanitarian grounds. The Russian Foreign Ministry said on August 28, that China had expressed its understanding of Russia's decision to recognize Georgia's breakaway regions of South Ossetia and Abkhazia. President Medvedev said recognition was necessary to protect the republics from Georgian acts of aggression, following the August 8 military offensive in South Ossetia. Medvedev urged the leaders at the summit in Dushanbe, to support Russia's role in Georgia, in order to "send a serious signal to those who are trying to justify the aggression that was committed".

However, in reality, the Russian military action in support of secession of two ethnic groups from a sovereign state grossly contradicts and undermines the very foundation and spirit of SCO framework which is based on fighting three evils namely "separatism, extremism and terrorism." In the case of Georgia, Russia is seen standing on the side of the separatists.

Russia-Georgia conflict created a serious dilemma for Chinese diplomacy as the Chinese government had, since 2006, considered South Ossetia and Abkhazian issues as internal affairs of Georgia. China had accepted the sovereignty of Georgia over these territories. Chinese political expediency rendered it unable to take a principled position in favor of Georgia. Chinese analysts were unable to voice their concerns over this issue. Chinese media also maintained a low coverage policy on Russia-Georgia conflict. While China seemed to be uncomfortable with the situation, in order to safeguard its long-term strategic interests with Russia, it decided to keep a low diplomatic profile on this issue at all forums, including UNSC. For China, the events in Georgia had set a negative precedence with serious implications for the regions/ territories where similar conditions exist. The case of Taiwan in particular has continued to inform Chinese strategic thinking. China is also of the view that it in Russia's fight with the EU+US, it should refrain from taking a definitive position. The only strategic advantage for China in the aftermath of the Russian invasion is that the Russian-Georgia is likely to restrain and delay NATO's eastward expansion and consequently provide China with an opportunity to consolidate its strategic interests in the Eurasian region. Russia and China also have common interests in Central Asian region which is extensively dealt in the next chapter.

Russia-China-India Triangle

The emerging triangle between Russia-India-China is being closely watched in the strategic and academic quarters of the West and the three countries involved. This idea was mooted by the then Russian Prime Minister Yevgeny Primakov at a time when India had been internationally isolated after its May 1998 nuclear tests. This was also the time when Russia was facing intense pressure from the West on the issue of human rights violation in Chechnya and on the establishment of true democratic system in Russia. The third component of the triangle China, was already on the hit lit of the US led West due to its ideological commitment to Marxism. The Thiamin massacre incident had made China almost untouchable internationally. China has also been facing constant pressure form the West on the Taiwan and Tibet issue.

Aware of the circumstances in which all three countries found themselves and the power aspirations which all these shared; Primakov gave a call to unite in the face of unnecessary intervention of the West in their internal matters. However, no triangular relation can take off and be sustained if each had problem with the other.

To analyze the possibility of this triangle actually materializing it is, therefore, important to study the kind of relation these states share with each other. In the first sect on swings in Sino-Soviet relation is briefly discussed. The disintegration of the Soviet Union created fresh opportunities for qualitatively different nation to develop between China and the successor Soviet states, especially Russia. The triangle can only be understood in this context. Thereafter the chapter focuses on the kind of relation developing between Russia and India and China and India. An analysis of the bilateral relations would indicate the possibilities of this triangle actually materializing. The last section of the chapter briefly highlights the implication this triangle will have on India.

a) The Soviet Times

Soviet Union and China were bound to each other as comrades resolutely devoted to working class and peasant revolutions. Soviet Union's assistance under the Stalin regime to Mao's revolution endeared the two, who after the success of the 1949 Chinese revolution, presented themselves as the impenetrable and expanding socialist world of the early 1950s. The comradeship however began to drift apart on several counts and there were many reasons that soured Soviet-China relations. Both wanted to establish their credentials as true Marxists. Gradually the two drifted away from each other though these two countries belonged to the same idea bloc there were strong difference between them. Khrushchev's de-Stalinization campaigns were amongst the first signs of discord. Chairman Mao opposed CPSU's new ideological formulations like peaceful co-existence and non-antagonistic contradictions between imperialism and socialism. Concepts used by Soviets for the third world like non-capitalist path of development and policy of support to the 'national bourgeois' were similarly opposed. The real issue behind the ideological discord was however, leadership and hegemony over the international communist movement and relations with the newly emerging countries of Asia and Africa. (Chenoy, April 2005: 11)

The Chinese and Russians had disagreements on internal matters as well. Chinese wanted assistance from the Soviets on their nuclear programme which was denied by the Soviets. The Chinese and Soviets became competitors in the space technology; Chinese needed more economic assistance for their modernization programmes that the overextended Soviet Union failed to provide. Soviets were critical of several Chinese policies including the Cultural Revolution; Chinese called the Soviets revisionists', an insult to those who believed themselves to be Marxists (Gorbachev, 1987: 10-12).

As, the Sino-Soviet dispute broke out in 1959 and became bitter after 1961, the Chinese and the Soviets saw themselves on opposite sides of major international disputes. During the Sino-Indian border clash in 1962 contrary to Chinese expectations, Soviets remained neutral and provided military equipments to India soon after that. That is incidence further caused damage between the two countries whose relations reached an all time low. The Soviets were critical of the Sino-US rapprochement and opening of trade relations between the two. China's border clashes with Vietnam in the 1980s, their support to Pol Pot's oppressive regime in Cambodia, were basis of Soviet critique of Chinese opportunism.

However, the tense relationship of two communist giants eased with the rise of Gorbachev as the Secretary General of CPSU in 1985. He made epoch making changes in the Soviet history by introducing 'Perestroika' and 'Glasnost'. Some have described him in Soviet history as 'reformer in hurry'. In the realm of international relations he introduced 'New Thinking' which stressed on a deidoelogised foreign policy.

In the words of Gorbachev, 'New Thinking' stood for:

> "We need normal international conditions for our internal progress. But we want a world free of war, without arms races, nuclear weapons and violence, not only because this is an optimal condition for our internal development. It is an objective global requirement that stems from the realities of the present day. The world is living in an atmosphere not only of nuclear threat, but also of us resolved major social problems of new stresses created by the scientific and technological advancement and by the exacerbation of global problems. Mankind today faces unprecedented problems and the future will hang in the balance, if joint solutions are not found. All countries are now more interdependent than ever before and the stockpiling of weapons especially nuclear missiles, makes the outbreak of a world war, increasingly more probable due to technical failure or human fallibility. Yet all living things on each would suffer". (Gorbachev, 1987: 10-12).

Under the slogan of 'New Thinking' Gorbachev's foreign policy was based on shared moral and ethical principles to solve global problems rather than on Marxist-Leninist concept of irreconcilable conflict between capitalism and communism. The historic meeting between Deng and Gorbachev lead to resolution of many outstanding problems between the two. The border dispute was resolved by demarcating the Usuri River; trade was opened up and threat perceptions to a large extent eliminated.

While relations were improving between the two countries, the Soviet Union itself collapsed in December 1991. It was a historical event of global significance. Relations between the two neighbours, Russia and China could not therefore, escape the global effects of this historical event (Imam, 1999: 379-402).

The new government of Russia appeared to ignore the need for further development of relations with China from the point where Gorbachev had left during his tenure. The reasons were obvious. President Yeltsin and his government were preoccupied with a series of domestic problems arising out the disintegration of Russia's domestic factors placed a very important role in the formulation of Russian foreign policy during the initial period. The economic crisis of the early 1990s produced national humiliation. Unemployment increased and a large number of people were pushed below poverty line. Between the 'Atlantists' and "Eurasians' model of foreign policy Russia went ahead with former in the hope that the west will provide huge aid to restructure the socialist model of economy into it capitalist one. But once the threat perception of Russia was eliminated the US emerged victorious in the Cold War. Neither West not the US paid much attention to admit Russia into Western world and help it economically. Instead, they started treating Russia as competitor in various field.

The bubble of 'Common European Home and one World From Vancouver to Vladivostok" etc. burst very soon and a disillusioned Russia turned her face towards the Third World and Asia which had been a natural ally of the erstwhile Soviet Union. So in the changed circumstances and policies countries like China, India, Iran got the top priority in Russian foreign policy list.

Soon, Kozyrev was replaced by ill academician Yevgeny Primakov as Russia's new foreign minister who tried to balance between the East and the West. In December 1998 he made an official visit to India. Primakov visited India at the time when India was internationally isolated for conducting nuclear tests a few months back. He proposed to formulate a triangle between three major Eurasian countries Russia-China-India to counter US hegemony and unilateralism in the world politics. According to him 'Russia favours the creation of a Moscow-Beijing-Delhi triangle and also it would be a good idea (SWB/SU/3416 B/5, December 22, 1998).

Before going into detail about the emerging triangle between the three, let us see how their individual relations are developing with each other.

b) Russia-India Relations

The legacy of strong mutually beneficial relations between Soviet Union and India weighed heavily on Indian expectations in developing relations with new Russia. Global events brought India and Soviet Union together in the fifties when the Cold War dominated international relations. India had identified itself with the Soviet Union World view just as Pakistan had with that of the USA. The general understanding was Indo-Soviet friendship being time tested. Indo-Russian equation would rot dramatically alter. End of Soviet Union, however, altered the international scenario completely. It heralded the end of the confrontational bloc politics (If the Cold War era and the weakening of ideologies. Free from ideological compulsion new Russia had new options (Shams-ud-din, 2001: 1)

After prolong dilly dallying and rescheduling his visit since 1992, Yeltsin finally arrived in New Delhi only in January 1993. President Yeltsin's belated visit to India in January 1993 was aimed to reassure New Delhi that Russia was not cold-shouldering India. But Russian leaders first visited South Korea in November 1992 and China in December 1992. Russian foreign policy it appeared was now being based on the maxim 'we do not have any permanent friends or foes, but we do have permanent interests'. Since 1993 Indo-Russian relations have been growing smoothly. Indian Prime Minister P. V. Narsimha Rao visited Moscow in 1994; during high visit President Yeltsin remarked that "there was no difference at all between the two countries on international and bilateral issues". The document signed during his visit promised for joint action by both countries against terrorism. The document supported all forms of cooperation, investment, joint enterprise, creation of conditions for economic initiative development of scientific technical cooperation, peaceful atom, cosmos, and laser technology (Chenoy,2005: 183-184).

Of the weapons Indian armed for the possesses around 70% of weapons is that of Soviet/Russian origin. Russia supplies cheap and reliable arms to India, unlike West and USA which always puts certain conditions before delivery of arms with higher price tag. India gave more importance to Russia than the USA because Russia had been an all\weather friend and both countries maintained close political, economic, nuclear and military relations.

Between 1992-96 India imported from Russia defense equipments worth $3.5 billion. Indian military and defence orders now sustain many defence industries in Russia, especially in St. Petersburg and Irkutsk which would otherwise have faced closure at the time of transition in the Russian economy. India is the only country with which Russia has a long term programme of military-technical cooperation, which was signed in 1994. The Soviet era Treaty of Friendship, Peace and Cooperation was renewed for another 10 years, during the then Defence Minister Mulayam Singh Yadav's visit to Moscow in December 2000. (Chenoy, 2001: 183-184) Russian spokesman stated that Russian Indian military cooperation would touch $4.5 billion in 2000 and $6.5 billion in the end of 2005.

The crucial and the most time testing moment in Indo-Russian relations came in May 1998 when India tested five nuclear bombs in Pokhran, Rajasthan and most of the influential countries imposed economic and many other kinds of sanctions on India. Although Russia disagreed with the West and USA that India should sign on CTBT and NPT and ratify it as soon as possible, but Russia opposed any kind of economic sanction against India, and refused to impose sanctions itself. Tremendous pressure was exerted by the USA led West on Russia to scrap all its agreements in nuclear cooperation with India and also stop technical support to India's two nuclear reactors under construction with Russian assistance at Kudnakulam, Tamilnadu. But Russia stood upto the Indian expectations and refused to company with US dictates. (Boquerat and Frederic: 2004:132-140).

Russia has constantly supported India's point of view on the issue of Kashmir in various international forums. It has also promised India to using veto power in UNSC if India would be pressurized on the Kashmir issue. As the reciprocal gesture India also always supported Russian stand on the Chechnya issue and criticized the West for interfering in Russia's internal matters on the pretext of addressing hum m rights violations.

India and Russia set up a joint working group on Afghanistan. As on many other issues their stance on this issue was similar. Together they made it possible for the Northern Alliance to keep afloat and thereby a counterforce against the Taliban was available when the American attack on Afghanistan took place. Their joint proposal of resistance also mooted by General Musharraf and virtually endorsed by the USA prevented the sneaking in of Taliban elements in the interim government formed subsequently in Afghanistan under the leadership of Hamid Karzai (Dutt, 2003: 18-19).

Russia is one of the states which promised to support for India for a permanent seat in the Security Council, And thus has demonstrated to the Indian foreign policy establishment its loyalty to Indian position and its understanding of India's strategic aspirations globally.

Another important land mark in the development of Indo-Russian ties was Prime Minister Primakov's visit at the end of 1998. The visit sparked off a debate following his references to an Indo-China-Russia strategic triangle. He remarked that "Russo-Indian relations are perhaps unique in diplomatic history of the past fifty years. Their strength has been tested by many turns and twists in the two countries political life and during the profound transformation of international system". He also rightly noted that cooperation between the two countries rests on a long established bread public consensus in both countries regarding the priority of Russian-Indian cooperation as a factor promoting national interests (Shams-ud-Din, p.8)

On March 22, 1999 India and Russia signed an agreement to train Indian defence personnel in key Russian defence establishment for maintaining advanced defence equipments. The 44,500 tonnes Kiev class Admiral Gorshkov aircraft carrier has been gifted to India by Russia. The Mig-29K Fulcrum aircrafts stand a better chance to be operated from this aircraft carrier.

Upgrading of MiG-29 Bis Fished Fighters, construction of 3 Kirvak class frigates of the Indian Navy modernizatie n foT -72 MBT, procurement of T -90s MBTs, for the Indian army and 8-300 antiballistic missiles systems were discussed. (Shams-ud-Din, p.8).

Russia-India-China Emerging Triangle: Myth or Reality

During his visit in December 1958, the former Russian Prime Minister Yevgeny Primakov, proposed a Russia-India-China strategic triangle, which envisaged closer strategic cooperation. He said that:

> If we succeed in establishing a strategic triangle, it will be very good a lot depend in the region on the policies perused by India, China and Russia. Further, this proposal was made in the framework of partnership between the three countries that could bring about greater stability not just in the region but the world.

The immediate response from Beijing on the proposed triangle was positive. The spokesperson of Chinese foreign ministry dubbed it as 'very positive thought' and 'would help in containing growing unilateralism in international politics'. India's response was cautious and rather lukewarm because she did not want to send wrong signals to the West by joining in bloc politics. In his speech then Prime Minister Vajpayee said 'Russia is a longstanding partner of India with which we have traditionally enjoyed friendly relations. At the same time, India is working on normalizing its relations with China' . Due to this cold response from India, speaking to the media Primakov explained that his earlier words on the possibility of forming a triangle between Russia-China-India were not official pI:) posal. He said "I wanted to say that such partnership could reliably stabilize the situation in the region and in the world". (SWB/SU/3417 B/4, December 23, 1998.)

In 1990s and after 9/11 USA loomed over the world as sole superpower ready to undertake unilateral action anywhere ranging from NATO led attack on Yugoslavia to bombing in Afghanistan to oust Talibans from power. The next states which form 'Axis of Evil' i.e. Iran, Iraq and North Korea are now on USA's hit list. Presence of US troops in Central Asia, Afghanistan, Pakistan, and

Taiwan close to the borders of Russia and China is posing grave threat to their security. Repercussions of these international developments are bound to affect the two countries.

The multi-ethnic and multi-cultural societies of Russia, India, and China have faced increasing pressure from 1he forces that seek to destroy their pluralistic societies. In India infiltration in Kargil was the culmination of years of infiltrations and terrorist activities. The terrorists have also attacked the highest symbol of Indian democracy, parliament. Russia's long bleeding problem of Chechnya has been further aggravated with the Western and US media and human right groups' intervention on the name of human rights violations. China is facing potential threat of secession in its Xinjiang province by Islamic extremists who are engaged with continuous low level warfare with Chinese authorities. There is growing feeling among the three countries that US alone should not set the agenda of global war against terror. The experience of Iraq also shows that the US polices can leave a bigger mess in the region, the effect of which has to be borne by neighbouring countries. (Joshi, 2003: 187-188).

Meanwhile as Twenty First Century progresses, Asia is likely to occupy a centre stage in the international system. While on the one hand Asia has seen economic prosperity it also has sources of danger. It stretches from Persian Gulf to Philippines contains sources of tel1sions such as global terrorism. In American perception the 'Axis of Evil' i.e., Iraq, Iran and North Korea are located in Asia. President Vladimir Putin has proposed that the arc of instability be converted into an arc of stability. To achieve this objective India, Russia and China can play vital role.

At broader level India, Russia and China agree that the world should be a multipolar one. China felt the pressures from the West after the Thiamin square massacre, the US relentless support to Taiwan and threat perception of China despite of years of normalization of US- Chinese relations, US sale of F -16s to Taiwan and promised Theater Missile Defense (TMD), forced Chinese to reconsider relations with the USA. With the development of National Missile Defence (NMD), US will get cutting edge on strategic position vis-a-vis Russia and China. Russia, with its huge nuclear arsenal, could live with the US NMD. From Chinese perspective, however, the same system could immediately render China's minimalist nuclear relations form obsolete. (Yu Bin, 2000:121-130).

The issue of NMD and its deployment in Asia (Japan and Taiwan) is bound to affect strategic balance in the region. India on the whole, has been supportive to President Bush's decision to go ahead with missile defense, although New Delhi has opposed unilateral abrogation of the ABM Treaty of 1971. China is worried about a US defensive shield that could make Taiwan more independent minded. Russia has objected to unilateral abrogation of ABM treaty and fears that, even Russian nuclear forces are in decay and decline, the US could be poised to take a great leap forward militarily.

Russia-India-China has ample possibility to play together a constructive role to build stability in Central Asian energy resources. Of the three, only Russia is more or less self-sufficient in oil and natural gas. About 70% of India's oil is imported, mostly from the Gulf. Central Asian alternative supplies are being actively considered. Beijing has already indicated its interest in an ambitious venture linking up Central Asia with its industrial heartland in the eastern provinces. China and Russia have made deals for supply of oil and natural gas through pipeline which could feed oil hungry China in the decades to come.

There are other interested players in the region, foremost and most influential being the USA. Due to presence of petroleum and hydrocarbons, the 'great game' in Central Asia has been revived. Russia, China, USA are the major players in this game and competing for lion's share in the Central Asian natural resources. India, though a marginal player in this game is trying to reduce her dependence on Gulf oil, and looking forward for supply of oil from Central Asia.

Russia, India and China can also combine to discuss and if necessary deal with terrorism. Islamic extremism in Kashmir,

Xinjiang and in Chechnya has grown over the years. Although US war on terrorism will help in reducing the problem, Washington clearly cannot do everything.

There has been a consensus between the three countries on the growing menace of terrorism. In April 1996, the 'Shanghai Five', a multilateral forum composed of China, Russia, Kazakhstan, Tajikistan and Kyrgyzstan, was created with the aim of fighting ethnic separatism as well as Islamic fundamentalism. In March 2000, a meeting was held in Astana, Kazakhstan, to determine a common position on these two issues. This was later confirmed in a joint declaration in July 2000 in Dushanbe followed by a decision to create an anti-terrorist centre in Bishkek, Kyrgyzstan. (Djalili, 2001: 64-65). Likewise, in October 2000, during President Putin's visit to Delhi, India and Russia reaffirmed their convergence of view on fighting terrorism, expressing their deep concern over the situation in Central Asia and Afghanistan for which they agreed to set up a working group. (Basu, vol. 24: 1764).

Although the period of study of this research work is 1991-2001, but it would be worth taking note of some of the recent developments vis-a-vis the triangle. Since the time of proposal of the triangle in December 1998 to 2001, by and large no concrete steps seem 10 have been taken was by the three concerned steps to realize it. But the more US unilateralism became blatant the more attractive the option seemed. As a result for the first time the three foreign ministers of Russia, China and India net on the sidelines of UN General Assembly meet at New York in 2002 to explore the 'triangle' possibility.

The approach continued to be en extremely cautious one. The three foreign ministers gave no media briefing for the press except that informally they let the press know that they had me' and that these meetings will continue. By comparison at the second 2003 New York meeting the difference in both their body language and press briefing could be clearly noticed. At the conclusion of their second meeting, three foreign ministers were ready to convey to the press that three states had. Adopted a common approach on Iraq favoring return to political process to ensure quick return of sovereignty to Iraqi people. (Singh, 2005: 14-16). This clearly had strong connotations for the USA, especially as all three of them had also refused to send troops to Iraq.

The 2004 meeting on the eve of the UN General Assembly session in New York could not occur due to change of government in New Delhi leading to some scheduling problems with the Indian establishment. Nevertheless, this was soon rectified and the three foreign ministers had their third 'trialogue' on strategic triangle on the sidelines of the Almaty meet of the 16 nation Conference on Interaction and Confidence Building Measures in Asia (CICA) in October 2004. In the press briefing all three countries agreed to strengthen a "collective approach" in world affairs. (Singh, 2005: 14-16)

On June 2, 2005 the three foreign ministers of Russia, China and India namely Sergei Lavrov, Li Zhaoxing and Natwar Singh had their first ever stand alone meeting at the port city of Vladivotosk in Russia's Far East. The presence of large number of Western journalists at this meeting indicated that the meet generated curiosity beyond these states. Most experts believe that a meeting solely for this purpose reflects the beginning of the new era in the evolution of the Russia-India-China triangle.

For various reasons, all three countries feel that they are under Western pressure. Russia because of NATO's eastward expansion, Chechnya issue, and more generally, because of perceived CS design on former Soviet republics, including Central Asia and Caspian Sea region. China is experiencing Western pressure on human rights issue and feels threatened by US arms sales to Taiwan and more generally, an East Asian security policy which moves towards greater use of Japan in balancing China. India is experiencing in concealed Western propensity to try to get involved on Kashmir issue and helping Pakistan to internationalising Kashmir issue; as well as the Western -mainly US attempt to limit country's nuclear and missile programme. (Heisbroug, 1999-2000: 5-19) India also accused US for pursuing 'double standard' on fighting with terrorism. India blames that terrorist outfits functioning in Pakistan with covert support of Pakistani establishment are posting grave threat to India's security, but US in eliminating only those terrorists who pose threat for her own interests and not that of India.

Implications for India

India on its side is also willing to engage in great power politics and is looking for international recognition it has been deprived since independence. Nehru wrote movingly of India's desire and its destiny to play a major role in the world politics. He hoped that it would not be military role, but one based on sound moral values. Today although there exists no "white paper" enunciating the objectives of the country's foreign policy, India still strives towards this goal. The most spectacular example of this new assertiveness, largely founded on the self-confidence generated by the relative success of the nuclear tests, is the claim for a permanent seat at the UNSC.

On the issue of triangle, it is only India that seems to be least under pressure to pursue this triangle. India has to carefully weigh its policy options and maintain a delicate balance between promoting strategic triangle and strengthening its engagement with the USA. Individually both Russia and China have maintained good relationship with the US and their trade volume are increasing rapidly with the US.

Fear persists at the bilateral level as well. To some Chinese analysts Russia still represents a potential threat and vice-versa is also true. Both Russia and India presume that in the short and medium term, China may pursue the policy of peace, but in the long term equations may change. China's overt and covert support to Pakistani nuclear and missile development programme pose a great security danger for India.

India-Russia-China can do some sensible things together in the military and geopolitical realm. There is very little prospect that they are going to be allies or even thoroughgoing strategic performers. Moreover there are number of areas where protocol, discussions and agreements might be reached which would enhance their security and contribute to the security of Asia. If the idea of triangle between them mean anything, it is probably means a relatively modest set of understanding on which their view coverage.

The Eurasian security in future will depend a lot on how these three largest countries harmonise their relationships. They represent world's most populous segment, rich with natural resources and are on a fast track to emerge as leading global economic power. The June 2, 2005 concluded meeting at Vladivostok recently solely for this purpose indicate that future of triangle is very promising and the picture will be clearer in the time to come. At the same time the future of triangle rests with how India and China solve their own long standing problem of border disputes.

To conclude, therefore, if Asia has to make any positive contribution towards the evolution of new global order and if world has to evolve an adequately representative framework for international security then, increasingly mutual cooperation of these three Asian powers amongst themselves and also their cooperation with other major players remains the most critical pre-requisite to all initiative:; in building the future world order.

Russia, China and India have great historical experience of dealing with such Western influences and preserving their Asian identity despite all challenges. The fundamentals of strategic triangle seem robust and clear and effort must be made to make it effective As of today Russia-India-China stand together in their support for evolving 'just and rational' new international order with democratization of international politics and multipolarization. Also all three have been suffering from transnational and cross-border terrorism and have not been comfortable with unipolar world led by the US. The trilateral cooperation among themselves holds the key of 'triangle' and how these three Asian giants resolve their internal disputes would be the deciding factor in the emergence of 'Eurasian triangle'.

To conclude, Russian and Chinese interests in Central Asia seems smooth but with growing Chinese influence in the region is the cause of concern for Russia. China has already surpassed Germany to become third largest economy in the world. China's fast growing economy needs continuous energy supply for which Central Asia is its natural choice. Russia treats Central Asia as its backyard and interests of both countries seems to be at odds here.

5 Conclusion

Russia being the largest country and China being the most populous country on the planet, both collectively are undoubtedly the two major powers of the international system. Russia being the successor of erstwhile Soviet Union wishes to regain the role once Soviet Union enjoyed whereas China being a communist country is also showing signs of new ambitions based on her history, population and military power and also her emergence as an important international economic actor.

China has embarked on an extensive modernization effort which aims exclusively at resisting aggression, curbing armed subversion and defending state sovereignty, unity and territorial integrity. Russia plays a vital role in the modernization of Chinese armed forces by providing them advanced weaponry on reasonable rate without any string attached.

Both Russia and China have greater common ground to chalk out their strategy to deal with outside world compare to the issues on which they are at odds. Russo-Chinese link is built on a number of shared concerns which includes:

- The struggle against US led unipolar hegemonism;
- unilateral humanitarian interventionism by passing UN;
- Islamic extremism and secessionism;
- opposition to NATO enlargement and inter-reference in the internal matters;
- opposition to NMD and TMD;

- opposition to US withdrawal from ABM Treaty of 1972
- restructuring of UN
- opposition to US led NATO forces to stay longer in the Central Asian region;
- near mutual acceptance of Russia's hegemony as a guarantor of order in Eurasia
- Strengthening the SCO
- Working together in the multilateral forums like WTO etc.

The Russian and Chinese economies are among the ten fastest growing economies in the world. Both have vast potentials to become the economic super power. Russian oil and gas pipelines are the life lines for the Western Europe. Russia is the second largest producer of crude oil after Saudi Arabia and it has the largest gas reserves. Whereas China is the energy hungry country with abundant cheap labour and have cutting edge in manufacturing industry. Both countries have ample scope to get benefitted from each other's expertise.

Russian arms sale consists major portion in Russo-Chinese trade. Russian defence industries are facing financial crunch in order to remain competitive in highly volatile defence equipment market to find its buyers. Here China can play vital role to meet much needed financial crunch by using its huge foreign exchange reserves with other countries like India and Iran. China is the largest arms buyer from Russia. China has acquired many advanced weaponry from Russia like SU-30 MKK fighter planes, Akula Class nuclear submarines etc. which have provided advantage to the Chinese armed forces.

The Putin-Hu declaration on the 'New World Order' in 21st Century on July 1, 2005 provided a sound base for further converting the relations between the two countries. Both agreed that 'All countries of the world must strictly abide by the principles of mutual respect for sovereignty and territorial integrity, mutual non-aggression, non-interference in internal affairs of each other, equality and mutual benefit and peaceful coexistence. Both attacked US 'double standards' in the war against terrorism (though without mentioning).

The declaration of 'New World Order in 21st Century' confirms that relations between two 'headed eagle' and 'dragon' have reached on its height. Both countries have gone very far and deep in their defence translations and no longer count each other as enemies. Their defence personnel, scientists, students are getting training in each other's establishments. Russia is building up nuclear reactors in China and has offered parternership in the state in the state owned space agency GLONASS which itself indicates the comfort level in their ever flourishing bilateral relations.

One of the prime reasons for developing close ties between Moscow and Beijing in the US factor, the common cause of concern for the both countries. US's continuous military and economic support to Taiwan and its huge military presence poses grave threat to the Chinese sovereignty. USA has also agreed to deploy TMD technology to Taiwan, which may virtually neutralize Chinese missile capabilities and would disturb the strategic balance in the region.

Russia is consistently under immense pressure from western human rights groups and media on the issue of human rights violations in the Chechnya war. These groups had virtually shut their eyes on Moscow Theatre tragedy and Beslan School crisis in which hundreds of Russian people lost their lives. It shows as if these human rights groups and media people are acting at the behest of their respective governments to settle their political goals with Moscow. When the issue of human rights violations by US forces comes from Iraq or Afghanistan, these groups keep their mouth shut.

To neutralize these double standards on terrorism, both Russia and China call for implementation of UN charter and International Laws globally without any fear or favour. The most frequent violator of international laws, Israel always go unpunished due to overt and covert support from the USA but a single incidence of Tianmen Square in China made her virtually untouchable in the international politics.

Initially there was some opposition within the Russian establishment to the entry of the US troops in Central Asia, an area of traditional Russian influence. However, subsequently, Moscow decided to allow air corridors, the use of its bases for the search and secure operations as well as sharing of intelligence regarding the terrorist networks operating in Afghanistan. Uzbekistan offered its airspace and bases to the US troops ahead of other CARs, whereas Moscow preferred to maintain the façade of coordinated stand of all the CIS states. Kyrgyzstan claimed that the granting of Manas air base was coordinated in advance with its partners in the CIS Collective Security Treaty.

Manas airbase of Kyrgyzstan is just 200 miles away from Chinese territory from where US troops can keep their eye on Chinese troop movements. Presence of US troops in such a close to Chinese border made security expert in Beijing uncomfortable. Beside military bases in Pakistan and Kyrgyzstan, US acquired military bases in Baghram and Kandahar in Afghanistan and bases of Khanabad in Uzbekistan.

Development of closer ties between Russia and US, especially after coming of Obama regime is causing concerns in Beijing. Before Obama regime, Bush administration worked closly with Russia especially after September 2001 terrorist attack.

After the September 11, 2001 attacks on New York and Washington and subsequent military action taken by US and NATO against Al-Queda and Talibans have radically altered the geopolitical situation in Central Asian Region. Russia and Central Asian republics acquired a prominence place in the US military strategy in Afghanistan military bases in Baghram and Kandahar in Afghanistan and the bases of Khanabad in Uzbekistan. It is believed that these facilities helped US military to quickly establish air superiority thought Central Asia and even to the Middle East.It is believed that in offering bases to the USA, the Central Asian States sought security against the threat of terrorist attacks as well as gain maneuvering space vis-à-vis Russia and China. CARs hoped to gain financially from the US presence.

The impact of post-September 11 developments on China has been the mixed one. China gained in so far as combating international terrorism became the number one task of the US policy. Prior to it economically and militarily growing China was increasingly being projected as emerging strategic rival of sole super power. China reluctantly, joined the international community in supporting the US war against terror but with certain conditions. China wanted UNSC to play central role in the war against terrorism as a guarantee against the US unilaterism. In fact China insisted that struggle against terrorism also includes the 'East Turkistan' terrorist forces or the Uighur separatist movement in Xinjiang province.

There is no doubt that the prospects of a prolonged US military presence in Central Asian region are not welcome to either Russia or China. Post September 11 developments in the region are seem as a set back to SCO, because SCO was created to forge Russia – China partenership in the Central Asia for jointly maintaining peace, stability and economic cooperation in the region and keep a check on the Western influence in the region.

Russian and Chinese interests also converge on the issue of eastward expansion of NATO. First time ever NATO crossed the border of a non-NATO remember country i.e. Afghanistan in the name of fight against terrorism. Both Russia and China opposed the bombing on Belgrade, the capital of Yugoslavia in 1999. Also the US B-2 bombers dropped bomb on Chinese embassy in Belgrade causing many casualties. These incidences proved beyond doubt that US led NATO forces are crossing their granted mandate in the name of fight against terrorism and in the name of humanitarian intervention. Russia and China have their own set of problems in Chechnya and Xinjiang respectively.

At the time when NATO bombing was on, the 50th anniversary celebrations of the founding of NATO took place in Washington in which all the former Soviet republics with exception of Russia participated. What aroused the further Russian and Chinese concern and even the concern in countries like India was the enunciation of new strategies doctrine of NATO that permitted use of force by it in regions beyond the areas of its traditional responsibility comprising the territories of its member states. So, now NATO forces could be used anywhere.

Against such unilateral hegemonism of the US and NATO. Russia-China wants a multipolar world with many power centres. The declaration between Yeltsin and Jiang Zemin in 1997 openly talked about establishment of multipolar world based on principles of Panchsheel. Both call for respect of State sovereignty, equality of states eschewing of pursuit of hegemony, non-interference in internal affairs of other states, an equitable and just economic order and the strengthening of UN. Both Russia and China also seeks to work closely with NAM and champion the cause of third world.

The major bone of contention in the smooth relation was border dispute which is now solved. China has not only settled in border dispute with Russia but also with the Central Asian Republics in a peaceful manner. With the border dispute gone there is no any serious issues left between Russia and China to doubt each other's intention.

Peaceful solution of Korean Peninsula problem is also in the priority list of Russia and China. The proposed NMD system of the USA is expressly aimed at providing defence against the 'rogue' states like Iran, Iraq and North Korea etc. The launch of Pyongyong's rocket over Japan in 1998 provided justification to US for such apprehensions. Russia and China therefore, have sought to minimize the perception of North-Korean threat. They favour a rapprochement between North and South Korea and one between US and North Korea.

To counter the eastward expansion of NATO and with drawl of US from ABM Treaty of 1972, President Putin made an overture to European Union and NATO to reach some compromise solution. He called upon to EU and NATO to join forces with Moscow and set up a joint anti-missile shield during his visit to Rome on 5th June, 2000. He said that such a system will avoid creating problems linked to an imbalance in the equilibrium of forces and ensures 100 percent security to European countries.

As far as economic ties between Russia and China are concerned, it lag behind political, diplomatic, strategic and military ties. It is apparent that the two countries are also to create economic interdependence. The economies of the two countries are mutually complementary. Russia is the major producer and supplier of energy while China is energy hungry and its needs are growing. Russia's main exports apart from defence equipments include fertilizer, steel, timber and machinery, while its main imports are consumer goods and food items.

There are some major pre-requisites for further growth in the scale and diversifications of Russo-Chinese economic collaboration. These are implementing joint programmes in the fuel and energy sector; stepping up cooperation in the field of investment; involving Russian companies in the strategy of accelerated development of China's western region; expanding cooperation between the two countries' border region and cooperation in the manufacturing sector and joint mastering of high technologies.

By strengthening trade with China, Russia will try to reduce its shortage of light industrial goods and electronics, create an economic infrastructure using cheap Chinese labour in the less developed areas of Russian Far East. Russia will also be able to reduce the financial crunch of its arms manufacturing units by selling weapons to China which includes more than $2 billion every year. Russia can also benefit by sending part of its well educated labour force to China to help create high technology industries and reduce the chronic unemployment among highly educated youths.

On the other hand China will get benefitted by sending a certain amount of its unskilled labour force to Russia to work in the unstaffed industries. The excess of labour force available in China is about 200 million. This arrangement will reduce some burden of unemployment among Chinese people. In addition,

China will have a chance to participate in the economic opening of oil fields resources in Russian Far East and Siberia.

Russia, India and China are multi-ethnic and multi-cultural societies and have faced increasing pressure from the forces that seek to destroy their pluralistic societies. All Russia, China and India are facing heat of human rights groups based in Western Europe and US on the issue of human rights violations in Chechnya, Xinjiang and Kashmir respectively. So there is growing feeling among the three countries that US alone should not set the agenda of global war against terror. The experience of Iraq also shows that the US policies can leave a bigger mess in the region, the effort of which has to be borne by neighbouring countries.

Not in the military but in the economic arena there can be the possibility to forge an alliance among Russia-China-India. As the 21st Century progresses, Asia is likely to occupy a centre stage in the international politics. While on one hand Asia is being seen as the engine of growth to the world economy, it has also sources of dangers. The danger stretches from Persian Gulf to Philippines in the form of global terrorism. In American dictum, the 'Axis of Evil' which includes countries like Iraq, Iran and North Korea are located in Asia. Putin had proposed that the arc of instability be converted in to arc of salability. To achieve this objective Russia, China and India can play a vital role.

Russia-China-India have ample possibilities to play together a constructive role to build stability in central Asian Energy resources. Of the three, only Russia is self-sufficient in oil and natural gas. About 70 percent of India's oil is being imported especially from Gulf region. Central Asian alternative supplies are being actively considered. Beijing has already taken the lead in tapping energy resources of Central Asia. Russia and China have made deals for the supply of oil and natural gas through pipelines which can feed oil hungry China in decades to come.

For various reasons, all three countries feel that they are under western pressure on various issues. Russia is under pressure of NATO's eastward expansion, Chechnya issue and more generally because of perceived US design on former Soviet republics including Central Asia and Caspian Sea. US is encircling Russia from all sides by signing treaties with anti-Moscow countries like GUAAM and fermenting anti-Russian feelings in erstwhile Soviet Union countries.

China is under severe pressure to spend more on defence sector because it feel threatened by US arms sales to Taiwan and more specifically East Asian Security policies of US administration which is moving towards greater use of Japan in balancing China. India is experiencing ill conceived Western propensity to try to get involved on Kashmir issue and helping Pakistan to internationalize Kashmir issue, also US is trying its best to roll back India nuclear and missile programme. India also accused US for pursuing 'double standard' on fighting with terrorism. India blames that terrorist outfits operating from Pakistani soil with overt and covert support of Pakistan is posing grave threat to India's security, but US is eliminating only those terrorists which pose threat to US interests.

To conclude, Russo-China relations are smoothly progressing in the post-cold war era where there is no ideological constraints remain and it is national interest which is the torch bearer in their individual relations. However, the issue of legal and illegal migration of Chinese to the Russian Far-East has the potential to derail their bilateral ties.

Appendices

Joint Declaration by the Russian Federation and the People's Republic of China

Beijing, China, December 2, 2002

I

The Heads of State of Russia and China, having comprehensively discussed the state of, and prospects for Russian-Chinese ties, declare that deepening of the relations of strategic partnership between the Russian Federation and the People's Republic of China is the only correct historic choice arising from the long-term interests of the two countries and their peoples and meeting the requirements for coping with challenges to the development of the world situation and international relations.

Over the last decade, bilateral relations have witnessed positive historic changes. In the new 21st century the sociopolitical and economic bases of Russian-Chinese relations have become ever firmer, mutual political trust has deepened, the traditional friendship between the two countries' peoples has grown stronger and mutually beneficial cooperation has produced substantial results. The close contacts between leaders of the two states play a guiding role for the development of bilateral relations.

The Heads of State of Russia and China concur that development of relations of good-neighborliness, friendship and cooperation and the deepening of strategic interaction between

Russia and China have extensive prospects and huge potential. The sides are determined to go on making untiring efforts to continually push forward and raise the level of friendly and mutually beneficial cooperation between the two countries.

The Heads of State of Russia and China affirm their readiness to strengthen further the exchange of high-level visits and the regular meeting mechanism between the two countries, to raise the level of mutual trust in the political and military fields and to exchange views continuously on major bilateral and international issues. The foreign affairs, defense, law enforcement, economic and scientific-technical agencies of the two countries will all heighten their coordination and cooperation. Friendly exchanges and businesslike cooperation between regions of the countries will be strengthened.

II

The year that has elapsed since the signing by the Heads of State of Russia and China of the Treaty of Good-Neighborliness, Friendship and Cooperation Between the Russian Federation and the People's Republic of China, of July 16, 2001, has entirely confirmed that this document has a historic and important practical significance and is a solid foundation for the healthy and stable development of good-neighborly and friendly relations between the two states. The Treaty is a program document possessing an enormous life-affirming force, aimed at ensuring the continuous deepening of bilateral relations, which opens up new horizons for the building-up of the strategic partnership between the two countries in all the directions without exception.

The Heads of State of Russia and China reiterate that no matter what changes take place in the international situation or in Russia and China, they are determined to adhere unswervingly to the course and principles set forth in the Treaty, continue to promote, expand, deepen and fill the relations of strategic partnership between the two countries with new content, coordinate the positions and support each other on issues of common concern, fully implement the great strategic idea that the two countries will "forever be good neighbors, friends and reliable partners and never be enemies," and meet the challenges of our time together with all peace-loving states and peoples all over the world.

The sides emphasize that the friendly relations of the two countries are a new type of state-to-state relations based on non-alignment and non-confrontation and which are not directed against third countries. The Heads of State of Russia and China are deeply convinced that the solid foundation laid by the Treaty will definitely elevate Russian-Chinese relations to a new, still higher level in this century.

The Heads of State of Russia and China point out that national independence, sovereignty and territorial integrity are the basic elements of international law, the underlying principles governing international relations, and the essential preconditions for each state's existence. It is the lawful right of every state to firmly condemn and strike against any designs or actions seeking to undermine the above-mentioned principles. Russia and China resolutely support each other's policy and actions in questions of maintaining state unity and territorial integrity.

The Russian side reiterates that the Government of the People's Republic of China is the sole legal government representing the whole of China, and that Taiwan is an integral part of China's territory. Russia will not establish any official relations or have any official contacts with Taiwan. Russia has always recognized that Tibet is an integral part of China. The Chinese side supports the efforts of the Russian side in fighting Chechen terrorists and separatists.

Russia and China will not allow the establishment or activities of any organization or group within their own territories that would inflict harm upon the sovereignty, security and territorial integrity of the two states.

The heads of the two states believe that the most favorable conditions have currently taken shape in order to reach a mutually acceptable solution to the question where the line of the Russian-

Chinese state boundary is to run on its two remaining non-agreed sections. In this connection the ministries of foreign affairs of the two countries are instructed to complete the process of border negotiations as soon as possible.

The definitive settlement of the historically inherited border question between Russia and China will have a historic significance for relations between the two countries for the strategic term and will exert an important stabilizing effect on the situation in the Asia-Pacific region and globally.

III

The Heads of State of Russia and China presume that strengthening and developing in every way the positive trends in trade and economic cooperation is of great importance to ensuring stable long-term progress in the whole range of Russian-Chinese relations.

The Heads of State of Russia and China believe that the mechanism of regular meetings between the Heads of Government of the two states has a great significance and highly assess its contribution to developing trade and economic cooperation between Russia and China over the long term.

The sides point out that for the purpose of ensuring the stable and predictable development of trade and economic relations active measures need to be taken to expand the scope of trade, improve its commodity pattern by increasing in it the proportion of high-technology, engineering and electronic products, along with other high value added products, to create favorable conditions for mutual access for goods, services and investments to the markets of the two states, to intensify technical, economic and investment cooperation, including the establishment of joint ventures, industrial partnerships, and technology transfer, to improve the system of handling trade transactions, including heightened cooperation in the area of banking settlements, crediting and insurance, to strengthen work in the legal, administrative, managerial and other fields so as to bring their trade regulations into conformity with international norms, and to enhance contacts between small and medium-sized businesses. The sides are determined to achieve a breakthrough in the development and qualitative growth of the whole range of bilateral trade and economic relations.

Taking into account the great significance of cooperation in the energy sphere for both sides, the Heads of State of Russia and China consider it important to ensure the prompt implementation of the existing agreements concerning the Russian-Chinese oil pipeline and gas pipelines as well as to coordinate the implementation of promising energy projects to ensure the long-term and stable nature of oil and gas supplies.

The sides agree that in the context of Russia's integration into the system of world economic ties as an equal member of the world economic and trade community its accession to the World Trade Organization (WTO) will be of special significance, and acknowledge that it is necessary to actively and constructively hold bilateral negotiations on the accession of Russia to the WTO and achieve an appropriate agreement on the basis of consideration of mutual interests, which will help to strengthen Russian-Chinese trade and economic relations. China declares its support for entry of the Russian Federation into the WTO, which will impart to this international organization a more universal character.

IV

The Heads of State of Russia and China presume that expanding friendly contacts and cooperation between the sides in the fields of education, culture, health, sports and media is instrumental in consolidating the social foundation of good-neighborliness, friendship and mutual trust between the two states. They attach great significance to the activities of the Russian-Chinese Committee of Friendship, Peace and Development and the improvement of its forms and methods of work.

In order to promote mutual understanding and cooperation between the peoples of the two countries, the sides intend to continue to take practical measures to stimulate mutual trips of citizens of Russia and China, including the steps to regularize and perfect the juridical basis of such contacts.

The Heads of State of Russia and China underscore the importance of developing cooperation in the field of law enforcement. The sides intend to expand cooperation in fighting against illegal migration.

The Heads of State of Russia and China note the necessity of taking further action to strengthen cooperation and improve the appropriate legal basis in the field of ecology and the protection of environment, paying attention to environmental cooperation in the border areas.

V

The criminal attacks of international terrorism in New York, Moscow, Bali and other areas of the world show that terrorism, separatism and extremism pose a serious threat to the security of sovereign states, as well as to world peace and stability. Factors causing uncertainty in global security have increased. The Heads of State of Russia and China maintain that there may be no double standards in addressing these problems, and that it is necessary to counter terrorism by the joint efforts of all states. Russia and China are determined to take purposeful and necessary practical steps, on a bilateral and multilateral basis, in the tough fight against terrorism in all its manifestations.

The sides reaffirm that the terrorists and separatists of Chechnya and "East Turkestan" are part and parcel of international terrorism. They must be condemned and made an object of joint struggle by all states of the world. For the purpose of the effective protection of the security and stability of their states and the promotion of peace and prosperity on the regional and even global levels, the sides will increase mutual support in the field of combating terrorism and intensify coordination and international cooperation in this area.

In June 2002, in St. Petersburg, the member states of the Shanghai Cooperation Organization (SCO) signed an agreement setting up a permanent SCO Regional Antiterrorist Structure. The

Heads of State of Russia and China highly evaluate the potential for antiterrorist cooperation of this organization and want it to start its practical work as soon as possible.

The sides also highly appreciate the activities of the Russian-Chinese Working Group on fighting terrorism, and especially stress that the constructive and confidential dialogue that has developed therein is fully in accord with the level of relations of strategic partnership existing between Russia and China.

VI

Since the events of September 11, 2001, the international situation has undergone deep and complex changes. International terrorism and other nontraditional challenges pose a serious threat to international peace and security. Local conflicts have not been extinguished, there persist the hotbeds of tension and instability and the gap between South and North has widened even more. Peace and the development of mankind are faced with challenges that cannot be ignored.

The Heads of State of Russia and China believe that the harmonious coexistence of all countries of the world and its diversity, the democratization of international relations will help to strengthen global stability and security. The sides hold that peace and development are the keynote of the contemporary epoch, that in the conditions of the strengthening of the key tendencies for the formation of a multipolar world and economic globalization the peoples of all countries are interested in shaping an equitable and rational new international political and economic order which would guarantee the ongoing development and equal security of all states.

Russia and China favor strengthening the central role of the United Nations as the principal mechanism for safeguarding international security and cooperation in a multipolar world, and advocate the further enhancement of the efficiency of the UN and, in particular, its Security Council.

The two sides believe that at a time of globalization and scientific and technical progress, countries are becoming increasingly more inter-dependent. It is necessary to formulate an overall strategy for sustainable development of the mankind. The military, political, economic, ecological and human contents related to international security are inter-linked and such a concept should form the basis of the overall strategy mentioned above.

The Heads of State of Russia and China believe the two sides' coordination on strategic stability issues is of great significance to fortifying international security and global and local stability. The two sides will cooperate within the framework of bilateral relations and related international forums; promote the formulation and adoption of effective measures in arms control, disarmament, and non-proliferation of weapons of mass destruction and their carriers. The two sides will make further efforts to advance their joint proposal on the conclusion of an international agreement on the prevention of deployment of weapons in outer space.

The two sides will continue their close coordination in resolving the issue of missile proliferation. They hold that it is necessary to further explore and advance the proposal for multilateral talks so as to formulate a legally binding agreement on global missile non-proliferation mechanism. The United Nations and other multilateral organizations should play a major role in this area. Russia and China are ready to continue bilateral dialogue on export control related to non-proliferation.

The two sides attach great importance to interstate cooperation on protection and promotion of human rights. They believe that there should be no "double standards" in this area, and stand against the use of human rights problems for imposing pressures in international relations.

The two sides stress it should become a norm of interstate relations to resolve regional conflicts by political and diplomatic means and through dialogues and negotiations.

The two sides maintain that the Iraq issue should be thoroughly resolved through political and diplomatic means on the basis of strictly observing resolutions of the UN Security Council. They are willing to further cooperate within the UN framework on this issue.

The two sides have a discussion on the Middle East situation and express grave concern over the prolonged Palestine-Israel confrontation. They believe that the use of force can never resolve their differences and a political solution conforms to the long-term interests of all nations. The goal of the political solution is the peaceful co-existence of Israel and Palestine as two countries within their safe and recognized boundaries.

VII

The Shanghai Cooperation Organization (SCO) has become an important factor in maintaining regional peace, security and stability, as well as a pillar in the future structure of a multipolar world. In the current complicated international situation, it is in the common interests of SCO member countries to inject new vigor into the organization so that it can take a more active part in regional and international affairs for the promotion of peace and prosperity in Asia and the creation of cooperative atmosphere for dialogues on an equal footing.

The Heads of State of Russia and China, therefore, maintain that it is of primary importance to strengthen cooperation within the framework of the SCO.

Russia and China are willing to work with the other member countries of the SCO to speed up the improvement of the SCO mechanism, set up the SCO Secretariat and Regional anti-terrorism structure at an early date, intensify the fight against terrorism, separatism and extremism and take measures to curb drug trafficking and other forms of cross-border crime, deepen the extensive cooperation of the sides in economic and cultural fields, and actively carry out exchanges and cooperation between the SCO and other international organizations and countries to safeguard peace and development of the region and the world as a whole.

VIII

The Heads of State of Russia and China hold that to strengthen multilateral cooperation in the field of security in the Asian-Pacific region is one of the key factors in consolidating global strategic stability. The two countries will strive to establish in the Asian-Pacific region an effective regional multilateral cooperation system to ensure stability and security in the region.

The Heads of State of Russia and China express concern over the prospects and possible results of cooperation between interested countries in establishing a theater missile defense system in East Asia on a bloc basis, and reiterate that such cooperation should not destroy regional and global security and stability. Both sides urge all interested countries to strengthen dialogue on the issue of theater missile defense systems in East Asia on a bloc basis. Russia and China will continue consultations on the issue within the bilateral framework.

The two sides have discussed Central Asian situation. They point out that it is crucial to maintain stability and security in the region.

Both sides point out that the Association of Southeast Asian Nations (ASEAN) plays a constructive role in establishing a new type of interstate relations in the Asia-Pacific region, and hold that the ASEAN Regional Forum is an effective mechanism for conducting political dialogue on regional security issues. Both sides reiterate that they will carry out close cooperation within the framework of the ASEAN Regional Forum.

Russia reiterates its positive attitude toward the further development of "ASEAN + 3" dialogue and cooperation mechanism. China will provide necessary assistance to Russia for the establishment of contacts between Russia and the mechanism in the fields of common concern.

Both sides hold that comprehensively advancing economic, trade, investment and technological cooperation within the framework of the Asia Pacific Economic Cooperation (APEC) is a major contribution to the stability and development in the Asia-Pacific region. Both sides are willing to conduct regular consultations on APEC affairs to exchange views and coordinate their positions.

Both sides speak highly of the Asia-Europe Meeting's contributions to pushing forward the further development of a new equal partnership between Asia and Europe. The Chinese side supports Russia's entry into the Meeting.

The Heads of State of Russia and China welcome the establishment of a nuclear-free area in related regions in Asia, and hold that such a nuclear-free area should fully take into consideration the interests and concerns of all countries.

The Heads of State of Russia and China support the continuation and advancement of the relaxation process in recent years on the Korean Peninsula, especially the dialogue and cooperation between the Democratic People's Republic of Korea (DPRK) and the Republic of Korea (ROK), and are for the normalization of relations between the DPRK and Japan and the implementation of the results achieved at the Pyongyang summit.

Both sides hold that it is crucial to peace and security in North-East Asia to maintain a nuclear-free status of the Korean Peninsula and the system for non-proliferation of weapons of mass destruction. Both sides emphasize that the United States and the DPRK should, as always, abide by all agreements reached before including the 1994 framework agreement, and realize, on this basis, the normalization of their relations in the principle of conducting constructive and equal dialogue for catering to mutual concerns. Both sides will continue to develop good-neighborly friendship and cooperation with the DPRK and the ROK so as to facilitate peace and prosperity in the region.

Both sides completely support the work done by the Afghan Interim Authority to bring the country's situation back to normal in line with the Agreement on Provisional Arrangements in Afghanistan Pending the Re-Establishment of Permanent Government Institutions signed in Bonn, the Loya Jirgah's (Grand

Assembly) decisions and resolutions adopted by the United Nations Security Council. Both sides express the concern over the instability of the Afghan situation, the rampant activities of the residual Taliban forces, the intensifying contradictions among different ethnic groups and the increasing output of drugs. Both sides stress that the UN's leading role in solving Afghan issues must be upheld.

The Heads of State of Russia and China declare that they are willing to continue to conduct intensive and mutually-trusted political dialogue, expand and deepen economic cooperation of mutual benefit, boost cooperation in international affairs, and consolidate the friendship between the peoples of the two countries.

President of the Russian Federation Chairman of the People's Republic of China

V.V. Putin **Jiang Zemin**

Shanghai Cooperation Organization Charter: (Xinhua)

The People's Republic of China, the Republic of Kazakhstan, the Kyrgyz Republic, the Russian Federation, the Republic of Tajikistan and the Republic of Uzbekistan being the founding states of the Shanghai Cooperation Organization (herein after SCO or the Organization),

Based on historically established ties between their peoples;

Striving for further enhancement of comprehensive cooperation;

Desiring to jointly contribute to the strengthening of peace and ensuring of security and stability in the region in the environment of developing political multi-polarity and economic and information globalization;

Being convinced that the establishment of SCO will facilitate more efficient common use of opening possibilities and counteracting new challenges and threats;

Considering that interaction within SCO will promote the realization of a huge potential of good neighborliness, unity and cooperation between States and their peoples;

Proceeding from the spirit of mutual trust, mutual advantage, equality, mutual consultations, respect for cultural variety and aspiration to joint development that was clearly established at the meeting of heads of six States in 2001 in Shanghai;

Noting that the compliance with the principles set out in the Agreement between the People's Republic of China, the Republic of Kazakhstan, the Kyrgyz Republic, the Russian Federation and the Republic of Tajikistan on Strengthening Confidence in the Military Field in the Border Area of 26 April, 1996, and in the Agreement between the People's Republic of China, the Republic of Kazakhstan, the Kyrgyz Republic, the Russian Federation and the Republic of Tajikistan on Mutual Reductions of Armed Forces in the Border Area of 24 April, 1997, as well as in the documents signed at summits of heads of the People's Republic of China, the Republic of Kazakhstan, the Kyrgyz Republic, the Russian Federation, the Republic of Tajikistan and the Republic of Uzbekistan in the period from 1998 to 2001, has made an important contribution to the maintenance of peace, security and stability in the region and in the world;

Reaffirming our adherence to the goals and principles of the Charter of the United Nations, other commonly acknowledged principles and rules of international law related to the maintenance of international peace, security and the development of good neighborly and friendly relations, as well as the cooperation between States;

Guided by the provisions of the Declaration on the Creation of the Shanghai Cooperation Organization of 15 June, 2001, has agreed as follows:

Article 1: Goals and Tasks

The main goals and tasks of SCO are:

To strengthen mutual trust, friendship and good neighborliness between the member States;

To consolidate multidisciplinary cooperation in the maintenance and strengthening of peace, security and stability in the region and promotion of a new democratic, fair and rational political and economic international order;

To jointly counteract terrorism, separatism and extremism in all their manifestations, to fight against illicit narcotics and arms trafficking and other types of criminal activity of a transnational character, and also illegal migration;

To encourage the efficient regional cooperation in such spheres as politics, trade and economy, defense, law enforcement, environment protection, culture, science and technology, education, energy, transport, credit and finance, and also other spheres of common interest;

To facilitate comprehensive and balanced economic growth, social and cultural development in the region through joint action on the basis of equal partnership for the purpose of a steady increase of living standards and improvement of living conditions of the peoples of the member States;

To coordinate approaches to integration into the global economy;

To promote human rights and fundamental freedoms in accordance with the international obligations of the member States and their national legislation;

To maintain and develop relations with other States and international organisations;

To cooperate in the prevention of international conflicts and in their peaceful settlement;

To jointly search for solutions to the problems that would arise in the 21st century.

Article 2: Principles

The member States of SCO shall adhere to the following principles:

Mutual respect of sovereignty, independence, territorial integrity of States and inviolability of State borders, non-aggression, non-interference in internal affairs, non-use of force or threat of its use in international relations, seeking no unilateral military superiority in adjacent areas;

Equality of all member States, search of common positions on the basis of mutual understanding and respect for opinions of each of them;

Gradual implementation of joint activities in the spheres of mutual interest;

Peaceful settlement of disputes between the member States;

SCO being not directed against other States and international organizations;

Prevention of any illegitimate acts directed against the SCO interests;

Implementation of obligations arising out of the present Charter and other documents adopted within the framework of SCO, in good faith.

Article 3: Areas of Cooperation

The main areas of cooperation within SCO shall be the following:

Maintenance of peace and enhancing security and confidence in the region;

Search of common positions on foreign policy issues of mutual interest, including issues arising within international organizations and international fora;

Development and implementation of measures aimed at jointly counteracting terrorism, separatism and extremism, illicit narcotics and arms trafficking and other types of criminal activity of a transnational character, and also illegal migration;

Coordination of efforts in the field of disarmament and arms control;

Support for, and promotion of regional economic cooperation in various forms, fostering favorable environment for trade and investments with a view to gradually achieving free flow of goods, capitals, services and technologies;

Effective use of available transportation and communication infrastructure, improvement of transit capabilities of member States and development of energy systems;

Sound environmental management, including water resources management in the region, and implementation of particular joint environmental programs and projects;

Mutual assistance in preventing natural and man-made disasters and elimination of their implications;

Exchange of legal information in the interests of development of cooperation within SCO;

Development of interaction in such spheres as science and technology, education, health care, culture, sports and tourism. The SCO member States may expand the spheres of cooperation by mutual agreement.

Article 4: Bodies

1. For the implementation of goals and objectives of the present Charter the following bodies shall operate within the Organization:

The Council of Heads of State;
The Council of Heads of Government (Prime Ministers);
The Council of Ministers of Foreign Affairs;
Meetings of Heads of Ministries and/or Agencies;
The Council of National Coordinators;
The Regional Antiterrorist Structure;
Secretariat.

2. The functions and working procedures for the SCO bodies, other than the Regional Antiterrorist Structure, shall be governed by appropriate provisions adopted by the Council of Heads of State.

3. The Council of Heads of State may decide to establish other SCO bodies. New bodies shall be established by the

adoption of additional protocols to the present Charter which enter into force in the procedure, set forth in Article 21 of this Charter.

Article 5: The Council of Heads of State

The Council of Heads of State shall be the supreme SCO body. It shall determine priorities and define major areas of activities of the Organization, decide upon the fundamental issues of its internal arrangement and functioning and its interaction with other States and international organizations, as well as consider the most topical international issues.

The Council shall hold its regular meetings once a year. A meeting of the Council of Heads of State shall be chaired by the head of State organizing this regular meeting. The venue of a regular meeting of the Council shall generally be determined in the Russian alphabetic order of names of the SCO member States.

Article 6: The Council of Heads of Government (Prime Ministers)

The Council of Heads of Government (Prime Ministers) shall approve the budget of the Organization, consider and decide upon major issues related to particular, especially economic, spheres of interaction within the Organization.

The Council shall hold its regular meetings once a year. A meeting of the Council shall be chaired by the head of Government (Prime Minister) of the State on whose territory the meeting takes place.

The venue of a regular meeting of the Council shall be determined by prior agreement among heads of Government (Prime Ministers) of the Member State.

Article 7: The Council of Ministers of Foreign Affairs

The Council of Ministers of Foreign Affairs shall consider issues related to day-to-day activities of the Organization, preparation of meetings of the Council of Heads of State and holding of consultations on international problems within the

Organization. The Council may, as appropriate, make statements on behalf of SCO.

The Council shall generally meet one month prior to a meeting of the Council of Heads of State. Extraordinary meetings of the Council of Ministers of Foreign Affairs shall be convened on the initiative of at least two member States and upon consent of ministers of foreign affairs of all other member States. The venue of a regular or extraordinary meeting of the Council shall be determined by mutual agreement.

The Council shall be chaired by the minister of foreign affairs of the member State on whose territory the regular meeting of the Council of Heads of State takes place, during the period starting from the date of the last ordinary meeting of the Council of Heads of State to the date of the next ordinary meeting of the Council of Heads of State.

The Chairman of the Council of Ministers of Foreign Affairs shall represent the Organization in its external contacts, in accordance with the Rules of Procedure of the Council.

Article 8: Meetings of Heads of Ministries and/or Agencies

According to decisions of the Council of Heads of State and the Council of Heads of Government (Prime Ministers) heads of branch ministries and/or agencies of the member States shall hold, on a regular basis, meetings for consideration of particular issues of interaction in respective fields within SCO.

A meeting shall be chaired by the head of a respective ministry and/or agency of the State organizing the meeting. The venue and date of a meeting shall be agreed upon in advance.

For the preparation and holding meetings the member States may, upon prior agreement, establish permanent or ad hoc working groups of experts which carry out their activities in accordance with the regulations adopted by the meetings of heads of ministries and/or agencies. These groups shall consist of representatives of ministries and/or agencies of the member States.

Article 9: The Council of National Coordinators

The Council of National Coordinators shall be a SCO body that coordinates and directs day-to-day activities of the Organization. It shall make the necessary preparation for the meetings of the Council of Heads of State, the Council of Heads of Government (Prime Ministers) and the Council of Ministers of Foreign Affairs. National coordinators shall be appointed by each Member State in accordance with its internal rules and procedures.

The Council shall hold its meetings at least three times a year. A meeting of the Council shall be chaired by the national coordinator of the member State on whose territory the regular meeting of the Council of Heads of State takes place, from the date of the last ordinary meeting of the Council of Heads of State to the date of the next ordinary meeting of the Council of Heads of State.

The Chairman of the Council of National Coordinators may on the instruction of the Chairman of the Council of Ministers of Foreign Affairs represent the Organization in its external contacts, in accordance with the Rules of Procedure of the Council of National Coordinators.

Article 10: Regional Antiterrorist Structure

The Regional Antiterrorist Structure established by the member States of the Shanghai Convention to combat terrorism, separatism and extremism of 15 June, 2001, located in Bishkek, the Kyrgyz Republic, shall be a standing SCO body.

Its main objectives and functions, principles of its constitution and financing, as well as its rules of procedure shall be governed by a separate international treaty concluded by the member States, and other necessary instruments adopted by them.

Article 11: Secretariat

Secretariat shall be a standing SCO administrative body. It shall provide organizational and technical support to the activities carried out in the framework of SCO and prepare proposals on the annual budget of the Organization. The Secretariat shall be headed by the Secretary-General to be appointed by the Council of Heads of State on nomination by the Council of Ministers of Foreign Affairs.

The Secretary-General shall be appointed from among the nationals of member States on a rotational basis in the Russian alphabetic order of the member States‘ names for a period of three years without a right to be reappointed for another period.

The Secretary-General deputies shall be appointed by the Council of Ministers of Foreign Affairs on nomination by the Council of National Coordinators. They cannot be representatives of the State from which the Executive Secretary has been appointed.

The Secretariat officials shall be recruited from among nationals of the member States on a quota basis.

The Secretary-General, his deputies and other Secretariat officials in fulfilling their official duties should not request or receive instructions from any member State and/or government, organization or physical persons. They should refrain from any actions that might affect their status as international officials reporting to SCO only.

The member States shall undertake to respect the international character of the duties of the Secretary-General, his deputies and Secretariat staff and not to exert any influence upon them as they perform their official functions. The SCO Secretariat shall be located at Beijing (the People's Republic of China).

Article 12: Financing

SCO shall have its own budget drawn up and executed in accordance with a special agreement between member States. This agreement shall also determine the amount of contributions paid annually by member States to the budget of the Organization on the basis of a cost-sharing principle.

Budgetary resources shall be used to finance standing SCO bodies in accordance with the above agreement. The member

States shall cover themselves the expenses related to the participation of their representatives and experts in the activities of the Organization.

Article 13: Membership

The SCO membership shall be open for other States in the region that undertake to respect the objectives and principles of this Charter and to comply with the provisions of other international treaties and instruments adopted in the framework of SCO.

The admission of new members to SCO shall be decided upon by the Council of Heads of State on the basis of a representation made by the Council of Ministers of Foreign Affairs in response to an official request from the State concerned addressed to the acting Chairman of the Council of Ministers of Foreign Affairs.

SCO membership of a member State violating the provisions of this Charter and/or systematically failing to meet its obligations under international treaties and instruments, concluded in the framework of SCO, may be suspended by a decision of the Council of Heads of State adopted on the basis of a representation made by the Council of Ministers of Foreign Affairs. If this State goes on violating its obligations, the Council of Heads of State may take a decision to expel it from SCO as of the date fixed by the Council itself.

Any member State shall be entitled to withdraw from SCO by transmitting to the Depositary an official notification of its withdrawal from this Charter no later than twelve months before the date of withdrawal. The obligations arising from participation in this Charter and other instruments adopted within the framework of SCO shall be binding for the corresponding States until they are completely fulfilled.

Article 14: Relationship with Other States and International Organisations

SCO may interact and maintain dialogue, in particular in certain areas of cooperation, with other States and international organizations.

SCO may grant to the State or international organisation concerned the status of a dialogue partner or observer. The rules and procedures for granting such a status shall be established by a special agreement of member States.

This Charter shall not affect the rights and obligations of the member States under other international treaties in which they participate.

Article 15: Legal Capacity

As a subject of international law, SCO shall have international legal capacity. It shall have such a legal capacity in the territory of each Member State, which is required to achieve its goals and objectives.

SCO shall enjoy the rights of a legal person and may in particular:

-conclude treaties;

-acquire movable and immovable property and dispose of it;

-appear in court as litigant;

-open accounts and have monetary transactions made.

Article 16: Decisions-Taking Procedure

The SCO bodies shall take decisions by agreement without vote and their decisions shall be considered adopted if no Member State has raised objections during the vote (consensus), except for the decisions on suspension of membership or expulsion from the Organization that shall be taken by "consensus minus one vote of the member State concerned".

Any member State may expose its opinion on particular aspects and/or concrete issues of the decisions taken which shall not be an obstacle to taking the decision as a whole. This opinion shall be placed on record.

Should one or several member States be not interested in implementing particular cooperation projects of interest to other member States, non-participation of the above said member States in these projects shall not prevent the implementation of such cooperation projects by the member States concerned and, at the same time, shall not prevent the said member States from joining such projects at a later stage.

Article 17: Implementation of Decisions

The decisions taken by the SCO bodies shall be implemented by the member States in accordance with the procedures set out in their national legislation.

Control of the compliance with obligations of the member States to implement this Charter, other agreements and decisions adopted within SCO shall be exercised by the SCO bodies within their competence.

Article 18: Permanent Representatives

In accordance with their domestic rules and procedures, the member States shall appoint their permanent representatives to the SCO Secretariat, which will be members of the diplomatic staff of the embassies of the member States in Beijing.

Article 19: Privileges and Immunities

SCO and its officials shall enjoy in the territories of all member States the privileges and immunities which are necessary for fulfilling functions and achieving goals of the Organisation.

The volume of privileges and immunities of SCO and its officials shall be determined by a separate international treaty.

Article 20: Languages

The official and working languages of SCO shall be Russian and Chinese.

Article 21: Duration and Entry into Force

This Charter shall be of indefinite duration.

This Charter shall be subject to ratification by signatory States and shall enter into force on the thirtieth day following the date of the deposit of the fourth instrument of ratification.

For a State which signed this Charter and ratified it thereafter it shall enter into force on the date of the deposit of its instrument of ratification with the Depositary.

Upon its entering into force this Charter shall be open for accession by any State.

For each acceding State this Charter shall enter into force on the thirtieth day following the date of receiving by the Depositary of appropriate instruments of accession.

Article 22: Settlement of Disputes

In case of disputes or controversies arising out of interpretation or application of this Charter member States shall settle them through consultations and negotiations.

Article 23: Amendments and Additions

By mutual agreement of member States this Charter can be amended and supplemented. Decisions by the Council of Heads of State concerning amendments and additions shall be formalized by separate protocols which shall be its integral part and enter into force in accordance with the procedure provided for by Article 21 of this Charter.

Article 24: Reservations

No reservations can be made to this Charter which contradict the principles, goals and objectives of the Organization and could prevent any SCO body from performing its functions. If at least two thirds of member States have objections the reservations must be considered as contradicting the principles, goals and objectives of the Organization or preventing any body from performing its functions and being null and void.

Article 25: Depositary

The People's Republic of China shall be the Depositary of this Charter.

Article 26: Registration

Pursuant to Article 102 of the Charter of the United Nations, this Charter is subject to registration with the Secretariat of the United Nations.

Done at Saint-Petersburg the seventh day of June 2002 in a single original in the Chinese and Russian languages, both texts being equally authoritative.

The original copy of this Charter shall be deposited with the Depositary who will circulate its certified copies to all signatory States.

Shanghai Cooperation Organization (SCO) Charter

The People's Republic of China, the Republic of Kazakhstan, the Kyrgyz Republic, the Russian Federation, the Republic of Tajikistan and the Republic of Uzbekistan being the founding states of the Shanghai Cooperation Organization (hereinafter SCO or the Organization),

Based on historically established ties between their peoples;

Striving for further enhancement of comprehensive cooperation;

Desiring to jointly contribute to the strengthening of peace and ensuring of security and stability in the region in the environment of developing political multi-polarity and economic and information globalization;

Being convinced that the establishment of SCO will facilitate more efficient common use of opening possibilities and counteracting new challenges and threats;

Considering that interaction within SCO will promote the realization of a huge potential of good neighborliness, unity and cooperation between States and their peoples;

Proceeding from the spirit of mutual trust, mutual advantage, equality, mutual consultations, respect for cultural variety and aspiration to joint development that was clearly established at the meeting of heads of six States in 2001 in Shanghai;

Noting that the compliance with the principles set out in the Agreement between the People's Republic of China, the Republic of Kazakhstan, the Kyrgyz Republic, the Russian Federation and the Republic of Tajikistan on Strengthening Confidence in the Military Field in the Border Area of 26 April, 1996, and in the Agreement between the People's Republic of China, the Republic of Kazakhstan, the Kyrgyz Republic, the Russian Federation and the Republic of Tajikistan on Mutual Reductions of Armed Forces in the Border Area of 24 April , 1997, as well as in the documents signed at summits of heads of the People's Republic of China, the Republic of Kazakhstan, the Kyrgyz Republic, the Russian Federation, the Republic of Tajikistan and the Republic of Uzbekistan in the period from 1998 to 2001, has made an important contribution to the maintenance of peace, security and stability in the region and in the world;

Reaffirming our adherence to the goals and principles of the Charter of the United Nations, other commonly acknowledged principles and rules of international law related to the maintenance of international peace, security and the development of goodneighborly and friendly relations, as well as the cooperation between States;

Guided by the provisions of the Declaration on the Creation of the Shanghai Cooperation Organization of 15 June, 2001,

Have agreed as follows:

Article 1: Goals and Tasks

The main goals and tasks of SCO are:

to strengthen mutual trust, friendship and good neighborliness between the member States;

to consolidate multidisciplinary cooperation in the maintenance and strengthening of peace, security and stability in the region and promotion of a new democratic, fair and rational political and economic international order;

to jointly counteract terrorism, separatism and extremism in all their manifestations, to fight against illicit narcotics and arms trafficking and other types of criminal activity of a transnational character, and also illegal migration;

to encourage the efficient regional cooperation in such spheres as politics, trade and economy, defense, law enforcement, environment protection, culture, science and technology, education, energy, transport, credit and finance, and also other spheres of common interest;

to facilitate comprehensive and balanced economic growth, social and cultural development in the region through joint action on the basis of equal partnership for the purpose of a steady increase of living standards and improvement of living conditions of the peoples of the member States;

to coordinate approaches to integration into the global economy;

to promote human rights and fundamental freedoms in accordance with the international obligations of the member States and their national legislation;

to maintain and develop relations with other States and international organizations;

to cooperate in the prevention of international conflicts and in their peaceful settlement;

to jointly search for solutions to the problems that would arise in the 21st century.

Article 2: Principles

The member States of SCO shall adhere to the following principles:

mutual respect of sovereignty, independence, territorial integrity of States and inviolability of State borders, non-aggression, non-interference in internal affairs, non-use of force or threat of its use in international relations, seeking no unilateral military superiority in adjacent areas;

equality of all member States, search of common positions on the basis of mutual understanding and respect for opinions of each of them;

gradual implementation of joint activities in the spheres of mutual interest;

peaceful settlement of disputes between the member States;

SCO being not directed against other States and international organizations;

prevention of any illegitimate acts directed against the SCO interests;

implementation of obligations arising out of the present Charter and other documents adopted within the framework of SCO, in good faith.

Article 3: Areas of Cooperation

The main areas of cooperation within SCO shall be the following:

maintenance of peace and enhancing security and confidence in the region;

search of common positions on foreign policy issues of mutual interest, including issues arising within international organizations and international fora;

development and implementation of measures aimed at jointly counteracting terrorism, separatism and extremism, illicit narcotics and arms trafficking and other types of criminal activity of a transnational character, and also illegal migration;

coordination of efforts in the field of disarmament and arms control;

support for, and promotion of regional economic cooperation in various forms, fostering favorable environment for trade and investments with a view to gradually achieving free flow of goods, capitals, services and technologies;

effective use of available transportation and communication infrastructure, improvement of transit capabilities of member States and development of energy systems;

sound environmental management, including water resources management in the region, and implementation of particular joint environmental programs and projects;

mutual assistance in preventing natural and man-made disasters and elimination of their implications;

exchange of legal information in the interests of development of cooperation within SCO;

development of interaction in such spheres as science and technology, education, health care, culture, sports and tourism.

The SCO member States may expand the spheres of cooperation by mutual agreement.

Article 4: Bodies

1. For the implementation of goals and objectives of the present Charter the following bodies shall operate within the Organization:

The Council of Heads of State;
The Council of Heads of Government (Prime Ministers);
The Council of Ministers of Foreign Affairs;
Meetings of Heads of Ministries and/or Agencies;
The Council of National Coordinators;
The Regional Antiterrorist Structure;
Secretariat.

2. The functions and working procedures for the SCO bodies, other than the Regional Antiterrorist Structure, shall be governed by appropriate provisions adopted by the Council of Heads of State.

3. The Council of Heads of State may decide to establish other SCO bodies. New bodies shall be established by the adoption of additional protocols to the present Charter which enter into force in the procedure, set forth in Article 21 of this Charter.

Article 5: The Council of Heads of State

The Council of Heads of State shall be the supreme SCO body. It shall determine priorities and define major areas of activities of the Organization, decide upon the fundamental issues of its internal arrangement and functioning and its interaction with other States and international organizations, as well as consider the most topical international issues.

The Council shall hold its regular meetings once a year. A meeting of the Council of Heads of State shall be chaired by the head of State organizing this regular meeting. The venue of a regular meeting of the Council shall generally be determined in the Russian alphabetic order of names of the SCO member States.

Article 6: The Council of Heads of Government (Prime Ministers)

The Council of Heads of Government (Prime Ministers) shall approve the budget of the Organisation, consider and decide upon major issues related to particular, especially economic, spheres of interaction within the Organization.

The Council shall hold its regular meetings once a year. A meeting of the Council shall be chaired by the head of Government (Prime Minister) of the State on whose territory the meeting takes place.

The venue of a regular meeting of the Council shall be determined by prior agreement among heads of Government (Prime Ministers) of the member States.

Article 7: The Council of Ministers of Foreign Affairs

The Council of Ministers of Foreign Affairs shall consider issues related to day-to-day activities of the Organization, preparation of meetings of the Council of Heads of State and holding of consultations on international problems within the Organization. The Council may, as appropriate, make statements on behalf of SCO.

The Council shall generally meet one month prior to a meeting of the Council of Heads of State. Extraordinary meetings of the Council of Ministers of Foreign Affairs shall be convened on the initiative of at least two member States and upon consent of ministers of foreign affairs of all other member States. The venue of a regular or extraordinary meeting of the Council shall be determined by mutual agreement.

The Council shall be chaired by the minister of foreign affairs of the member State on whose territory the regular meeting of the Council of Heads of State takes place, during the period starting from the date of the last ordinary meeting of the Council of Heads of State to the date of the next ordinary meeting of the Council of Heads of State.

The Chairman of the Council of Ministers of Foreign Affairs shall represent the Organization in its external contacts, in accordance with the Rules of Procedure of the Council.

Article 8: Meetings of Heads of Ministries and/or Agencies

According to decisions of the Council of Heads of State and the Council of Heads of Government (Prime Ministers) heads of branch ministries and/or agencies of the member States shall hold, on a regular basis, meetings for consideration of particular issues of interaction in respective fields within SCO.

A meeting shall be chaired by the head of a respective ministry and/or agency of the State organizing the meeting. The venue and date of a meeting shall be agreed upon in advance.

For the preparation and holding meetings the member States may, upon prior agreement, establish permanent or ad hoc working groups of experts which carry out their activities in accordance with the regulations adopted by the meetings of heads of ministries and/or agencies. These groups shall consist of representatives of ministries and/or agencies of the member States.

Article 9: The Council of National Coordinators

The Council of National Coordinators shall be a SCO body that coordinates and directs day-to-day activities of the Organization. It shall make the necessary preparation for the meetings of the Council of Heads of State, the Council of Heads of Government (Prime Ministers) and the Council of Ministers of Foreign Affairs. National coordinators shall be appointed by each member State in accordance with its internal rules and procedures.

The Council shall hold its meetings at least three times a year. A meeting of the Council shall be chaired by the national coordinator of the member State on whose territory the regular meeting of the Council of Heads of State takes place, from the date of the last ordinary meeting of the Council of Heads of State to the date of the next ordinary meeting of the Council of Heads of State.

The Chairman of the Council of National Coordinators may on the instruction of the Chairman of the Council of Ministers of Foreign Affairs represent the Organization in its external contacts, in accordance with the Rules of Procedure of the Council of National Coordinators.

Article 10: Regional Antiterrorist Structure

The Regional Antiterrorist Structure established by the member States of the Shanghai Convention to combat terrorism, separatism and extremism of 15 June, 2001, located in Bishkek, the Kyrgyz Republic, shall be a standing SCO body.

Its main objectives and functions, principles of its constitution and financing, as well as its rules of procedure shall be governed by a separate international treaty concluded by the member States, and other necessary instruments adopted by them.

Article 11: Secretariat

Secretariat shall be a standing SCO administrative body. It shall provide organizational and technical support to the activities carried out in the framework of SCO and prepare proposals on the annual budget of the Organization.

The Secretariat shall be headed by the Secretary-General to be appointed by the Council of Heads of State on nomination by the Council of Ministers of Foreign Affairs.

The Secretary-General shall be appointed from among the nationals of member States on a rotational basis in the Russian alphabetic order of the member States' names for a period of three years without a right to be reappointed for another period.

The Secretary-General deputies shall be appointed by the Council of Ministers of Foreign Affairs on nomination by the Council of National Coordinators. They cannot be representatives of the State from which the Executive Secretary has been appointed.

The Secretariat officials shall be recruited from among nationals of the member States on a quota basis.

The Secretary-General, his deputies and other Secretariat officials in fulfilling their official duties should not request or receive instructions from any member State and/or government, organization or physical persons. They should refrain from any actions that might affect their status as international officials reporting to SCO only.

The member States shall undertake to respect the international character of the duties of the Secretary-General, his deputies and Secretariat staff and not to exert any influence upon them as they perform their official functions.

The SCO Secretariat shall be located at Beijing (the People's Republic of China).

Article 12: Financing

SCO shall have its own budget drawn up and executed in accordance with a special agreement between member States. This agreement shall also determine the amount of contributions paid annually by member States to the budget of the Organization on the basis of a cost-sharing principle.

Budgetary resources shall be used to finance standing SCO bodies in accordance with the above agreement. The member States shall cover themselves the expenses related to the participation of their representatives and experts in the activities of the Organization.

Article 13: Membership

The SCO membership shall be open for other States in the region that undertake to respect the objectives and principles of this Charter and to comply with the provisions of other international treaties and instruments adopted in the framework of SCO.

The admission of new members to SCO shall be decided upon by the Council of Heads of State on the basis of a representation made by the Council of Ministers of Foreign Affairs in response to an official request from the State concerned addressed to the acting Chairman of the Council of Ministers of Foreign Affairs.

SCO membership of a member State violating the provisions of this Charter and/or systematically failing to meet its obligations under international treaties and instruments, concluded in the framework of SCO, may be suspended by a decision of the Council of Heads of State adopted on the basis of a representation made by the Council of Ministers of Foreign Affairs. If this State goes on violating its obligations, the Council of Heads of State may take a decision to expel it from SCO as of the date fixed by the Council itself.

Any member State shall be entitled to withdraw from SCO by transmitting to the Depositary an official notification of its withdrawal from this Charter no later than twelve months before the date of withdrawal. The obligations arising from participation in this Charter and other instruments adopted within the framework of SCO shall be binding for the corresponding States until they are completely fulfilled.

Article 14: Relationship with Other States and International Organizations

SCO may interact and maintain dialogue, in particular in certain areas of cooperation, with other States and international organizations.

SCO may grant to the State or international organization concerned the status of a dialogue partner or observer. The rules and procedures for granting such a status shall be established by a special agreement of member States.

This Charter shall not affect the rights and obligations of the member States under other international treaties in which they participate.

Article 15: Legal Capacity

As a subject of international law, SCO shall have international legal capacity. It shall have such a legal capacity in the territory of each member State, which is required to achieve its goals and objectives.

SCO shall enjoy the rights of a legal person and may in particular:

- conclude treaties;
- acquire movable and immovable property and dispose of it;
- appear in court as litigant;
- open accounts and have monetary transactions made.

Article 16: Decisions-Taking Procedure

The SCO bodies shall take decisions by agreement without vote and their decisions shall be considered adopted if no member State has raised objections during the vote (consensus), except for the decisions on suspension of membership or expulsion from the Organization that shall be taken by "consensus minus one vote of the member State concerned".

Any member State may expose its opinion on particular aspects and/or concrete issues of the decisions taken which shall not be an obstacle to taking the decision as a whole. This opinion shall be placed on record.

Should one or several member States be not interested in implementing particular cooperation projects of interest to other member States, non-participation of the above said member States in these projects shall not prevent the implementation of such cooperation projects by the member States concerned and, at the same time, shall not prevent the said member States from joining such projects at a later stage.

Article 17: Implementation of Decisions

The decisions taken by the SCO bodies shall be implemented by the member States in accordance with the procedures set out in their national legislation.

Control of the compliance with obligations of the member States to implement this Charter, other agreements and decisions adopted within SCO shall be exercised by the SCO bodies within their competence.

Article 18: Permanent Representatives

In accordance with their domestic rules and procedures, the member States shall appoint their permanent representatives to the SCO Secretariat, which will be members of the diplomatic staff of the embassies of the member States in Beijing.

Article 19: Privileges and Immunities

SCO and its officials shall enjoy in the territories of all member States the privileges and immunities which are necessary for fulfilling functions and achieving goals of the Organization.

The volume of privileges and immunities of SCO and its officials shall be determined by a separate international treaty.

Article 20: Languages

The official and working languages of SCO shall be Russian and Chinese.

Article 21: Duration and Entry into Force

This Charter shall be of indefinite duration.

This Charter shall be subject to ratification by signatory

States and shall enter into force on the thirtieth day following the date of the deposit of the fourth instrument of ratification.

For a State which signed this Charter and ratified it thereafter it shall enter into force on the date of the deposit of its instrument of ratification with the Depositary.

Upon its entering into force this Charter shall be open for accession by any State.

For each acceding State this Charter shall enter into force on the thirtieth day following the date of receiving by the Depositary of appropriate instruments of accession.

Article 22: Settlement of Disputes

In case of disputes or controversies arising out of interpretation or application of this Charter member States shall settle them through consultations and negotiations.

Article 23: Amendments and Additions

By mutual agreement of member States this Charter can be amended and supplemented. Decisions by the Council of Heads of State concerning amendments and additions shall be formalized by separate protocols which shall be its integral part and enter into force in accordance with the procedure provided for by Article 21 of this Charter.

Article 24: Reservations

No reservations can be made to this Charter which contradict the principles, goals and objectives of the Organization and could prevent any SCO body from performing its functions. If at least two thirds of member States have objections the reservations must be considered as contradicting the principles, goals and objectives of the Organization or preventing any body from performing its functions and being null and void.

Article 25: Depositary

The People's Republic of China shall be the Depositary of this Charter.

Article 26: Registration

Pursuant to Article 102 of the Charter of the United Nations, this Charter is subject to registration with the Secretariat of the United Nations.

Done at Saint-Petersburg the seventh day of June 2002 in a single original in the Chinese and Russian languages, both texts being equally authoritative.

The original copy of this Charter shall be deposited with the Depositary who will circulate its certified copies to all signatory States.

Treaty of Good-Neighborliness and Friendly Cooperation between the Russian Federation and the Peoples Republic of China (2001)

The Russian Federation and the People's Republic of China (hereafter known as the "contracting parties"), in view of the historical tradition of good-neighbourliness and friendship between the people of Russia and China, hold that the Russian-Chinese Joint Declarations and Statements signed and adopted by the heads of states of the two countries from 1992 to 2000 which are of great significance to the development of bilateral relations, firmly believe that to consolidate the friendly and good neighbourly ties and mutual cooperation in all fields between the two countries is in conformity with the fundamental interests of the peoples of the two countries and conducive to the maintenance of peace, security and stability in Asia and the world, reiterate the obligations committed by each party in accordance with the Charter of the United Nations and other international treaties of which it is a signatory, with the hope of promoting and establishing a just and fair new world order based on universally recognized principles and norms of international laws, endeavour to enhance relations between the two countries to a completely new level, determined to develop the friendship between the people of the two countries from generation to generation, have reached agreement as follows:

Article 1

In accordance with universally recognized principles and norms of international laws and on the basis of the Five Principles of mutual respect of state sovereignty and territorial integrity, mutual non-aggression, mutual non-interference in each other's internal affairs, equality and mutual benefit and peaceful co-existence, the contracting parties shall develops the strategic cooperative partnership of good-neighborliness, friendship and cooperation and equality and trust between the two countries from a long-term view and in a comprehensive manner.

Article 2

In handling their mutual relations, the contracting parties will neither resort to the use of force ;or the threat of force nor take economic and other means to bring pressure to bear against the other. The contracting parties will only solve their differences through peaceful means by adhering to the provisions of the "United Nations Charter" and the principles and norms of universally recognized international laws.

The contracting parties reaffirm their commitment that they will not be the first to use nuclear weapons against each other nor target strategic nuclear missiles against each other.

Article 3

The contracting parties respect each other's choice for the course of political, economic, social and cultural development in line with their nation's actual conditions so as to ensure a long-term and stable development of relations between the two countries.

Article 4

The Chinese side supports the Russian side in its policies on the issue of defending the national unity and territorial integrity of the Russian Federation.

The Russian side supports the Chinese side in its policies on the issue of defending the national unity and territorial integrity of the People's Republic of China.

Article 5

The Russian side reaffirms that the principled stand on the Taiwan issue as expounded in the political documents signed and adopted by the heads of states of the two countries from 1992 to 2000 remain unchanged. The Russian side acknowledges that there is only one China in the world that the People's Republic of China is the sole legal government representing the whole of China and that Taiwan is an inalienable part of China. The Russian side opposes any form of Taiwan's independence.

Article 6

The contracting parties point out with satisfaction that each has no territorial claim on the other and both are resolved to make active efforts in building the border between the two countries into one where ever-lasting peace and friendship prevail. The contracting parties will adhere to the principles of non-encroachment upon territories and national boundaries as stipulated in international laws and strictly observe the national boundary between the two countries.

The contracting parties shall continue to hold talks on the pending boundary alignment of the sectors which China and Russia have not yet arrived at an agreement through consultations. Prior to the settlement of these issues, the two sides will maintain the status quo in such boundary sectors.

Article 7

In accordance with the current agreements, the contracting parties shall adopt measures to increase trust between their militaries and reduce military forces in the border areas. The contracting parties shall expand and deepen confidence building measures in the military field so as to consolidate each other's security and strengthen regional and international stability.

The contracting parties shall make efforts to ensure its own national security in accordance with the principle of maintaining reasonable and adequate weapons and armed forces.

The military and military technology cooperation of the contracting parties carried out in accordance with the relevant agreements are not directed at third countries.

Article 8

The contracting parties shall not enter into any alliance or be a party to any bloc nor shall they embark on any such action, including the conclusion of such treaty with a third country which compromises the sovereignty, security and territorial integrity of the other contracting party. Neither side of the contracting parties shall allow its territory to be used by a third country to jeopardize the national sovereignty, security and territorial integrity of the other contracting party.

Neither side of the contracting parties shall allow the setting up of organizations or gangs on its own soil which shall impair the sovereignty, security and territorial integrity of the other contrasting party and their activities should be prohibited.

Article 9

When a situation arises in which one of the contracting parties deems that peace is being threatened and undermined or its security interests are involved or when it is confronted with the threat of aggression, the contracting parties shall immediately hold contacts and consultations in order to eliminate such threats.

Article 10

The contracting parties shall employ and perfect the mechanism for regular meetings at all levels, above all the summit and high-level meetings, to conduct periodic exchanges of views and co-ordinate their stand on bilateral ties and on important and urgent international issues of common concern so as to reinforce the strategic cooperative partnership of equality and trust.

Article 11

The contracting parties stand for the strict observation of universally acknowledged principles and norms of international laws and oppose any action of resorting to the use of force to bring pressure to bear on others or interfering in the internal affairs of a sovereign state under all sorts of pretexts and both are ready to make positive efforts to strengthen peace, stability, development and cooperation throughout the world.

The contracting parties are against any action which may constitute a threat to international stability, security and peace and will conduct mutual co-ordination with regard to the prevention of international conflicts and bringing about their political settlement.

Article 12

The contracting parties shall work together for the maintenance of global strategic balance and stability and make great efforts in promoting the observation of the basic agreements relevant to the safeguard and maintenance of strategic stability.

The contracting parties shall actively promote the process of nuclear disarmament and the reduction of chemical weapons, promote and strengthen the regimes on the prohibition of biological weapons and take measures to prevent the proliferation of weapons of mass destruction, their means of delivery and their related technology.

Article 13

The contracting parties shall strengthen their cooperation in the United Nations and its Security Council as well as other United Nations Special Agencies. The contracting parties shall work to reinforce the central role of the United Nations as the most authoritative and most universal world organization composed of sovereign states in handling international affairs, particularly in the realm of peace and development and guarantee the major responsibility of the UN Security Council in the area of maintaining international peace and security.

Article 14

The contracting parties shall energetically promote the consolidation of stability of the surrounding areas of the two countries, create an atmosphere of mutual understanding, trust and cooperation, and promote efforts aimed at setting up a multilateral co-ordination mechanism which complies with the actual situation of the above-mentioned areas on issues of security and cooperation.

Article 15

In accordance with the two countries' inter-governmental agreements concerned and other documents relating to the handling of creditor's rights and liabilities, each side of the contracting parties recognizes the lawful right of ownership of the assets and other properties which belong to the other side and which are located within the territory of the other contracting party.

Article 16

On the basis of mutual benefit, the contracting parties shall conduct cooperation in such areas as economy and trade, military know-how, science and technology, energy resources, transport, nuclear energy, finance, aerospace and aviation, information technology and other areas of common interest. They shall promote economic and trade cooperation in border areas and local regions between the two countries and create necessary and favorable conditions in this regard in accordance with the laws of each country.

The contracting parties shall energetically enhance and develop exchanges and cooperation in culture, education, health, information, tourism, sports and legal matters.

In accordance with their national laws and international treaties of which they are a party, the contracting parties shall protect and maintain intellectual property rights, including copyright and other relevant rights.

Article I7

The contracting parties shall conduct cooperation in world financial institutions, economic organizations and forums, and in line with the rules and regulations of the above-mentioned institutions, organizations and forums, make efforts to promote the participation of a contracting party in the above-mentioned institutions of which the other contracting party is already a member (or member state).

Article 18

The contracting parties shall cooperate in promoting the realization of human rights and fundamental freedom in accordance with the international obligations each is committed and the national laws of each country.

In line with the international obligations each of the contracting parties is committed and the laws and regulations of each country, the contracting party shall take effective measures to guarantee the legal rights and interests of legal persons and natural persons of the other contracting party who reside within its territory, and provide the necessary legal assistance over civil and criminal matters.

The departments concerned of the contracting parties, in accordance with relevant laws, shall conduct investigation and seek a solution to the problems and disputes arising from the process of carrying out cooperation and business activities by the legal persons and natural persons within the territory of the other side of the contracting parties.

Article 19

The contracting parties shall carry out cooperation in the protection and improvement of the environment, prevention of cross-border pollution, the fair and rational use of water resources along the border areas and the use of biological resources in the northern Pacific and boundary river areas; make joint efforts in protecting rare floras, faunas and the natural ecosystem, and conduct cooperation in preventing the outbreak of major accidents arising from natural disasters or due to technical reasons and eliminating their after—effects .

Article 20

The contracting parties, in accordance with the laws of each country and the international obligation each has committed, shall actively cooperate in cracking down terrorists, splittists and extremists, and in taking strong measures against criminal activities of organized crimes, illegal trafficking of drugs, psychotropic substances and weapons. The contracting parties shall conduct cooperation to crack down on illegal immigration, including the crack down on illegal transportation of natural persons via its territory.

Article 21

The contracting parties attach great importance to the exchanges and cooperation between the central (federal) legislative organs and law enforcement agencies of the two countries.

The contracting parties shall promote with great efforts the exchanges and cooperation between the judicial organs of the two countries.

Article 22

This Treaty neither affects the rights and obligations of the contracting parties in other international treaties of which they are a party to it, nor is it directed against any third country.

Article 23

To implement the present Treaty, the contracting parties shall actively promote the signing of accords in specific realms which are of interests to both sides.

Article 24

This Treaty needs to be ratified and shall come into force from the date of the exchange of instruments of ratification. The exchange of instruments of ratification shall take place in Beijing.

Article 25

The term of validity of the present treaty is twenty years. If neither side of the contracting parties notify the other in writing of its desire to terminate the treaty one year before the treaty expires, the treaty shall automatically be extended for another five years and shall thereafter be continued in force in accordance with this provision.

Done in Moscow on July 16, 2001 in two copies, each in the Russian and Chinese languages, both texts being equally authentic.

Representative of the Russian Federation	**Representative of the People's Republic of China**
Vladimir Putin	**Jiang Zemin**

Bibliography

Primary Sources

"Border agreement among Russia, China and Mongolia", ITAR-TASS World Service, 24 June 1996, translated in Foreign Broadcast Information Services Central Eurasia, Vo1.96, No. 124, 26 June 1996, p.10.

"Declaration of Defense ministers of SCO" *News from Russia*, Vol. 3, No.14, April 7, 2000, pp.5-6.

"Jiang Zemin's speech in Moscow, Sept. 1994" as reported in *Beijing Review*, Vol.37, No.38, Sept.1994, p.l0

"Joint Declarations concerning the fundamentals of Relations between China and Russia, signed in Beijing on Dee 19, 1992", *People's Daily*, Dec. 19, 1992, p.14.

"Putin and Hu Jintao signed the agreement", *News from Russia*, Vol. 3, No. 10, Oct, 2005, pp. 15-16.

"Putin's Visit of Beijing and Sign of Joint Statement" *CDPSP*, Vo1. 21, No. 29, August 2000, pp. 4-5.

"Remarks (Regarding the dangers inherent in the military unipolar post-cold war world dominated by the USA) of foreign ministers Yevgeney Primakov and Qian Qichen" SWB FE/2775 G4 21 Nov. 1996.

"Russia -China Agreement on Humanitarian Intervention" *News From Russia*, Vol. 3, No.49, Dec.8, 2000, pp.22-23.

"Russia-China Signed Agreement on Oil Pipeline", *Strategic Digest*, Vo1.35, No.12, Dec. 2005, pp. l696-1697.

"Speech of visiting Chinese president Jiang Zemin delivered to the Russian state Duma on April 23, 1997", *People's Daily*, April 24, 1997.

"The Russian foreign policy concept approved by president Vladimir Putin" June 28,2000, www.1u.mid.rulns-osndcc.nsf

"Joint Statement by the Ministers of Foreign Affairs of the Member States of the Shanghai Cooperation Organization." Beijing, January 7, 2002, at http://missions.itu.int/~kazaks/eng/sco/sco06.htm.

Hu Jintao's visit to Russia and address to press "Hu in Russia for Summit" *CDPSP*, Vol. 57, No.27, Aug.2005.pp.5 -6.

Ministry of Foreign Affairs (2001), "Chinese Diplomatic Year Book", Beijing: World Affairs Press, 2001, p. 272.

News from Russia, December 17, 1999, p. 7. Prime Minister Vladimir Putin's Statement at a conference of the Security Council of Russia in the Kremlin on December 15, 1999.

Putin and Hu Jintao sign agreement on "economic cooperation", *News from Russia*, Vol. 8, No. 12, Dec. 1, 2005, p. 16.

Putin's speech in China "SCO Are Not Spearheaded Against Any Other Country" *News From Russia*, Vol. 6, No. I6, May 2003; pp.25-26.

The Treaty between Russia and China on "Friendship and Cooperation", *Current Digest of Post-Soviet Press (CDPSP)*, Vol. 53, No. 29, August 15, 2001, pp. 1-4.

United Nations Office for Disarmament Affairs (2003), "UN Register for Conventional Arms", [Online: web] Accessed on 23 March, 2010, URL:http//www.disarmament.un.org/ UN_REGISTER.nsf.

Secondary Sources

Adomeit, Hannes (1995), "Russia as Great Power in World Affairs: Images and Reality" *International Affairs*, 71(1): 35-68.

Ahmed, A.K.N. (1999), "Economic liberalisation in China and Russia: Contrasting Experience" *Mainstream*, 37(42): 6-9.

Akaha Tsuneo (1996), "Russia and Asia in 1995: Bold Objective and Limited Means", *Asian Survey*, 36(10): 100-108.

Alekseev, Mikhail A. and C. Richard Hofstetter (2006), "Russia, China and the Immigration Security Dilemma", *Political Science Quarterly*, 121(1): 23-43.

Ambrosio, Thomas (2005), "*Challenging America's Global Preeminence: Russia's Quest for Multipolarity*", Chippenham, Wiltshire: Antony Rose.

Amin Saikal and William Maley (1995), "*Russia in Search of its Future*", Cambridge: Cambridge University Press.

Anderson Jennifer (1999), "*The Limits of Sino-Russian Partnership*", London: IISS.

Andrew, Martin (2006), "PLA Doctrine on Securing Energy Resources in Central Asia", *China Brief*, 6(11): 89-98.

Aneja, Atul (2000), "China's Multi-Pronged Strategy to counter Separatism in Xinjiang. *The Hindu*, Chennai, September 16, 2000.

Aron, Leon and Kenneth Jonser (1994), "*The Emergence of Russian Foreign Policy*", Washington D.C: US Institute of peace.

Bajpai, Kanti and Mattoo, A. (1996), "*Securing India: Strategic Thought and Practice*", New Delhi: Manohar.

Bakayev, Anwar (2000), "Kirgiz Defence Industry Ready to Work for Russia", *Moscow News*, Moscow, November 1-7, 2000.

Bakshi, Jyotna (2002), "Shanghai Co-operation Organization (SCO) before and after September 11", *Strategic Analysis* 26(2): 268–69.

Bakshi, Jyotsan (1999), "Russian Policy Towards Central Asia", *Strategic Analysis*, 85(4): 1585-1586.

Bakshi, Jyotsana (2000), "Russia – China Military-Technical Cooperation", *Strategic Analysis*, 24(4): 643-661.

Bakshi, Jyotsna (2001), "Sino-Russian Strategic Partnership in Central Asia: Implications for India", *Strategic Analysis*, 25 (2) 174-176.

Bakshi, Jyotsna (2002), "Post Cold War Sino-Russian Relations: All Indian Perspective" *Strategic Analysis*, 26(1): 80-117.

Bakshi, Jyotsna (2004), "*Russia-China Relations: Relevance for India*", New Delhi: Shipra, IDSA.

Banerji, AX., and Bhattacharya P. (2001), *"Peoples Republic of China at Fifty: Politics Economy and Foreign Relations"*, New Delhi: Lancer.

Basu, Baidya Bikas (1998), "Russian National Security Thinking", *Strategic Analysis*, 24(7): 1285-1305.

Batra, R.K. and Khetan, A (2004), "Russia-India- China: Energy Cooperation", *China Report*, 40(2): 169-84.

Bazhanov, J.P. (1998), "Evolution of Russian Foreign Policy in the 1990s", *Review of International Affairs*, 49 (1063-64): 15-18.

Beng, Phar Kim and V. Y. W. Li (2005), "China's Energy Dependence on the Middle East", *The China and Eurasia Forum Quarterly*, 3(3): 19.

Bhakshi, Jyotsna (2004), "*Russia-China Relations: Relevance for India*", New Delhi (IDSA): SIPRA.

Bialer, Seweryn (1986), "*The Soviet Paradox: External Expansion, Internal Decline*", London: LB. Tauris.

Bilal, S. and M. Olarreaga (1998), "Regionalism, Competition Policy and Abuse of Dominant Position" *Journal of World Trade*, 32(3): 153-66.

Black, J.L. (2004), "*Vladmir Putin and the New World Order Looking East, Looking West*", New York: Rowman and Littlefield.

Blagov, Sergei (2005), "Russia Pledges to Up Trade With China", *Eurasia Daily Monitor*, November 7, 2005.

Blagov, Sergei. (2002), "US, Russia Marching on Central Asia", *Asia Times*, Dec. 7, 2002.

Blank, Stephen (1998), "Which way for Sino-Russian Relations", *Orbis*, 2(15): 4-22.

Blank, Stephen J. (1997), "Russia and China in Central Asia", in Stephen J. Blank and Alvin Z. Rubinstein Durham (eds.), *Imperial Decline: Russia's Changing Role in Asia*, N.C.: Duke Univ. Press.

Blank, Stephen J. (1997), "*The Dynamics of Russian Weapons Sales to China*", Carlisle, Penna: Strategic Studies Institute, U.S. Army War College.

Boquerat, G. and Grare, Frederic (2004), "*India-China, Russia Intricacies of an Asian Triangle*", New Delhi; India Research Press.

Bowker, Mike (1997), "*Russian Foreign Policy and The End of Cold War*", Brookfield: Dartmouth Publishing Company Ltd.

Brezhnev, L.I. (1969), "For Stregthening the Solidarity of Communists, for a New Upswing in the Anti-Imperialist Struggle" *Current Digest of the Soviet Press*, vol. 21: 10-16.

Brill, Olcott Martha. (2003), "Taking Stock of Central Asia", *Journal of International Affairs*, 56(2): 7-23.

Brodie, Jonathan (1999), "China Moves to Buy More Russian Aircraft, Warships and Submarines", *Jane's Defence Weekly*, 32(2): 22-37.

Burles, Mark. (1999), "*Chinese Policy Towards Russia and the Central Asian Republics*", Santa Monica, CA: RAND.

Buszynski, Leszek (2004), "Russia and the CIS in 2003", *Asian Survey,* 44(1): 158-67.

Buszynski, Leszek. (2006), "Oil and Territory in Putin's Relations with China and Japan", *The Pacific Review,* 19(3): 288-312.

Buszynski, Robert H. (2003), "The Arms Trade in Russian Chinese Relations: Identity, Domestic Politics, and Geopolitical Reasining", *International Studies Quarterly,* Vol. 47, p. 712-35.

Buszyuski L (1992-93), "Russia and Asia Pacific Region", *Pacific Affair,* 65(4): 86-109.

Buszyuski, Leszek (1995), "Russia and West: Towards Renewed Geopolitical Rivalry?", *Survival,* 37(3): 104-25.

Calder, Kent E. (2001), "The New Face of Northeast Asia", *Foreign Affairs* 80(1): 108.

Cheng, J.Y.S. (2004), "Challenges to China's Russian Policy in Early 21st Century", *Journal of Contemporary Asia,* 34(4): 480-502.

Chenoy, A.M. (2001), "The Phases in Indo-Russian Relations" in Shamsuddin (eds.), *India and Russia: Towards strategic Partnership,* New Delhi: Lancer's Book.

Chenoy, A.M. (2005), "Russia-India-China: Revisioning the International Political System", *World Focus* (April, 2005), p. 11-26.

Chikahito Harada (1997), "Russia and North East Asia", *Adelphi Paper 3l0,* pp.11-8l.

Christofferson, Gaye (1996), "Nesting the Sino-Russian Border and the Tumen Project in the Asia Pacific: Heilongjiang's Regional Relations", *Asian Perspective,* 20(2): 265-99.

Christopher, Bluth (2000), "*The Nuclear Challenge: US-Russian Strategic Relations After the Cold War*", Hants: Ashgate Publishing Limited.

Chufrin, G. (1999), "*Russia and Asia: The emerging Security Agenda*", New York: Sipri OUP.

Chufrin, Gennady (1999), "Asia as a Factor in Russia's international Posture", in Gennady Chufrin (eds.), *Russia and Asia: The Emerging Security Agenda,* London: SIPRI, OUP.

Cirincione, J. (2000), "The Asian Nuclear Chain", *Foreign Policy,* 118(1): 120-136.

Cohen, Ariel (2001), "The Russia-China Friendship and Cooperation Treaty: A Strategic Shift in Eurasia?", *Backgrounder* No. 1459, {Online: web] Accessed on 18 June, 2009, URL:http//www.hertiage.org/research/russianandeurasia/bg1459.cfm.

Cornell, Svante E., Johanna Popjanevski, and Niklas Nilsson (2008), "Russia's War in Georgia: Implications for Georgia and the World", Central-Asia Caucus Institute & Silk Road Studies Program, [Online:web] Accessed on 3 August, 2008, URL:http//www.silkroadstudies. org/new/docs/silkroadpapers/0808Georgia.

Crane, Keith and William Overholt (2005), "*Modernizing China's Military: Opportunities and Constraints*", Santa Monica, Calif.: RAND Corporation.

Crankshaw, E. (1963), *"The New Cold War: Moscow vs. Peking"*, Harmondsworth: Penguin.

Crocker, C.A (2003), "Engaging Failing States", *Foreign Affairs*, 182(5): 32-44.

Cutler, Robert M. (2000), "Kazakhstan-Xinjiang Pipeline: On Hold Forever?" *Central Asia– Caucasus Analyst*, 32(12): 22-34.

Cutler, Robert M. (2001), "The Shattering of the Sino-Russian Entente over the Shape of Central Asia", *Central Asia–Caucasus Analyst*, 2(5): 51-69.

Dahl, Erik. (2006), "Interview with China's NDRC Vice Director Zhang Guobao", *Interfax-China, March 8, 2006.*

Davisha K. and Parrot B. (1994), "*Russia and New States of Eurasia: The Politics of upheaval*", Cambridge: Cambridge University Press.

Dawish, Adid and Davisha, Karen (1995), "*The Making of Foreign Policy in Russia and the New States of Eurasia*", New York: M.C. Sharpe.

Denda, Milorad (2000), "Partnership on Long Term Basis", *Review of International Affairs*, 51(1096): 2l-23.

Deve Murarka (1997), "Russia and China: A Hollow Alliance", *Economic and Political Weekly*, pp. 1 955-19 58.

Dittmer, Lowell. (2001), "The Sino-Russian Strategic Partnership", *Journal of Contemporary China*, 10(28):24-34.

Donaldson R.H. and Nogee J. L. (1988), "*The Foreign Policy of Russia. Changing Systems, Enduring Interest*", New York: M. E. Sharpe.

Donaldson, Robert H. (2003), "The Arms Trade in Russian Chinese Relations: Identity, Domestic Politics, and Geopolitical Reasoning", *International Studies Quarterly*, (47): 712.

Dutt, V.P. (2003), "Puttin's Russia and India: Overview" in V.D. Chopra (eds.), *New Trends in Indo-Russian Relations,* New Delhi: Kalpaz.

Ellison, H.J. (1982), "*The Sino-Soviet Conflict*", Seattle: University of Washington Press.

Ellison, Herbert J. and Bruce A. Acker. (1996), "The New Russia and Asia: 1991-1995", *NBR Analysis,* 7(1):10.

Felgengaur, P. (1997), "An Uneasy Partnership: Sino-Russian Defence Cooperation and Arms Sales" in A. Pierre and D. Trenin (eds.) *Russia in the World Arms trade,* Washington: Carnegie Endowment for International Peace.

Flynn, Kevin. (2000), "Chinese Migration Alarms Border Patrol." *The Moscow Times,* Moscow, [Online: web] Accessed on June 1, 2009, URL:htttp//www.themoscowtimes.com/stories/2000/07/01/004.html.

Frank Peter (1995), "Russian Decides" *World Today,* 51(7): 139-42.

Frische, Klaus (1995), "Russia Refocuses on China", *Aussen Politik,* 46(4): 376-83.

Garnet, Sherman W. (1998), "*Limited Partnership*", Report of the Study Group on Russia-China Relations, Washington DC: Carnegie Endowment for International Peace.

Garnett, W.S (1998), "*Limited Partnership: Russia China Relations in a Changing Asia*", Washington: Russian and Eurasian Program Carnegie Endowment for International Peace.

Gerald Segal (1992), "China and Disintegration of the Soviet Union", *Asian Survey,* 32(9): 848-868.

Gertz, Bill and Rowan Scarborough (1999), "Inside the Ring: Russia-China Ties", *Washington Times,* Washington D.C., 3 September 1999.

Gidadhubli, R.G. (1998), "Russia: Resolving Financial Crisis", *Economic and Political Weekly,* 33(22): 11-17.

Gilbert Rozman (1998), "Sino-Russian Relation in the 1990s: A Balance Sheet", Post *Soviet Affairs,* l4 (2): 93-113.

Gill, G. and Slider, D. (1993), "*The Politics of Transition: Shaping a Post-Soviet Future*", Cambridge: Cambridge University Press.

Glacer C. L and Fetter S. (2001), "NMD and Future of US Nuclear Weapons Policy", *International Security*, 26(1): 7I -74.

Glumicic, Dragan (2000), "Foreign Policy Initiatives of the Russian Federation", *Review of International Affairs*, 51(1096): 18-20.

Golsman M. I. (1992), "*What Went Wrong with Perestroika*", New York: W.W. Norton.

Gorbachev, Mikhail (1987), "*Perestroika: New Thinking for our Country and the World*", London: Collins.

Gorodetsky, Gabriel (1994), "*Soviet Foreign Policy 1971-1991: A Perspective*", London: Frank Cass.

Grachev, Andrei S. (1995), "*Final Days: The Inside Story of Collapse of the Soviet Union*", Boulder: West-view Press.

Grare, Frederic and Mattoo, Amitabh (2001), "*India and ASEAN' The Politics of India's Look East Policy*", New Delhi: Manohar.

Grover, V. K (2002), "Strategic Triangle", *India Quarterly*, 58(1): 21-26.

Gu, Zuewu (1993), "China's Policy Towards Russia", *Aussen politik*, 44(3): 288-97.

Guo, Sujian and Shiping Hua, (eds.) (2008), "New Dimensions of China's Foreign Policy", Lanham, Md.: Lexington Books.

Hanlou, O.M (2000), "Why China Can Not Conquer Taiwan", *International Security*, 25(2): 51-86.

Harada, Chikahito (1997), "*Russia and North-East Asia*", Adelphi Paper 310, Oxford, U.K.: Oxford Univ. Press for the International Institute for Strategic Studies.

Harris, Lillina Craing (1993), "Xinjiang, Central Asia, and the Implicatoins", *The China Quarterly*, (March, 1993) pp. 112-119.

Harris, Stuart and Klintworth, Garry (1995), "*China as a Great Power: Myths, Realities and Challenges in Asia-Pacific Region*", Melbourne: Longman.

Holloway, Nigel and Charles Bicker (1997), "Brothers in Arms", *Far Eastern Economic Review* (March 13, 1997), p. 20.

Huntington, S. P. (1991), "*The Third Wave: Democratization in the Late Twentieth Century*", Norman: University of Oklahoma Press.

Rogachev, Igor (1997), "Russia-China: The Principles and Parameters of Partnership", *Far Eastern Affairs*, 3: 25.

Ivanov, Igor, (2002), "*The New Russian Diplomacy*", Washington D.C: The Nixon Centre and Brookings Institution Press.

Ivanov, Igor, (2000), "The Missile Defence Mistake Undermining Strategic Stability and the ABM Treaty", *Foreign Affairs*, 79(5): 15-20.

Imam, Zafar (1991), "*Soviet Foreign Policy 1917-1990*", New Delhi: Sterling Publishers.

Imam, Zafar (1992), "How and Why Soviet Union Disintegrated", *International Studies*, (Oct-Dec. 1992), pp. 379-402.

Jaffe, Amy Myers and Steven W. Lewis (2002), "Beijing's Oil Diplomacy," *Survival*, 44(1): 125–26.

Jiali Ma (2003), "Strengthening the Role of UNO Cooperation of India-China and Russia in UN", *China Report*, 39(3): 385-92.

Jingjie, L. (2000), "Pillars of the Sino-Russian Partnership", *Orbis*, 44(4): 527-539.

Jullie Rahm (2001-02), "Russia-India-China: A New Strategic Triangle for a New Cold War?", *Parameters*, 39(4): 94-98.

Kanet Roger E, and Vrozhemiekin Alexander (1997), "*Foreign Policy of Russian Federation*", London: Macmillan.

Kaser, Michael (1997), "Economic Transition in Six Central Asian Economies", *Central Asian Survey*, 19(1): 5-31.

Katz, Mark (2006), "Primakov Redux? Putin's Pursuit of 'Multipolarism' in Asia", *Democracy*, 14(4): 144-52.

Katz, Mark (2006), "The Shanghai Cooperation Organization", in Iwashta Akihiro (eds.), *Toward a New Dialogue on Eurasia: The Shanghai Cooperation Organization and Its Partners*, Hokkaido University: Slavic Research Center.

Kausik, Devendra (2003), "Triangle for Peace and Prosperity", *World Focus*, 24(9): 44-48.

Kavet, R.E. and A.V. Kozhmiakin (1997), "The Foreign Policy of the Russian Federation", London: MacMillan.

Kerr, David (1996), "Opening and Closing the Sino-Russian Border: Trade, Regional Development and Political Interest in North – East Asia", *Europe Asia studies*, 48(6): 31-44.

Kerr, David (1998), "Problems in Sino-Russian Economic Relations", *Europe-Asia Studies*, 50(7): 1133-1156.

Kerr, David. (2005), "The Sino-Russian Partnership and US Policy Toward China and North Korea: From Hegemony to concert in Northeast Asia", *International Studies Quarterely*, 49(3): 417-434.

Kim, S.S (1994), "*China and the World Chinese' Foreign Relations in the Post-Cold War Era*", San Francisco: Westview Press.

Koblentz, Gregory (1997), "Viewpoint: Theater Missile Defense and South Asia: A Volatile Mix", *Nonproliferation Review*, 4(3): 56-76.

Kozyrev (1992), "Offers Draft Foreign Policy Guidelines", *The Current Digest of the Post-Soviet Press*, 44(8): 14-17.

Kryzheva, Olga (2000), "Russia-China Arms Trade Growing" *Weekly Defense Monitor* (Centre for Defence Information), 4(5): 5-17.

Kuijper, Hans (2004), "Proposal to Solve Taiwan Problem", *China Report*, 40(2): 189-208.

Kuliev, Avdy (2000), "Jiang Continues Central Asian Tour With stop in Turkmenistan", *Eurasia Insight*, [Online: web] Accessed on October 18, 2009, URL:http//www.eurasianet.org.

Lagando, Alice. (2001), "Putin won't side with Beijing against shield." *Washington Times*, 19 July, 2001.

Lam, Willy Wolf (2001), "Combating American Hegemony", [Online: web] Accessed on June 20, 2009, URL:http//www.cnn.com.

Larion, V. and A Rubtsova (2001), "At the Crossroads: Russian – Chinese Border Interaction", in D. Papademetriou and D. Meyers (eds.), *Caught in the Middle*, Washington, D.C.: Carnergie Endowerment for International Peace.

Laszek Buszynski (1992), "*Russian and Asia-Pactfic Region*", Banberra: Australian National University Press.

Lawrence, Susan W. (2000), "Where Beijing Fears Kosovo", *Far Eastern Economic Review*, Moscow, September 7, 2000.

Lederer, Ivo (1962), "*Russian Foreign Policy: Essays in Historical Perspective*", New Haven: Yale University.

Leo, Cooper (1999), "*Russia and One World. New States of Play one International Stage*", London: Macmillan.

Levin, Michael (2008), "*The Next Great Clash: China and Russia vs. the United States*", Westport, Conn.: Praeger Security International.

Li, Jingjie (2000), "Pillars of Sino-Russian Partnership", *Orbis,* 44(4): 528-539.

Lijun, Sheng (2001), "*China's Dilemma: The Taiwan Issue*", London/New York: I.B. Tauris.

Lo, Bobo (2002), "*Russian Foreign Policy in the Post-Soviet Era: Reality, Illusion and Mythmaking*", New York: Palgrave Macmillan.

Lo, Bobo (2003), "Vladmir Putin and the Evolution of Russian Foreign Policy", London: Blackwell pub.

Lo, Bobo (2004), "Long Sunset of Strategic Partnership: Russia's Evolving China Policy", *International Affairs,* 50(2): 295-309.

Lounev, S.I (2002), "Russia-India: Political Cooperation in the Sphere of Global, Regional and Bilateral Relations", *China Report,* 38(1): 109-11.

Lukin Alexander (1998), "Image of China in Russian Border Regions", *Asian Survey,* 38(9): 821-15.

Malcom Neil, (1994), "New Russian Foreign Policy", *World Today,* 50(2): 29-32.

Malcom, Neil (1994), "*Russia and Europe An End to Confrontation?*", London: Royal Institute of International Affairs.

Malik Hafeez (1997), "*Role of US, Russia and China in the world Order*", London: Macmillan.

Malley, William D. O' and Roger N. McDermott (2003), "The Russian Air Force in

Mathews, M. (1986), "*Poverty in the Soviet Union*", Cambridge: Cambridge University Press.

Mehrotra, O.N. (2001), "Sino-Russian Relations in the Current Period", *World Focus,* 22(4): 9-17.

Menon, Rajan (1997), "The Strategic Convergence between Russia and China", *Survival,* 39(2): 101-125.

Menon, Rajan (1997), "The Strategic Convergence between Russia and China", *Survival,* 39(2): 105–106.

Menon, Rajan and Charles E. Ziegler (2000), "The Balance of Power and U.S. Foreign Policy Interests in the Russian Far East", *NBR Analysis* 11(5): 2-17.

Menon, Rajan and Charles E. Ziegler (2002), "The Balance of Power and US Foreign Policy Interest in the Russian Far East" in Thorton J and Ziegler

E.C. (eds.), *Russia's Far East a region at risk*, London; University of a Washington Press.

Mikheev, Vasily V. (1999), "Russian-Chinese Strategic Cooperation: The Migration Problem in Perspective", *BIISS- Journal*, 20(3): 374-406.

Miller, John (1993), "*Mikhail Gorbachev and End of Soviet Power*", London: Macmillan.

Moltz, Clay (1995), "Regional Tensions in Russo-China Rapprochement", *Asian Survey*, 35(36): 23-54.

Mosbahi, Mohiaddin (1994), "*Russia and Third World in Post Soviet Era*", Gainesville: University of Florida Press.

Myasnikov, V.S (2003), "Russia- India-China: Cooperation in 21st Century", *China Report*, 39(3): 34-60.

Myasnikov, Vladimir (2002), "Strategic Interaction between Russia and China, China Report", 38(l): 43-55.

Nathan, A.J. and Ross R.S. (1997), "*The Great Wall and The Empty Fortress; China's Search for Identity*", New York: W. W. Norton.

Nathan, Andrew J. and Robert S. Ross (1997), "*The Great Wall and the Empty Fortress: China's Search for Security*, New York: W. W. Norton.

Nelson, Harvey W. (1998), "*Power and Insecurity: Beijing Moscow and Washington, 1949-1988*", London: Lynne Reinner Publishers.

Norling, Nicklas (2007), "China and Russia: Partners with Tensions", *Policy Perspectives*, 4(1): 33-48.

Novichkov, Nikolai (2000), "Russia's Deputy PM Reveals Rescue Plan", *Jane's Defence Weekly*, 19 July, 2000.

Pan, Esther. (2006), "Backgrounder: Sino-Russian Energy Ties", *Council on Foreign Relations*. Washington DC, [Online: web] Accessed on April 5, 2009, URL: http//www.cfr.org/publication/10363/sinorussian_energy_ties.html.

Peng, Yuen (2001), "11 September' Incident and Sino-U.S. Relations", *Chinese Defence Analyst*, 20 November, 2001.

Peuch, Jean-Christophe and Paul Basken (2002), "China, Russia Voice Concern over U.S. Bases in Central Asia", *Bloomberg News*, [Online: web] Accessed on January 11, 2008, URL:http://www.globalsecurity.org/org/news/2002/020111-attack01.htmindex.html.

Philip, E.C. and Rhinelander J.B (2001), "NMD and ABM Treaty", *World Policy Journal*, 18(3): 12-18.

Pillsbury, Michael (2000), "*China and Debates the Future Security Environment*", Washington DC: National Defence University Press.

Pipe, Caroline K. (1998), "*Russia and World 1917-1991*", London: Arnold.

Pomfret, John (2000), "China, Russia Solidifying Military Ties", *Washington Post,* Washington, 10 February 2000.

Qimao, Chen (1999), "Sino-Russian Relationship after the Break Up of the Soviet Union" in Chaufrin Gennady (eds.), *Russia and Asia: Emerging Security Agenda,* New York: SIPRA, OUP.

Rahr, Alexander (1994), "*Russia and Europe: An End of Confrontation?*", London: The Royal Institute of International Affairs.

Raja Mohan, (1996), "China-Russia sign 14 Accords", *World Focus,* 17(4): 14.

Rajan, M.S. (1964), "*India in World Affairs 1954-1956*", Bombay: Asia Publishing House.

Ranganathan, C.V. (2002), "Towards an Understanding of the Bases of Cooperation Between Russia-India-China", *China Report*, 38(1): 43-55.

Rappal, M.V (2002), "China Joins the Grea. Game", *World Focus,* 23(6): 14-16.

Rasgotra M. and Chopra V.D. (1997), "*Imlia's Relation with Russia and China*", New Delhi: Gyan Publishing House.

Rasgotra, M. (1998), "*India's Relation with 'he Russia and China: A New Phase*", New Delhi: Gyan Publication .

Ray, J.K. (2000), "*Asia Annual 2000*", Delhi: Shipra.

Ritu Mathur (2000), "TMD in the Asia Pacific: A View From China", *Strategic Analysis,* 25(8): 1455-1466.

Rodman, Peter W. (2000), "Between Friendship and Rivalry", Ted Galen Carpenter and James A. Dorn (eds.) *China's Future: Constructive Partner or Emerging Threat?* Washington, D.C.: CATO Institute.

Rogachev, Igor (1997), "Russia-China: The principles and parameters of partnership", *Far Eastern Affairs,* no. 3: 25.

Roger E. Kanet (1992), "*Soviet Foreign Policy in Transition*", Cambridge: Cambridge University Press.

Rozman, Gilbert (1998), "Sino-Russian Relations in 1990s: A Balance Sheet", *Post Soviet Affairs*" 14(2): 3-113.

Rozman, Gilbert (2000), "New Sino-Russian American Triangle", *Orbis*, 44(4): 541-56.

Rozman, Gilbert. (1998), "Sino-Russian Relations: Will the Strategic Partnership Endure?", *Democracy*, 6(2):56-82.

Ruisheng, C. (2002), "Some observation on the international situation since September 11", *China Report*, 38(1): 331-335.

Ruishong, Chang (2002), "Areas of Possible Political Cooperation Between China, Russia and India in the \Jew Century", *China Report*, 38(1): 87-94.

Rumer, Boris (2002), "The Powers in Central Asia," *Survival*, 44(3): 61–62.

Russia and China, Can Bear Love a Dragon? *The Economist*, April 26, 1997, p. 19.

Saiget, Robert J. (2000), "*China, Russia beef up cooperation on Ethnic Separatism, Taiwan, Terrorism*", Hong Kong: AFP.

Sakwa Richard (1990), "*Gorbachev and His Reforms 1989-90*", New York: Philip Allan.

Sakwa, Richard (2003), "Putin's Foreign Policy: Transforming the East" in Garbriel Gorodetsky (eds.), *Russia Between East and West: Russian Foreign Policy on the Threshold of 21st Century*, London: Frankcass.

Sergounin, Alexander (1999), "*Sino-Russian Military-Technical Cooperation: Incentives, Major Programs, Security Implications*", Taipei: IPSS.

Sergounin, Alexander A. and Sergei V Subbotin (1997), "Sino-Russian Military Cooperation: Russian Perspective", *Spotlight on Regional Affairs*, 16(10): 19-37.

Sevastyanov, Sergey (2000), "Russian Reforms: Implications for Security Policy and the Status of the Military in the Russian Far East", *NBR Analysis*, 11(4): 3-19.

Shambaugh, David (2000), "Sino-American Strategic Relations: From Partners to Competitors", *Survival*, 42(1): 97-l15.

Shambaugh, David (2000), "China's Military Views the World: Ambivalent Security", *International Security*, 24(3): 72-89.

Shambaugh, David (2002), "*Annual Report on the Military Power of the People's Republic of China*", Washington, D.C.

Shambaugh, David (2003), "*Modernizing China's Military: Progress, Problems, and Prospects*, Berkeley: University of California Press.

Shaumian, T.L. (2003), "Geopolitical Changes in Central Asia and Positions of Russia, China and India" *China Report,* 38(3): 361-363.

Sherarman, Peter (1995), "*Russian Foreigr. Policy Since 1990*", San Francisco: Westview Press.

Sherman, Gamett W. (2000), "Limited Partnership" in Sherman W. Garnett (eds.), *Rapprochement or rivalry? Russia China Relations in Changing Asia,* Washington DC: Carnegie Endowment for International Peace.

Shichor, Yitzhak. (2006), "Fact and Fiction: A Chinese Documentary on Eastern Turkestan Terrorism", *The China and Eurasia Forum Quarterly,* 4(2):23-37.

Singh, Jasjit (1999), "Trends in Defence Expenditure" *Asian Strategic Review,* 1998-99, p. 47-64.

Singh, Rai (2001), "Chinese Foreign Policy Directions in Regard to Russia", *India Quarterly,* 57(1): 161-170.

Singh, Swaran (1996), "Sino-Russian Techno-Military Cooperation" *Asian Strategic Review,* 1995-1996, p. 182-204.

Singh, Swaran (1998), "Jiang- Yeltsin Summit", *Strategic Analysis,* 21(10): 1583-87.

Singh, Swaran (1999), "Russia-China-India: Time to Revive the Strategic Triangle Concept", *Mainstream,* 37(42): l0-12.

Singh, Swaran (2003), "India-China-Russia: A Strategic Triangle?", *World Focus,* 24(1): 9- 17.

Sisci, Francesco (2001), "Shanghai Spirit May Yet Haunt Asia", *Asia Times,* [Online:web] Accessed on 21 June, 2008, URL:http//www.atimes.com.

Sisci, Franceso (2001), "China Eyes Silk Road All the Way to the US", *Asia Times,* [Online: web] Accessed on 11 April. 2009, URL:http// www.tew.org.

Slank, Stephen (1995), "Russia's Real drive to the South" *Orbis,* 39(3): 22-45.

Solzhenitsyn, A. (1991), "*Rebuilding Russia*", London: March.

Stobdan, P (1996), "Shanghai Treaty: Readjusting the Frontiers", *Strategic Analysis,* 19(3): 513-20.

Tan, Chung (1999), "Russo-Sino-Indian Strategic Triangle: Signal missed in India", *Economic and Political Weekly,* 12(1): 12-13.

Ted, Apopf (1999), "*Understanding of Russian Foreign Policy*", Pennsylvania: Pennsylvania State University.

Titarenko, Michail L, (2001), "Russia end China: Partners for Peace", *World Affairs*, 5(4): 38-45.

Tremin, Dmitri (1999), "*Russia's China Problem*", Washington: Carnegic Endowment for International Peace.

Trenin, Dmitri (2003), "The China Factor: Challenge and Chance for Russia", in Garnett, (eds.), *Rapprochement or Rivalry*, Washington DC: Blackwell.

Trenin, Dmitri. (2002), "*The End of Eurasia: Russia on the Border between Geopolitics and Globalization*", Washington, D.C.: Carnegie Endowment for International Peace.

Tsyganov, Yuri V. (1999), "Russia and China: What is in the pipeline" in Gennady Chufrin (eds.), *Russia and Asia: The Emerging Security Agenda*, London: SIPRI, OUP.

Tsyplakov, Sergei and Evgeny Popov (2003), "Russian-Chinese Trade and Economic Cooperation: Current Problems and Outlook", *Far Eastern Affairs*, 31(3): 65-78.

Umbach, Frank. (2004), "The Wounded Bear and the Rising Dragon: The Sino-Russian Relationship at the Beginning of the 21st Century, A View from Europe", *Asia Europe Journal*, 2(1):126-142.

Vilya Gelbras (2003), "Chinese Migration to the Russian Far East", in Tsuneo Akaha (eds.), *Human Flows across National Borders in Northeast Asia*, Monterey, CA: Center For East Asian Studies, Monterey Institute of International Studies.

Voskresensski, A.D. (2003), "*Russia and China: A theory of inter-State Relation*", London and New York: Routledge Curzon.

Voskressenski, Alexei D. (1997), "The Perception of China by Russia's Foreign Policy Elit", *Issues and Studies*, 33(3): 18-33.

Wang, Lijiu (2000), "New Starting Poilt, New Challenges: Sino-Russian Relations in New Century", *Strategic Digest*, pp.1557-1563.

Webber, MarK (1996), "The International Politics of Russia and the Successor States", Manchester: Manchester University Press.

Weede, Erich. (2003), "China and Russia: On the Rise and Decline of Two Nations", *International Interactions*, 29(4):59-67.

White, S. (1993), "*After Gorbachev*", Cambridge: Cambridge University Press.

Wishnick, Elisabeth (2001), "*Mending Fences, The Evolution of Moscow's China Policy from Brezhnev to Yeltsin*", Seattle, Wash.: University of Washington Press.

Wishnick, Elizabeth (2001), "Russia and China: Brothers Again?" *Asian Survey*, 41(5): 797-821.

Wohlforth, W. (1993), "*The Elusive Ealanc?: Power and Perceptions During the Cold War*", Ithaca & New York: Cornell University Press.

Xing, G. (1996), "China and Central Asian States: A New Relationship", *East European and Central Asian Studies*, no. 6: 58-64.

Xuejun, Li and A. Taklev, (2001), "*Sino-Rusian Relationship: a Search at the Turn of the Century*", Beijing: China Nationality Press.

Yakovlev, A.G (2002), "Triangle (f Russia-China India: Prospects and Contrast", *China Report*, 38(1): 101-113.

Yeltsin, Boris (1994), "*The View From Kretvzlin*", London: Harper Collins.

Yi, Tung (2000), "Russian Experts said helping PRC make high tech weaponry" *People's Daily*, Sept. 6, 2000.

Yu Guozheng (2000), "*The Russian Far East in Sino-Russian Relations*", Changchum, China.

Yu, Bin (1993), "Sino-Russian Military Relations: Implications for Asia-Pacific Security", *Asian Survey*, 33(3); 302-16.

Yuan, Jing-dong (1998), "Threat Perception and Chinese Security Policy after the Cold War", *Pacific Focus*, 8(1): 55-78.

Yuryev, Mikhail (1999), "Japan: An Asian Member of NATO?", *National Gazette* (Internet version), 29 May 1999.

Zhammian, T.L (2003), "Geopolitical Changes in Central Asia and Position of Russia, China and India", *China Report*, 39(3): 360-363.

Zhikharev, Sergey (1995), "Russia and China Will Make Friends by Borders", *Commercial Daily*, 25 August, 1995.

Zhu, Lisheng (2000), "Problem of the Intelligentsia and Radicalism in Higher Education under Stalin and Mao", *Europe Asia Studies*, 3(2): 1489-1513.

Ziegler, Charles E. (1993), "Foreign Policy and East Asia: Learning and Adaptation in the Gorbachev Era", Cambridge Soviet Paperbacks, Cambridge: Cambridge University Press.

Index

A

AA-2 air-to-air missiles 181
AA-8 air-to-air missiles 181
ABM 55
ABM Agreement 103
ABM Treaty of 1972 45, 103, 108, 151
Afghanistan 23
AK-47 144
Al-Queda 288
Aleksander Shokhin 35
American military ships to Hongkong 104
American-Chinese consultations on human rights 104
Andrei Kozyrev 28, 58
Anti-Ballistic Treaty of 1972 68
Anti-U.S. Cooperation 202
Areas of Common Concern 66
Arkadii Volskii 33
Arms Factor 118
Arms Sales to China 81
ASEAN 94, 165
ASEAN Regional Forum 70, 303
Asia Pacific 89
Asia Pacific Economic Cooperation 303
Asian-Pacific Ocean region 38
Association of Southeast Asian Nations (ASEAN) 303
Atlantists 28
Atlantists firmly 28

B

B-2 bomber 68
Baku-Tbilisi-Ceyhan (BTC) 156
Beijing Summit 31
Bilateral dialogue on human rights 42
Bishkek Declaration of August 1999 45
Border Stability and Arms Control 190
Brezhnev 24, 25
British and American troops in Lebanon and Jordan 18

C

Caspian Sea 123
CBM-2 agreement 79
Central Asia 24, 36
Chechnya 45, 66, 100

China card 70
China-Georgia Relations 266
China's 11th Five Year Plan 128
China's Approach to the NATO Expansion 87
China's economic development 35
China's foreign policy 34
China's Policy towards Central Asia 221
China's Strategy 232
Chinese Communist Party's Military Commission 48
Chinese Diaspora 129
Chinese Emigration 130
Chinese engagement in Central Asia 163
Chinese migrants 139
Chinese National Petroleum Company 152
Chinese tourists and traders 169
Chinese-American dialogue 93
Chinese-Russian border 134
CIS 29, 36, 43, 46, 122
Civilizational barrier 147
Clinton 21
Cold War 20
Collective Security 239
Common European Home 274
Commonwealth of independent states (CIS) 20
Confidence Building Measures in Asia (CICA) 281
Constructive partnership 60
Cooperation Organization 156
CPSU 17
Criminal Law of the People's Republic of China 132
CSTO 122

D

Dalai Lama escape to India 19
Defence Cooperation 172
Deng 25
Deng Xiaoping 23, 25, 34, 77, 116
DF-31 intercontinental ballistic missile 186
Dmitry Medvedev 162
Duma 152
Dushanbe 268
Dushanbe Summit 218

E

Eritrea 100
Ethiopia 100
EU 28, 165
Eurasian security 283
Eurasists 29, 58
Euro-Americocentrism 31

F

Far East 32, 80
forces 24

G

G-8 economic group 126
Gazprom 47
Geopolitical Cooperation between Russia and China 197
Georgia 126
Gorbachev 25, 34
Gorbachev period 21

H

Historical Background 14
Hu Jintao 116 156
Huns 129

I

Identity crisis 111
IL-76 144
IL-78 144
India-Russia-China 283
India's active policy in favour of nuclear disarmament 19
Islamic Extremism and Terrorism 228
Islamic Movement of Uzbekistan (IMU) 244
ITAR-TASS 45

J

Jiang 156

K

Khrushchev 18, 25
Kosovo 45
Kosovo war 70
Kozyrev 31, 32
Krai 138
Kremlin 23

L

Leftists 73
Li Peng's trip to Moscow 42
Line of Actual Control (LAC) 238

M

Mao 20
Mao Zedong 15, 16, 17
Marshall Aid Plan 58
Marxism-Leninism 22
MI-17 helicopters 181
MI-60 helicopters 143
MID 31
Mikhail Titarenko 33
Military Doctrine 230
Military parity between the USSR 25
Military technology 25
Moscow and Beijing 13, 96
Moscow State Institute for International Relations 212
Moscow-Beijing military-technical cooperation 22
Moscow-Beijing-Delhi 274
Moscow's China policy 13
Moskit' surface-to-surface missiles 51
Multipolar 97
Multipolar World 0rder 66, 99, 114
Munich Conference on Security Policy 115

N

NAFTA 165
National People's Congress (NPC) 34
NATO 6, 43, 53, 54, 63, 67, 68, 70, 78
NATO Eastward Expansion 67
NATO's Involvement in Kosovo 97
New Delhi 160
New National Security Concept 230
New World Order 44, 112
NMD 55
North Caucasus 156
North Korea 28

O

Oblast 138
OECD 157
Operation Foreigner 42

Operation Iraqi Freedom 153
Ossetia 126

P

Pavel Grachev 32
Pavel Yudin 18
Peace Mission 2007 122
peaceful rise 117
People's Liberation Army 163
Peoples Republic of China (PRC) 29
PLA 83
Pokhran 31
Poland and Hungary 17
Politics-Sanghai Co-operation Organization 120
Potential Rivalry between Russia and China 234
PRC 17, 29
Putin 156

R

Rapprochement 23
Rightist 72
Rose Revolution 126
RSFSR 31
Rubezh-2008 123
Russia and China in Central Asia 209
Russia-China Conflict 263
Russia-China relations 173
Russia-China Security Dialogue 74
Russia-China-India Triangle 269
Russia-Chinese Summit 38
Russia-Georgia Crisis 267
Russia-India Relations 274
Russia-India-China 279
Russia-India-China Emerging Triangle 277
Russia-NATO Founding Act 91
Russian Air Force 46
Russian Ambassador to the USA 58
Russian diplomacy 31
Russian Federation's relations with China 65
Russian Foreign Policy 20, 21, 26, 31, 32, 33, 41, 43, 48, 53, 70
Russian foreign policy in Asia 39
Russian policies towards China during Yeltsin Regime 31
Russian weapons 172
Russian-Chinese border 82, 106
Russian-Chinese summit 75
Russian-Chinese Treaty on Friendship 78
Russia's defence and security policies 172
Russia's Maritime Territory 219
Russia's security policy 172
Russo-China bilateral Treaty of Friendship and Co-operation 28
Russo-China partnership 63
Russo-China rivalry 62
Russo-China trade relations 167
Russo-Chinese relations 14

S

S-300 surface-to-air missile 143
SAFTA 165
Sanghai Cooperation Organization 55
SCO 6
SCO Energy Club 256
Sergei Gonchavov 29
Sergei Karaoglanov 49
Sergei Stepashin 181